STAR WARS LEGACY

VOLUME II

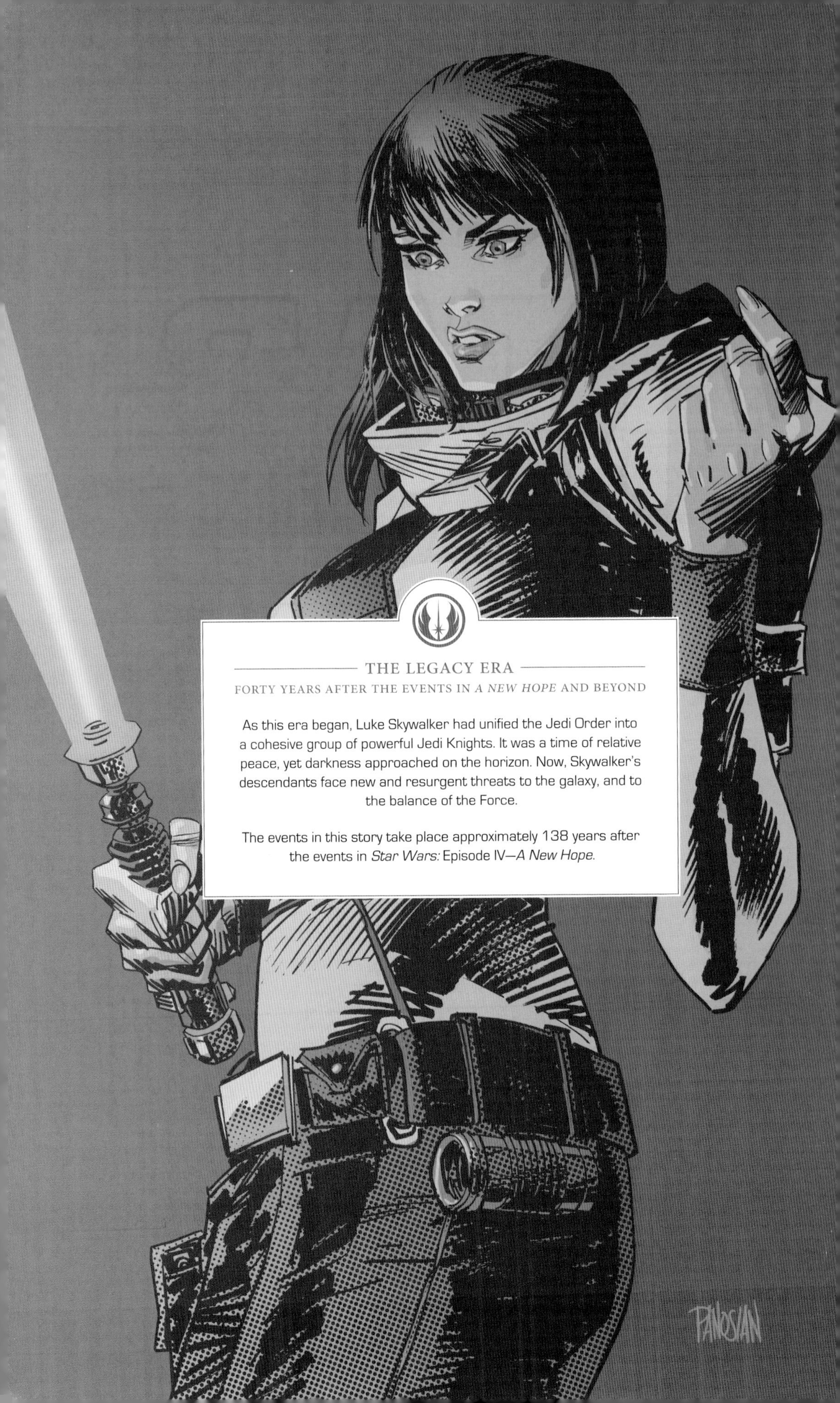
PANOSYAN

THE LEGACY ERA

FORTY YEARS AFTER THE EVENTS IN *A NEW HOPE* AND BEYOND

As this era began, Luke Skywalker had unified the Jedi Order into a cohesive group of powerful Jedi Knights. It was a time of relative peace, yet darkness approached on the horizon. Now, Skywalker's descendants face new and resurgent threats to the galaxy, and to the balance of the Force.

The events in this story take place approximately 138 years after the events in *Star Wars:* Episode IV—*A New Hope*.

BOOK 2
OUTCASTS OF THE BROKEN RING

VOLUME II

SCRIPT
CORINNA BECHKO   GABRIEL HARDMAN

ART
BRIAN ALBERT THIES

COLORS
RACHELLE ROSENBERG

LETTERING
MICHAEL HEISLER

FRONT COVER ART
AGUSTIN ALESSIO

DARK HORSE BOOKS   LUCAS BOOKS

PRESIDENT AND PUBLISHER
MIKE RICHARDSON

COLLECTION DESIGNERS
JIMMY PRESLER AND **SANDY TANAKA**

EDITOR
RANDY STRADLEY

ASSISTANT EDITOR
FREDDYE LINS

NEIL HANKERSON EXECUTIVE VICE PRESIDENT   TOM WEDDLE CHIEF FINANCIAL OFFICER
RANDY STRADLEY VICE PRESIDENT OF PUBLISHING   MICHAEL MARTENS VICE PRESIDENT OF
BOOK TRADE SALES   ANITA NELSON VICE PRESIDENT OF BUSINESS AFFAIRS   SCOTT ALLIE
EDITOR IN CHIEF   MATT PARKINSON VICE PRESIDENT OF MARKETING   DAVID SCROGGY VICE
PRESIDENT OF PRODUCT DEVELOPMENT   DALE LaFOUNTAIN VICE PRESIDENT OF INFORMATION
TECHNOLOGY   DARLENE VOGEL SENIOR DIRECTOR OF PRINT, DESIGN, AND PRODUCTION
KEN LIZZI GENERAL COUNSEL   DAVEY ESTRADA EDITORIAL DIRECTOR   CHRIS WARNER SENIOR
BOOKS EDITOR   DIANA SCHUTZ EXECUTIVE EDITOR   CARY GRAZZINI DIRECTOR OF PRINT AND
DEVELOPMENT   LIA RIBACCHI ART DIRECTOR   CARA NIECE DIRECTOR OF SCHEDULING   TIM WIESCH
DIRECTOR OF INTERNATIONAL LICENSING   MARK BERNARDI DIRECTOR OF DIGITAL PUBLISHING

SPECIAL THANKS TO JENNIFER HEDDLE, LELAND CHEE, TROY ALDERS, CAROL ROEDER,
JANN MOORHEAD, AND DAVID ANDERMAN AT LUCAS LICENSING.

ART ON PAGES 2 AND 6 BY DAN PANOSIAN

This volume collects issues #6–#10 of the Dark Horse comic-book series *Star Wars: Legacy* Volume II.
Published by Dark Horse Books
A division of Dark Horse Comics, Inc.
10956 SE Main Street, Milwaukie, OR 97222

DarkHorse.com StarWars.com

International Licensing: 503-905-2377

To find a comics shop in your area, call the Comic Shop Locator Service toll-free at 1-888-266-4226.

Library of Congress Cataloging-in-Publication Data
Bechko, Corinna, 1973-
Star Wars Legacy II. Volume II, Book II, Outcasts of the broken ring / script, Corinna Bechko, Gabriel Hardman ; art, Brian
Albert Thies ; colors, Rachelle Rosenberg ; lettering, Michael Heisler ; front cover art, Agustin Alessio.
     pages cm
Summary: "Ania Solo and Imperial Knight Jao Assam break with the Galactic Triumvirate to track down the Sith Darth
Wredd. The trail leads Ania and Jao to a dead planet–and another Sith Lord and his army of pirates"– Provided by publisher.
ISBN 978-1-61655-310-4 (v. 2) – ISBN 978-1-61655-381-4 (v. 3)
1. Star Wars fiction–Comic books, strips, etc. 2. Graphic novels. I. Hardman, Gabriel. II. Title. III. Title: Outcasts of the broken
ring.
PN6728.S73B444 2014
741.5'973–dc23
                    2013050883

First edition: May 2014
ISBN 978-1-61655-310-4

10 9 8 7 6 5 4 3 2 1
Printed in China

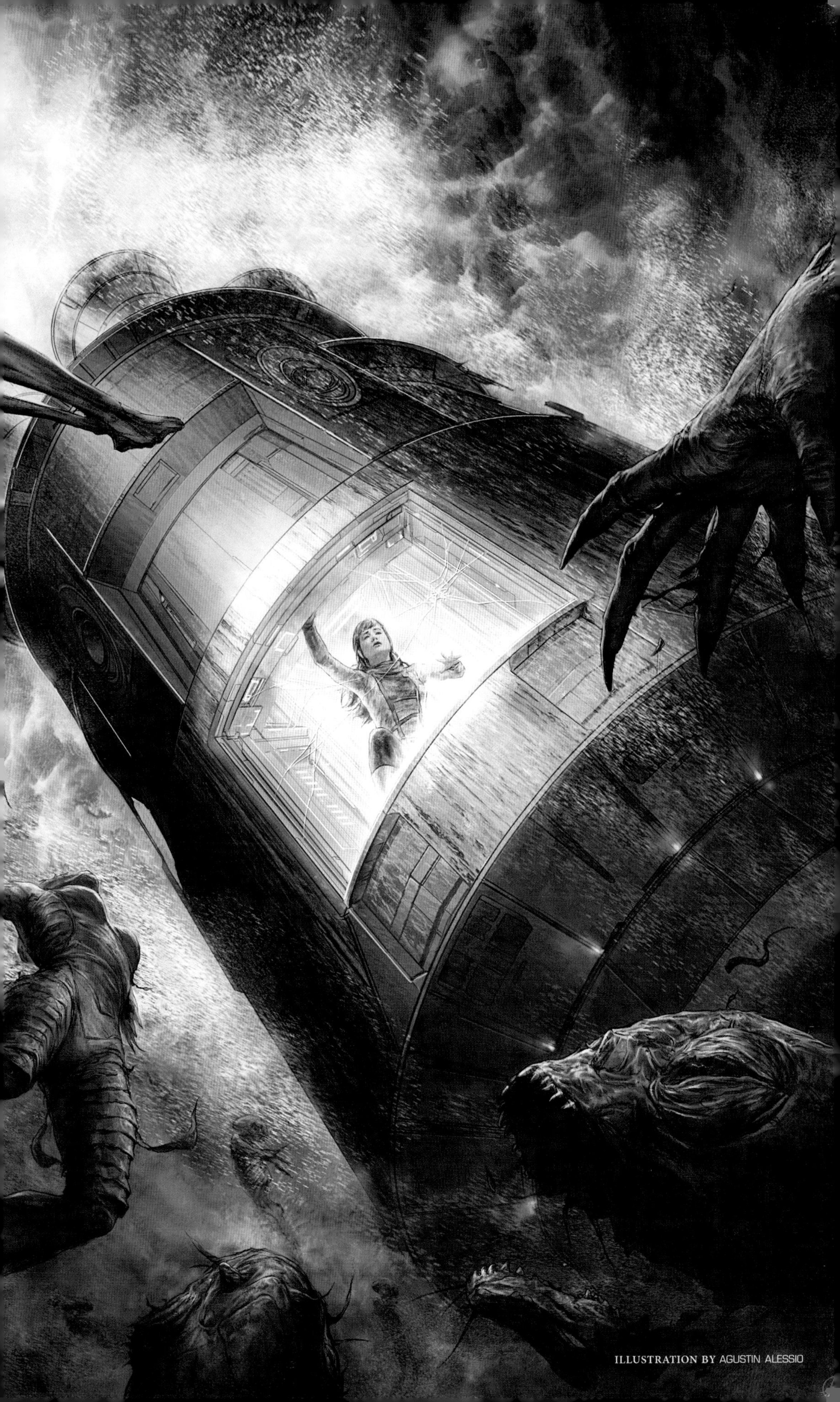

ILLUSTRATION BY AGUSTIN ALESSIO

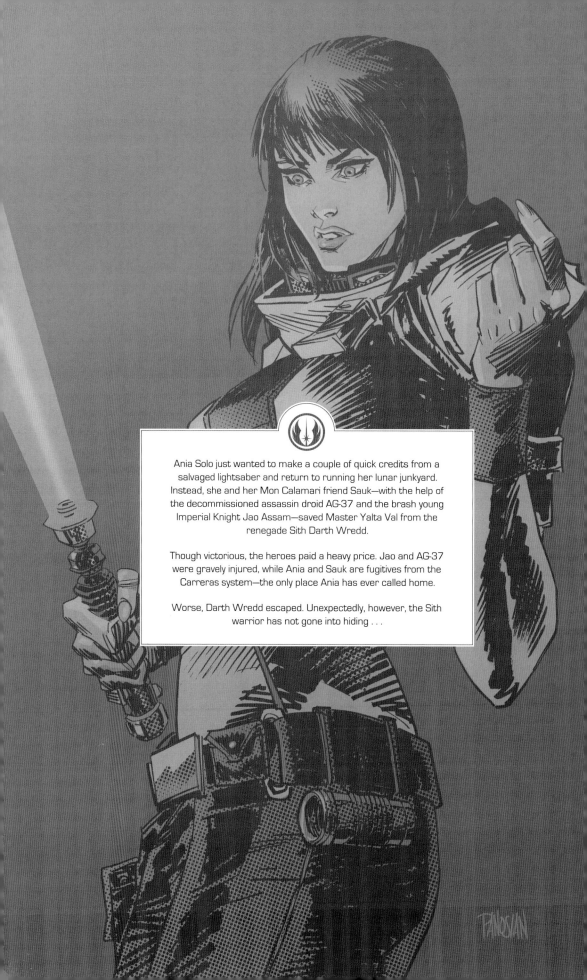

Ania Solo just wanted to make a couple of quick credits from a salvaged lightsaber and return to running her lunar junkyard. Instead, she and her Mon Calamari friend Sauk—with the help of the decommissioned assassin droid AG-37 and the brash young Imperial Knight Jao Assam—saved Master Yalta Val from the renegade Sith Darth Wredd.

Though victorious, the heroes paid a heavy price. Jao and AG-37 were gravely injured, while Ania and Sauk are fugitives from the Carreras system—the only place Ania has ever called home.

Worse, Darth Wredd escaped. Unexpectedly, however, the Sith warrior has not gone into hiding . . .

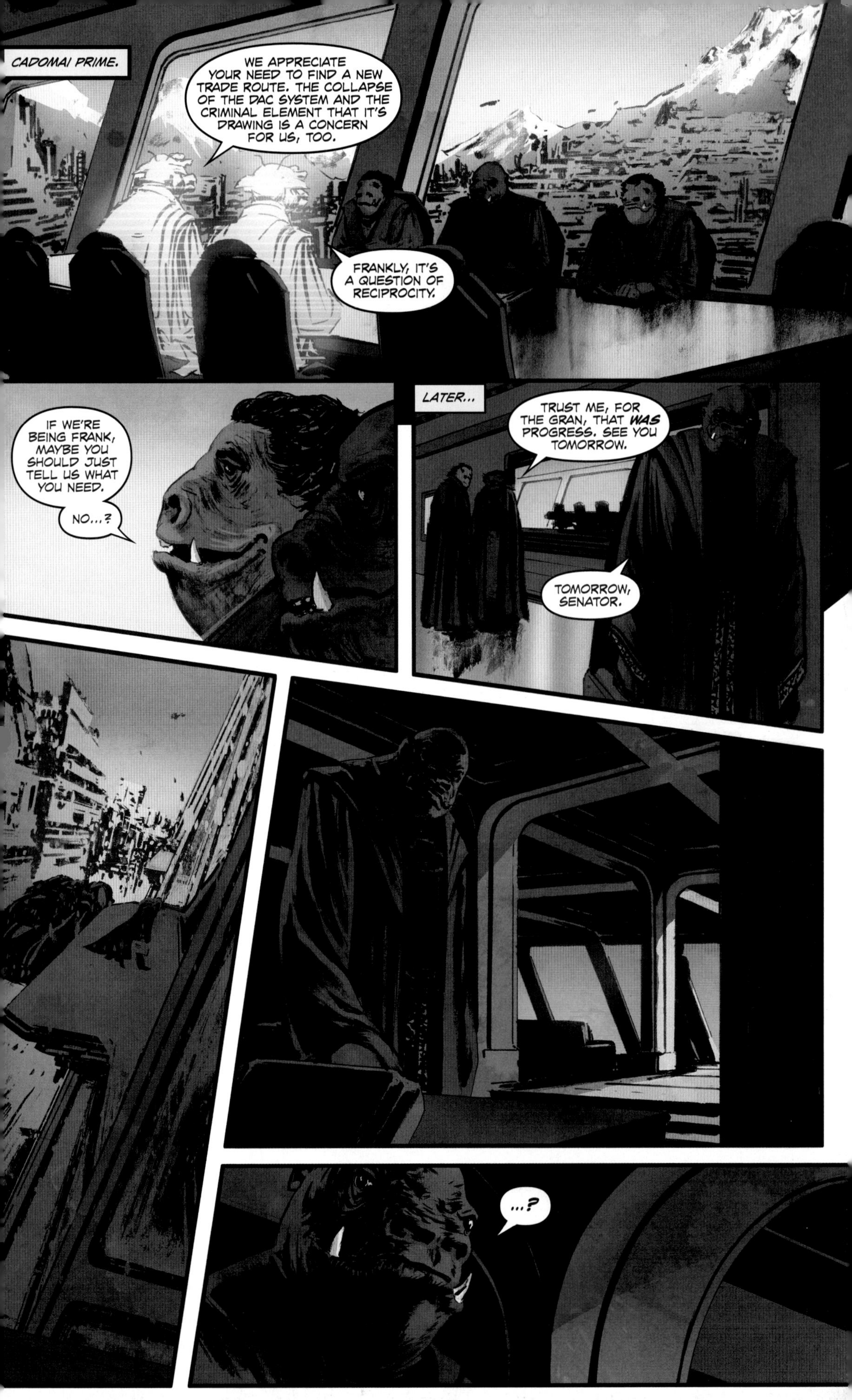

CADOMAI PRIME.
WE APPRECIATE YOUR NEED TO FIND A NEW TRADE ROUTE. THE COLLAPSE OF THE DAC SYSTEM AND THE CRIMINAL ELEMENT THAT IT'S DRAWING IS A CONCERN FOR US, TOO.
FRANKLY, IT'S A QUESTION OF RECIPROCITY.
IF WE'RE BEING FRANK, MAYBE YOU SHOULD JUST TELL US WHAT YOU NEED.
NO...?
LATER...
TRUST ME, FOR THE GRAN, THAT *WAS* PROGRESS. SEE YOU TOMORROW.
TOMORROW, SENATOR.
...?

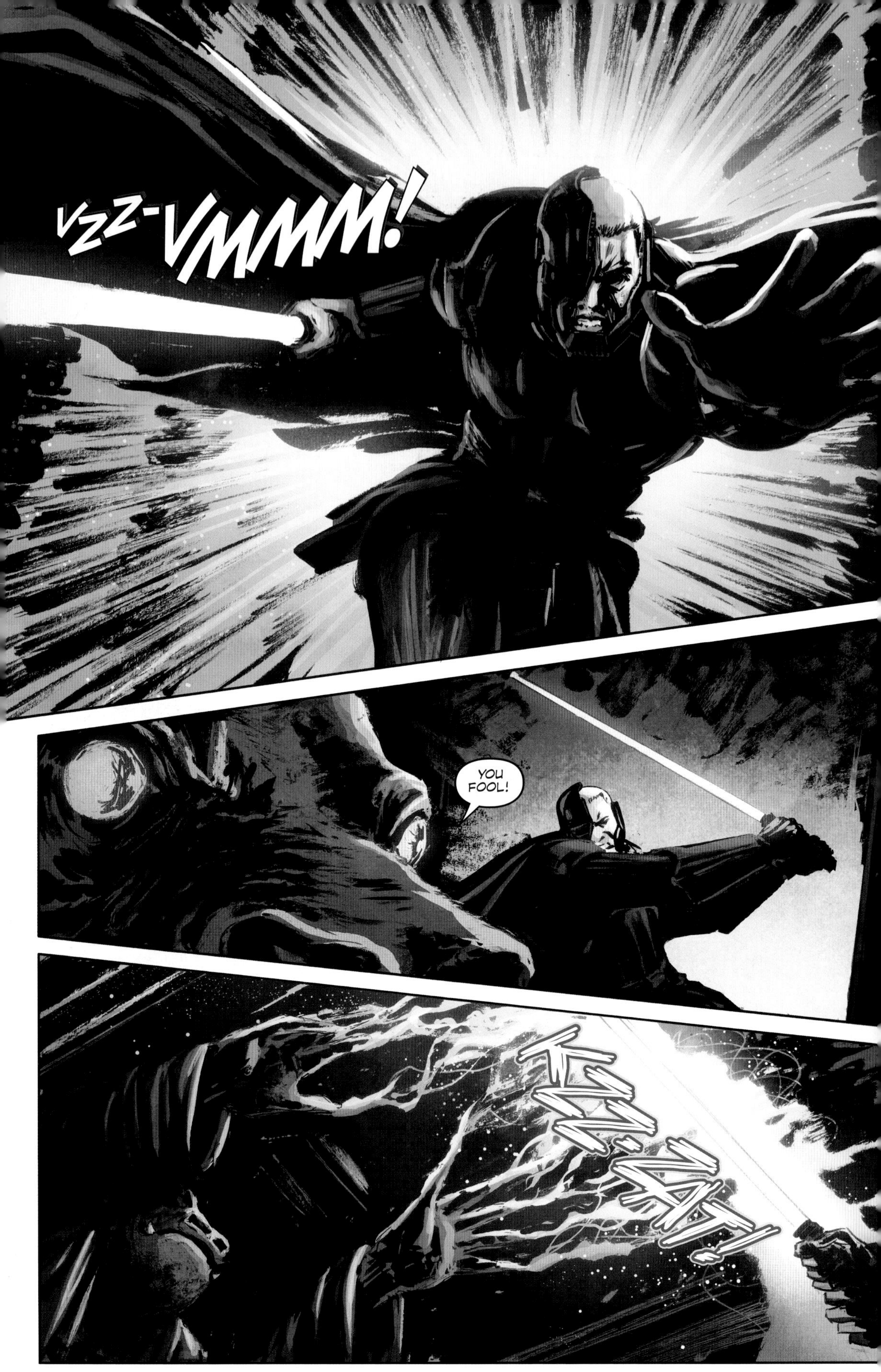
VZZ-VMMMM!
YOU FOOL!
KZZ-ZAT!

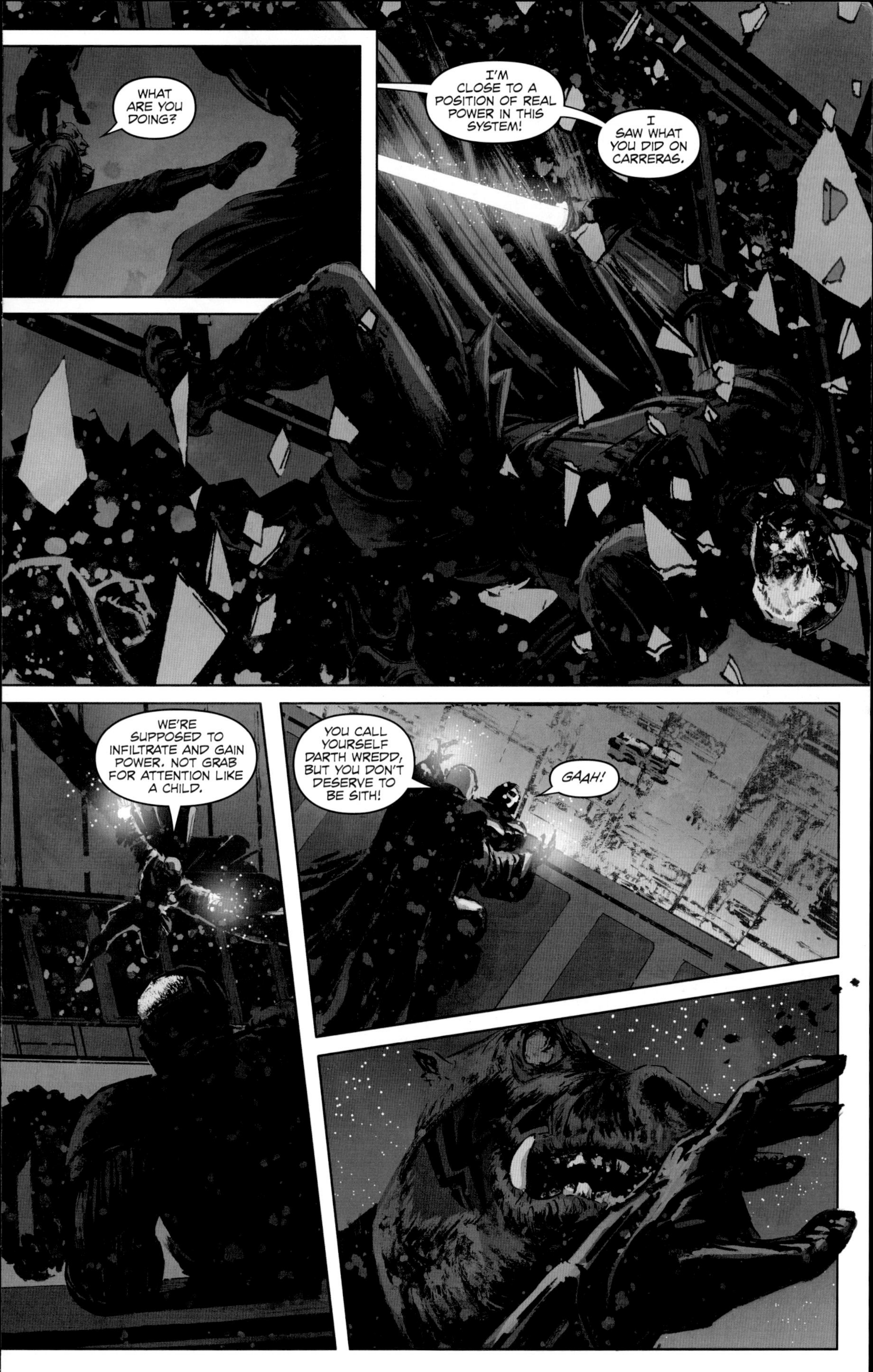
WHAT ARE YOU DOING?
I'M CLOSE TO A POSITION OF REAL POWER IN THIS SYSTEM!
I SAW WHAT YOU DID ON CARRERAS.
WE'RE SUPPOSED TO INFILTRATE AND GAIN POWER. NOT GRAB FOR ATTENTION LIKE A CHILD.
YOU CALL YOURSELF DARTH WREDD, BUT YOU DON'T DESERVE TO BE SITH!
GAAH!

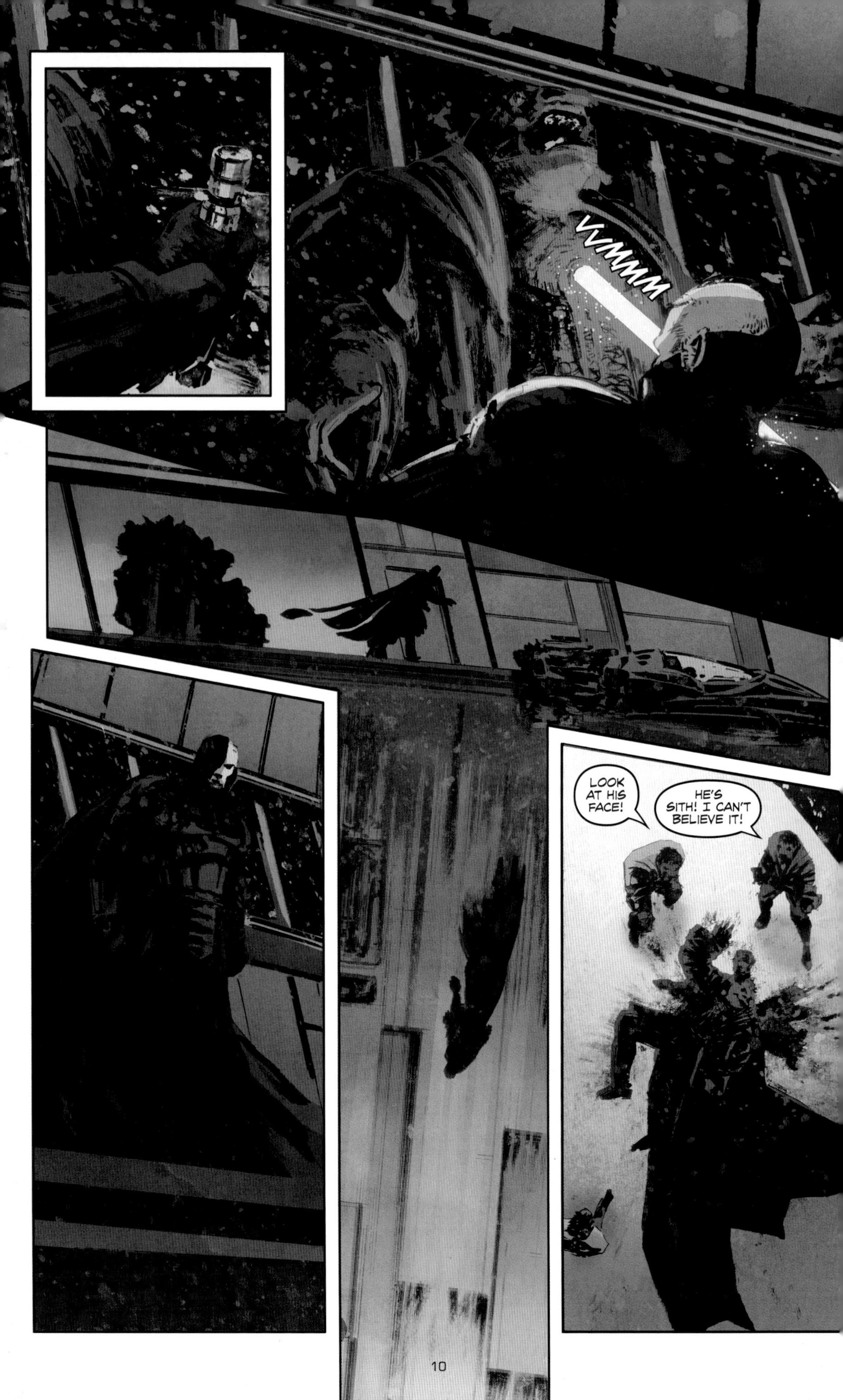
VVMMM
LOOK AT HIS FACE!
HE'S SITH! I CAN'T BELIEVE IT!

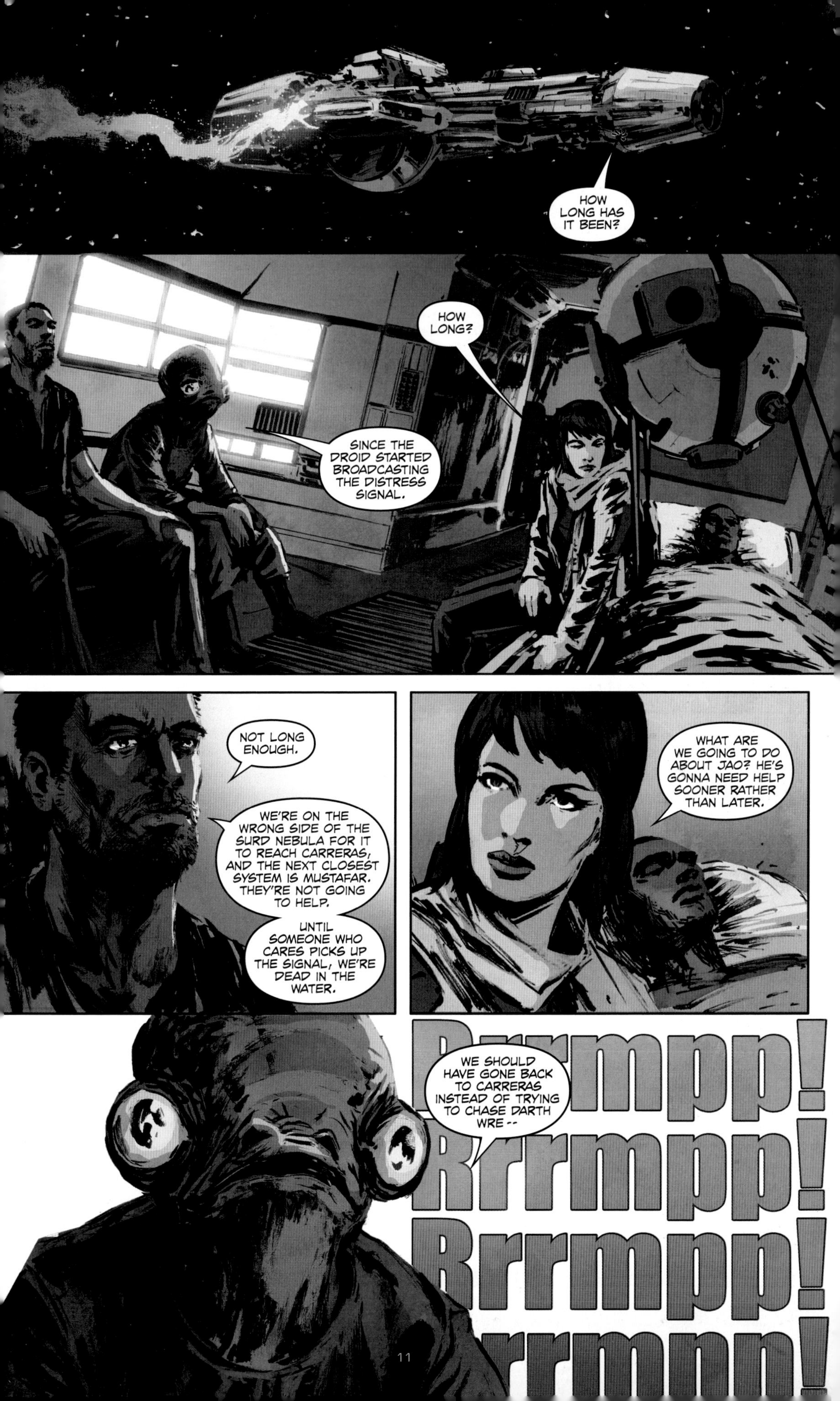

HOW LONG HAS IT BEEN?
HOW LONG?
SINCE THE DROID STARTED BROADCASTING THE DISTRESS SIGNAL.
NOT LONG ENOUGH.
WE'RE ON THE WRONG SIDE OF THE SURD NEBULA FOR IT TO REACH CARRERAS, AND THE NEXT CLOSEST SYSTEM IS MUSTAFAR. THEY'RE NOT GOING TO HELP.
UNTIL SOMEONE WHO CARES PICKS UP THE SIGNAL, WE'RE DEAD IN THE WATER.
WHAT ARE WE GOING TO DO ABOUT JAO? HE'S GONNA NEED HELP SOONER RATHER THAN LATER.
WE SHOULD HAVE GONE BACK TO CARRERAS INSTEAD OF TRYING TO CHASE DARTH WRE--
Rrrmpp!
Rrrmpp!
Rrrmpp!

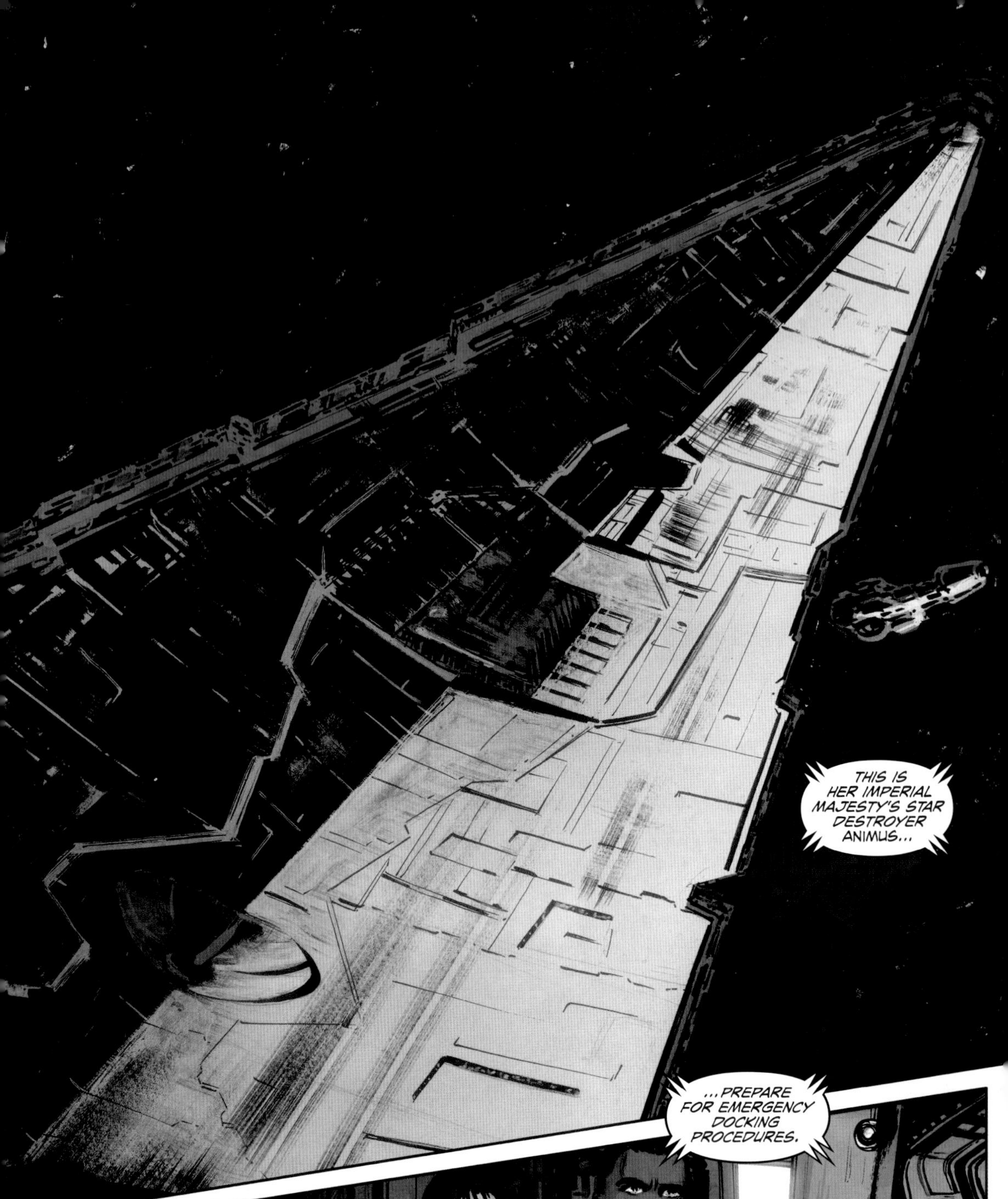
THIS IS HER IMPERIAL MAJESTY'S STAR DESTROYER ANIMUS...
...PREPARE FOR EMERGENCY DOCKING PROCEDURES.

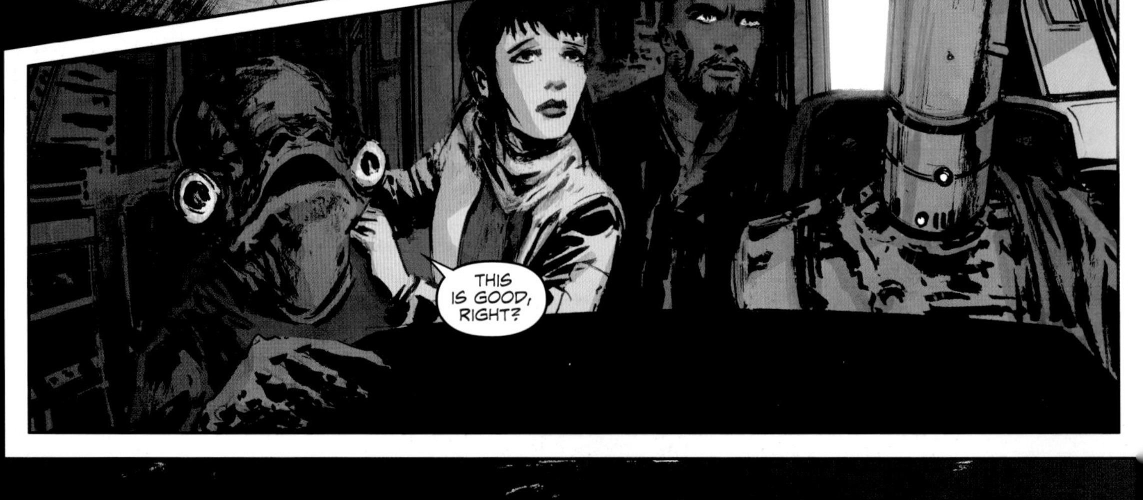
THIS IS GOOD, RIGHT?

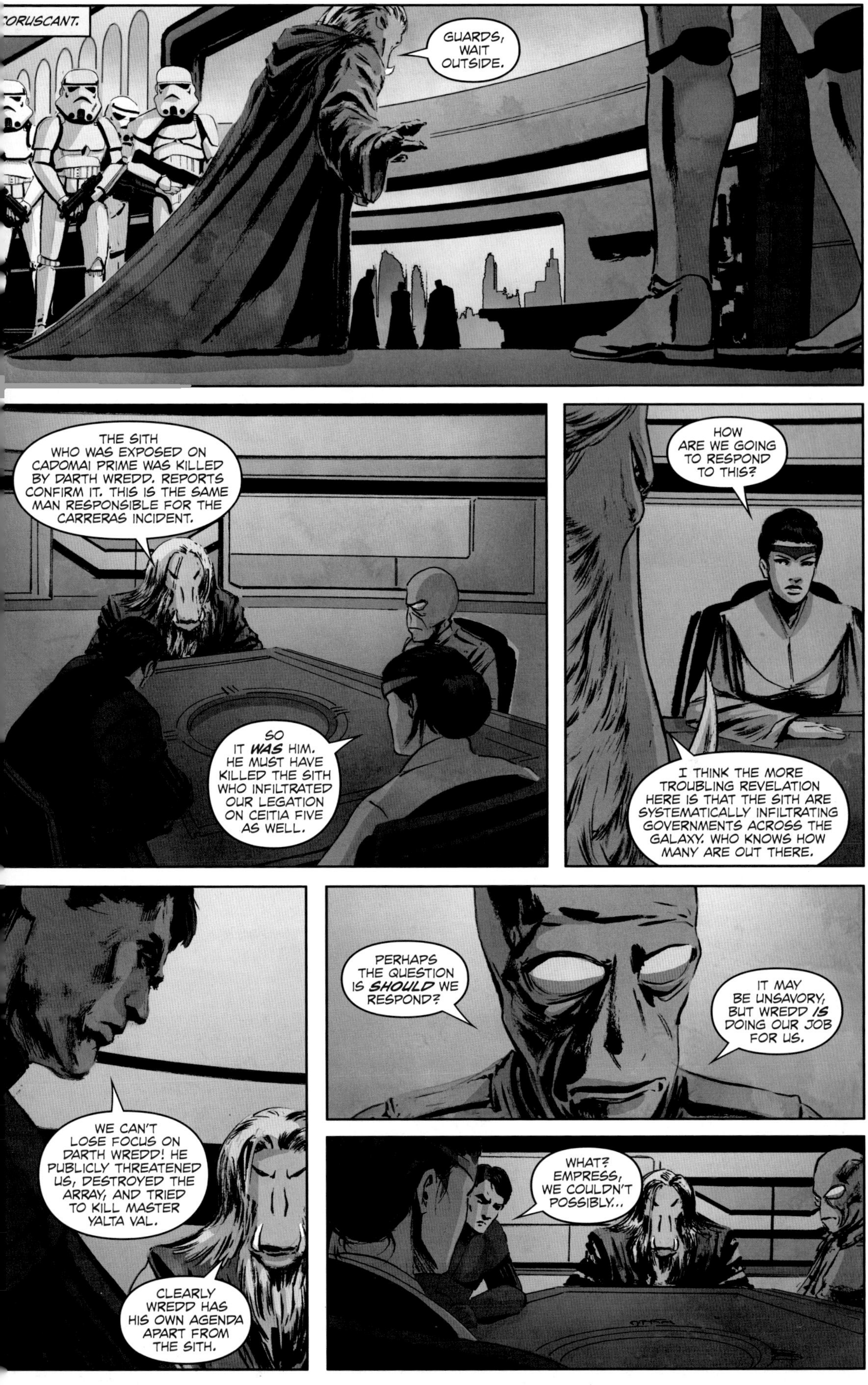
CORUSCANT.
GUARDS, WAIT OUTSIDE.
THE SITH WHO WAS EXPOSED ON CADOMAI PRIME WAS KILLED BY DARTH WREDD. REPORTS CONFIRM IT. THIS IS THE SAME MAN RESPONSIBLE FOR THE CARRERAS INCIDENT.
SO IT ***WAS*** HIM. HE MUST HAVE KILLED THE SITH WHO INFILTRATED OUR LEGATION ON CEITIA FIVE AS WELL.
HOW ARE WE GOING TO RESPOND TO THIS?
I THINK THE MORE TROUBLING REVELATION HERE IS THAT THE SITH ARE SYSTEMATICALLY INFILTRATING GOVERNMENTS ACROSS THE GALAXY. WHO KNOWS HOW MANY ARE OUT THERE.
WE CAN'T LOSE FOCUS ON DARTH WREDD! HE PUBLICLY THREATENED US, DESTROYED THE ARRAY, AND TRIED TO KILL MASTER YALTA VAL.
CLEARLY WREDD HAS HIS OWN AGENDA APART FROM THE SITH.
PERHAPS THE QUESTION IS ***SHOULD*** WE RESPOND?
IT MAY BE UNSAVORY, BUT WREDD ***IS*** DOING OUR JOB FOR US.
WHAT? EMPRESS, WE COULDN'T POSSIBLY...

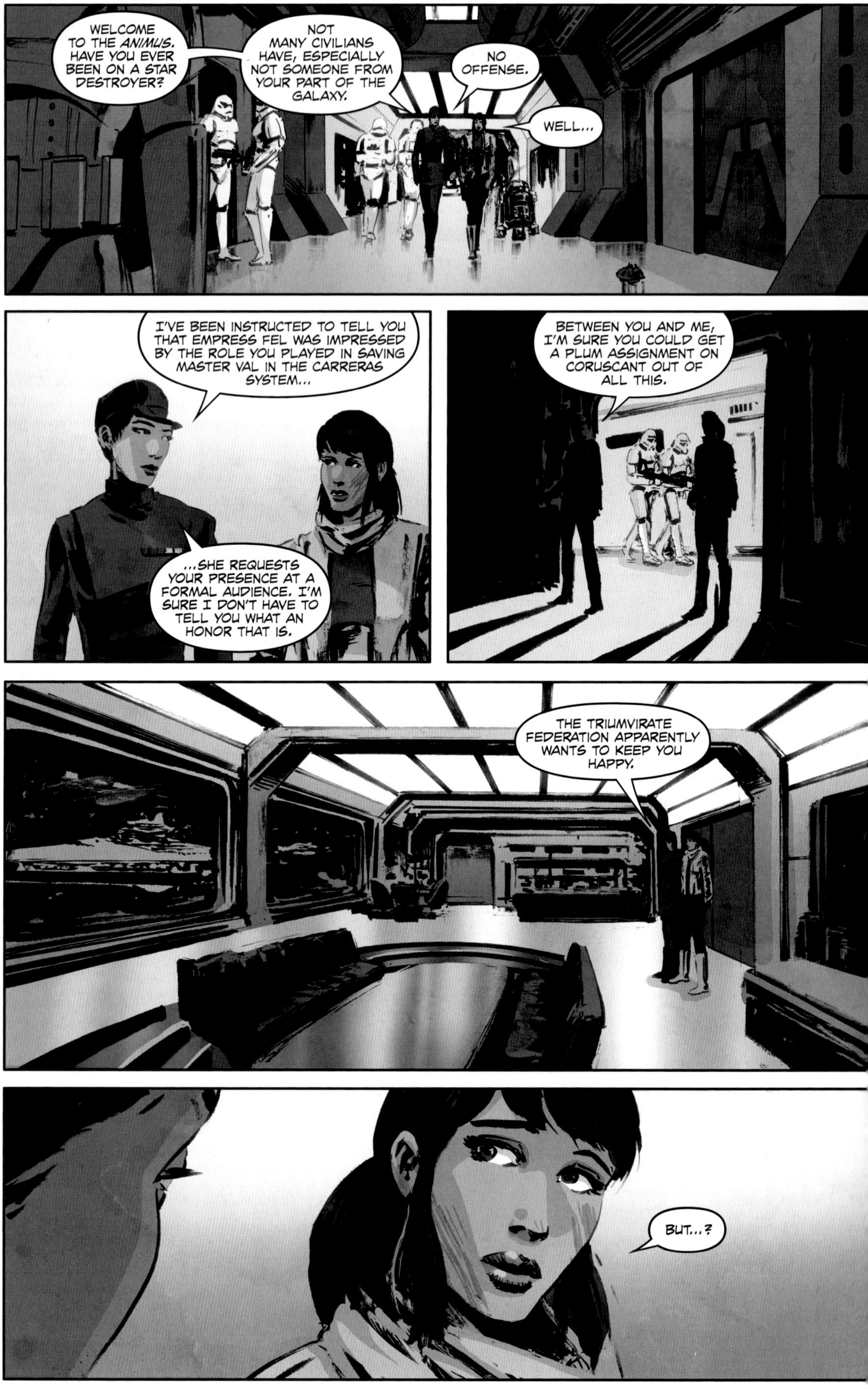
WELCOME TO THE *ANIMUS*. HAVE YOU EVER BEEN ON A STAR DESTROYER?
NOT MANY CIVILIANS HAVE, ESPECIALLY NOT SOMEONE FROM YOUR PART OF THE GALAXY.
NO OFFENSE.
WELL...
I'VE BEEN INSTRUCTED TO TELL YOU THAT EMPRESS FEL WAS IMPRESSED BY THE ROLE YOU PLAYED IN SAVING MASTER VAL IN THE CARRERAS SYSTEM...
...SHE REQUESTS YOUR PRESENCE AT A FORMAL AUDIENCE. I'M SURE I DON'T HAVE TO TELL YOU WHAT AN HONOR THAT IS.
BETWEEN YOU AND ME, I'M SURE YOU COULD GET A PLUM ASSIGNMENT ON CORUSCANT OUT OF ALL THIS.
THE TRIUMVIRATE FEDERATION APPARENTLY WANTS TO KEEP YOU HAPPY.
BUT...?

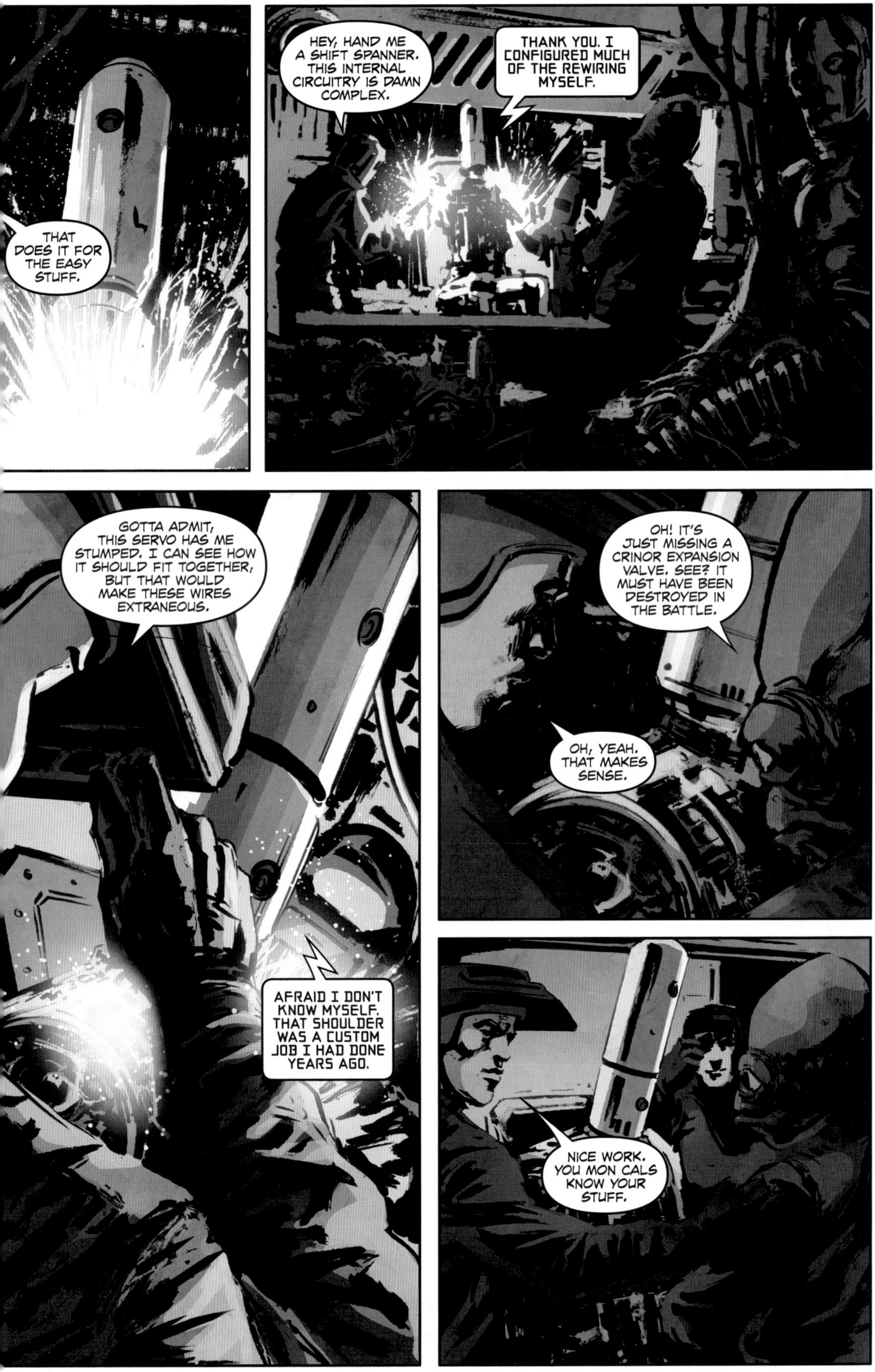
THAT DOES IT FOR THE EASY STUFF.
HEY, HAND ME A SHIFT SPANNER. THIS INTERNAL CIRCUITRY IS DAMN COMPLEX.
THANK YOU. I CONFIGURED MUCH OF THE REWIRING MYSELF.
GOTTA ADMIT, THIS SERVO HAS ME STUMPED. I CAN SEE HOW IT SHOULD FIT TOGETHER, BUT THAT WOULD MAKE THESE WIRES EXTRANEOUS.
AFRAID I DON'T KNOW MYSELF. THAT SHOULDER WAS A CUSTOM JOB I HAD DONE YEARS AGO.
OH! IT'S JUST MISSING A CRINOR EXPANSION VALVE. SEE? IT MUST HAVE BEEN DESTROYED IN THE BATTLE.
OH, YEAH. THAT MAKES SENSE.
NICE WORK. YOU MON CALS KNOW YOUR STUFF.

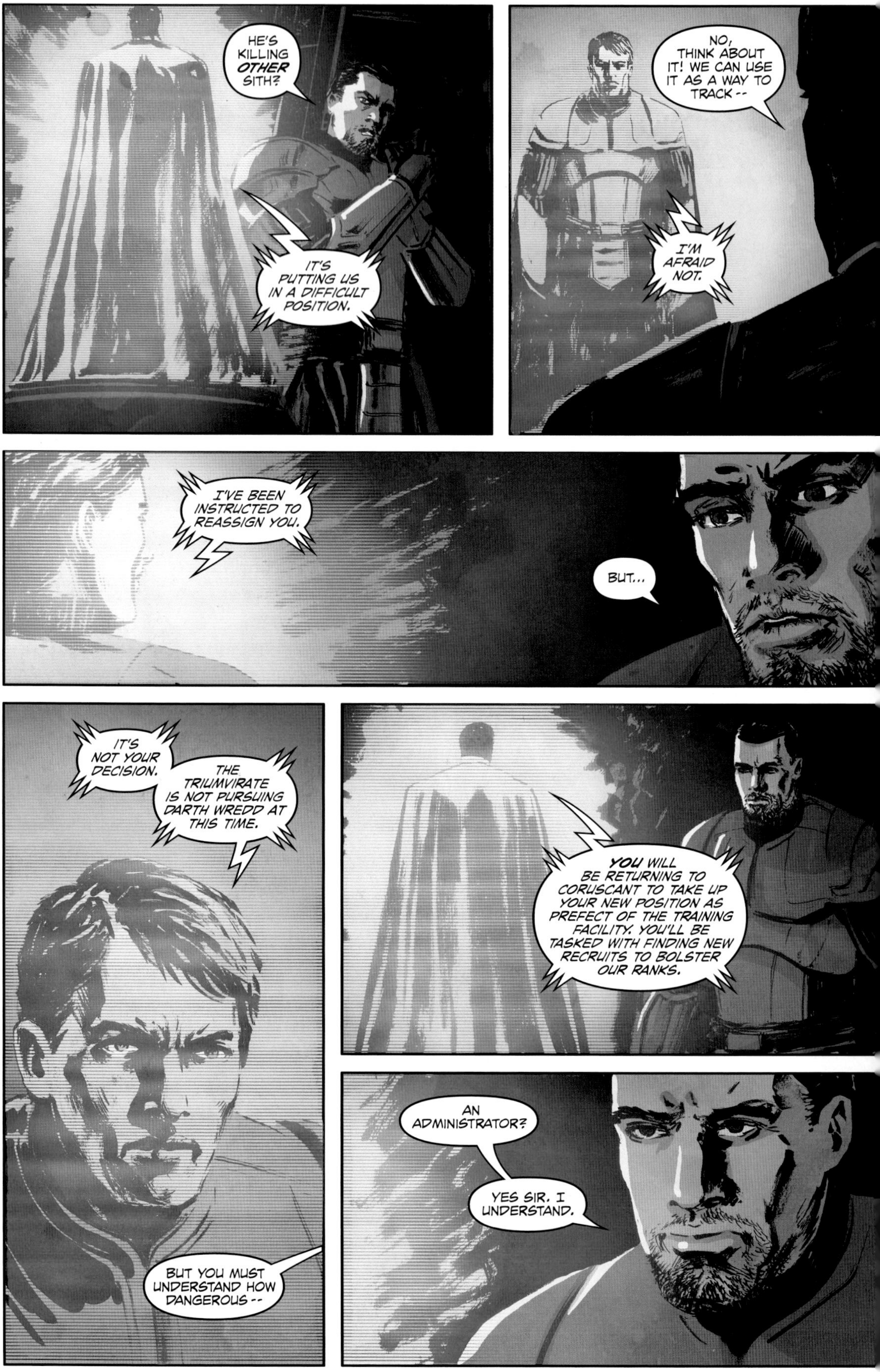
HE'S KILLING OTHER SITH?
IT'S PUTTING US IN A DIFFICULT POSITION.
NO, THINK ABOUT IT! WE CAN USE IT AS A WAY TO TRACK --
I'M AFRAID NOT.
I'VE BEEN INSTRUCTED TO REASSIGN YOU.
BUT...
IT'S NOT YOUR DECISION.
THE TRIUMVIRATE IS NOT PURSUING DARTH WREDD AT THIS TIME.
BUT YOU MUST UNDERSTAND HOW DANGEROUS --
YOU WILL BE RETURNING TO CORUSCANT TO TAKE UP YOUR NEW POSITION AS PREFECT OF THE TRAINING FACILITY. YOU'LL BE TASKED WITH FINDING NEW RECRUITS TO BOLSTER OUR RANKS.
AN ADMINISTRATOR?
YES SIR. I UNDERSTAND.

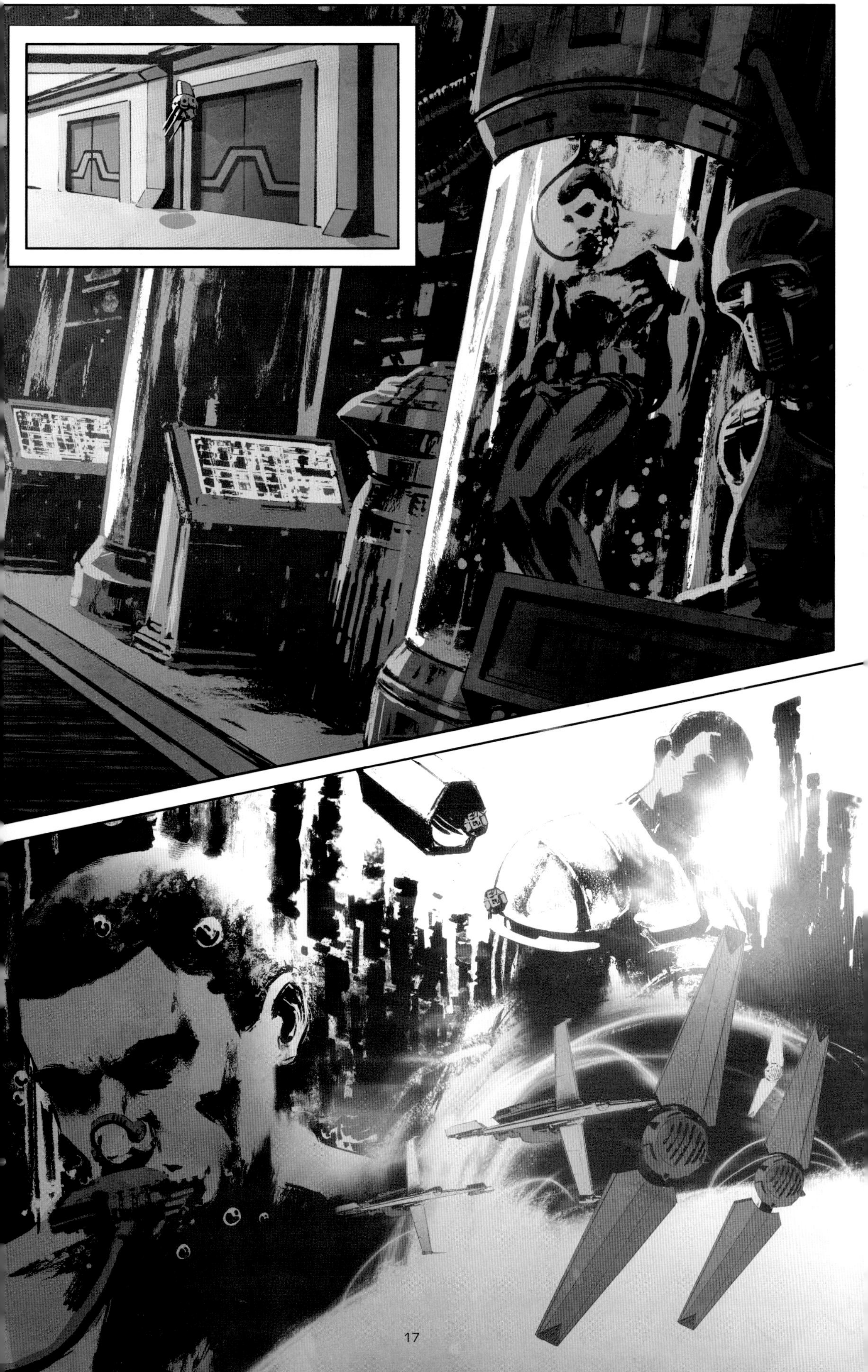

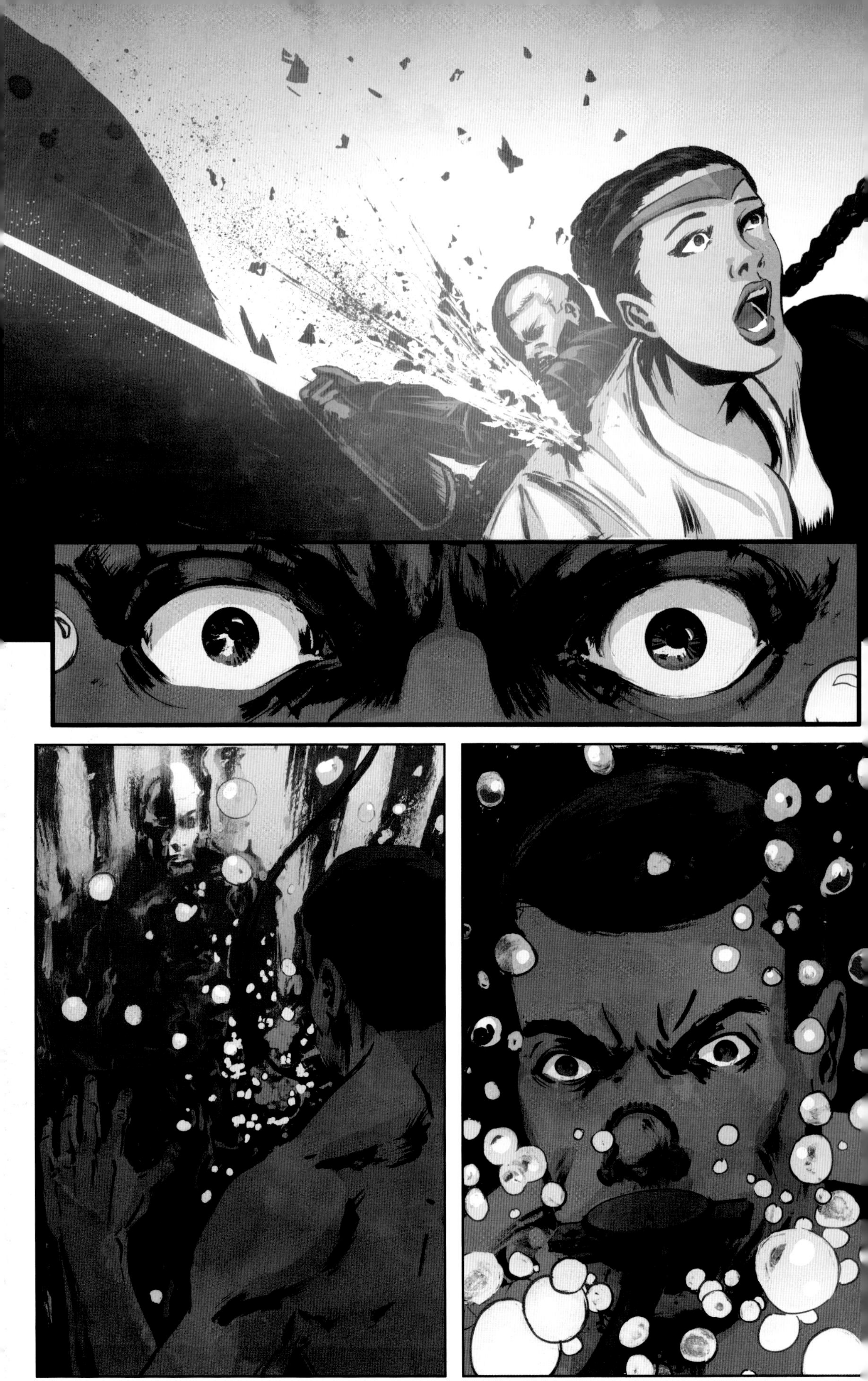

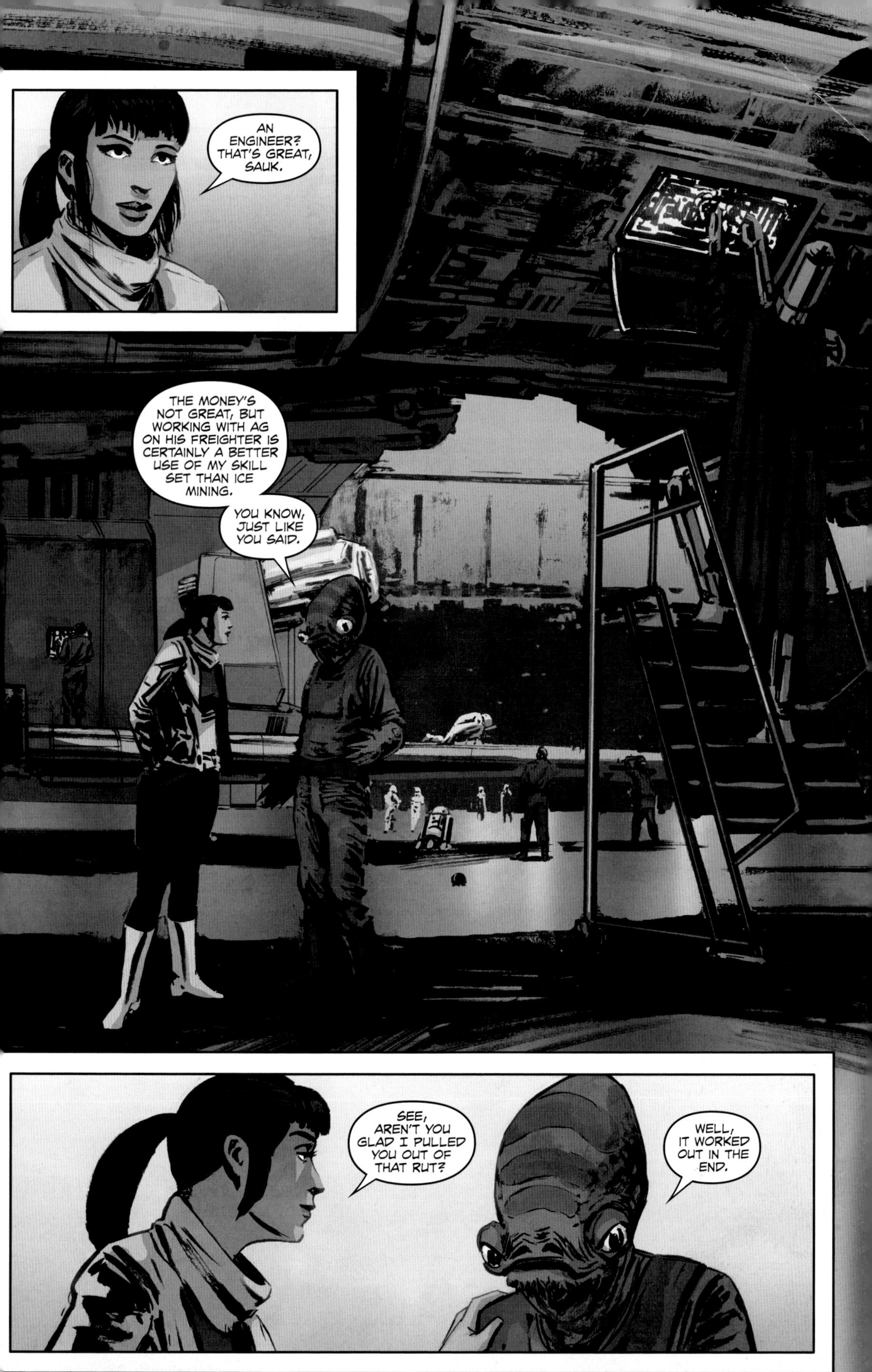
AN ENGINEER? THAT'S GREAT, SAUK.
THE MONEY'S NOT GREAT, BUT WORKING WITH AG ON HIS FREIGHTER IS CERTAINLY A BETTER USE OF MY SKILL SET THAN ICE MINING.
YOU KNOW, JUST LIKE YOU SAID.
SEE, AREN'T YOU GLAD I PULLED YOU OUT OF THAT RUT?
WELL, IT WORKED OUT IN THE END.

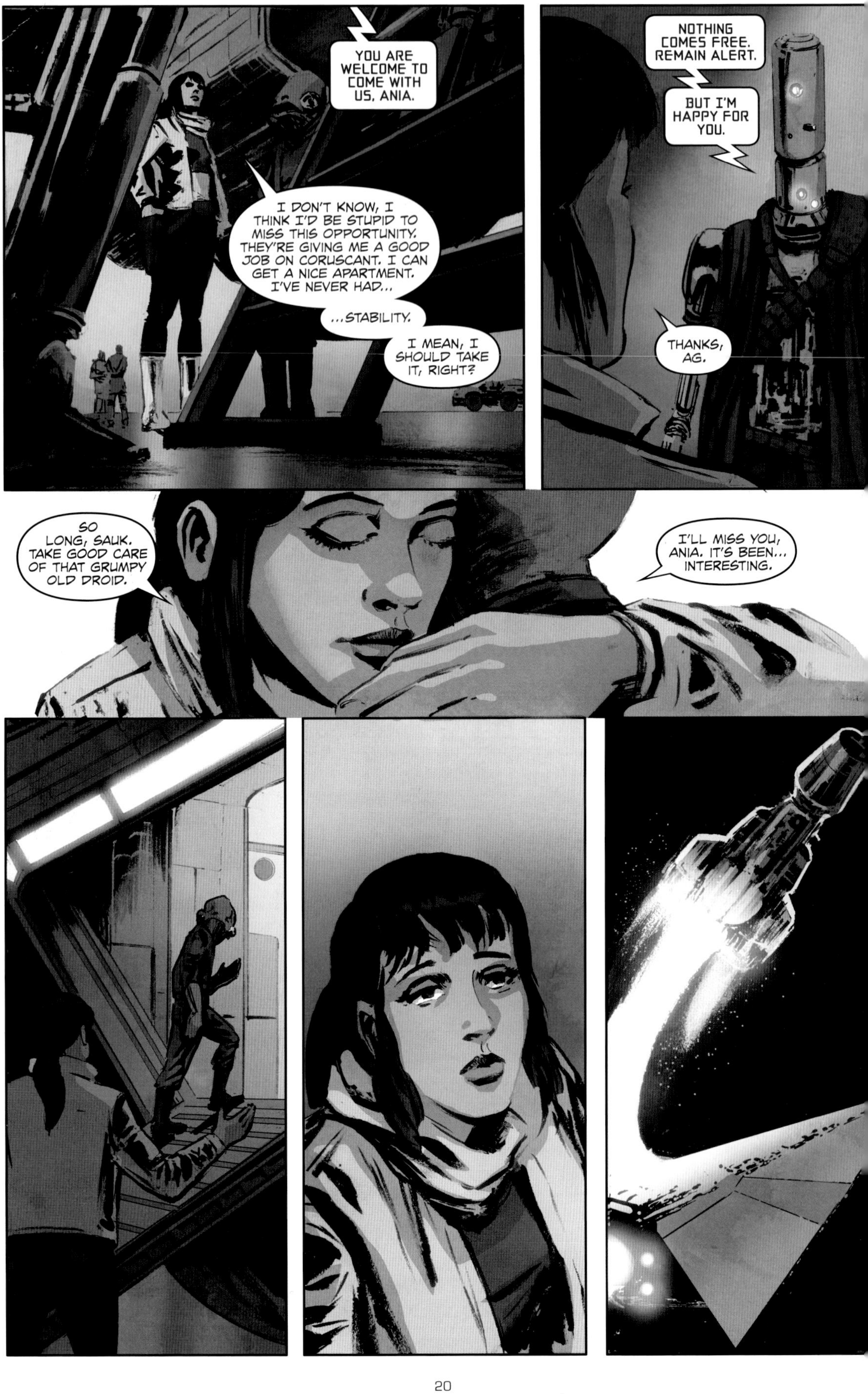
YOU ARE WELCOME TO COME WITH US, ANIA.
I DON'T KNOW, I THINK I'D BE STUPID TO MISS THIS OPPORTUNITY. THEY'RE GIVING ME A GOOD JOB ON CORUSCANT. I CAN GET A NICE APARTMENT. I'VE NEVER HAD...
...STABILITY.
I MEAN, I SHOULD TAKE IT, RIGHT?
NOTHING COMES FREE. REMAIN ALERT.
BUT I'M HAPPY FOR YOU.
THANKS, AG.
SO LONG, SAUK. TAKE GOOD CARE OF THAT GRUMPY OLD DROID.
I'LL MISS YOU, ANIA. IT'S BEEN... INTERESTING.

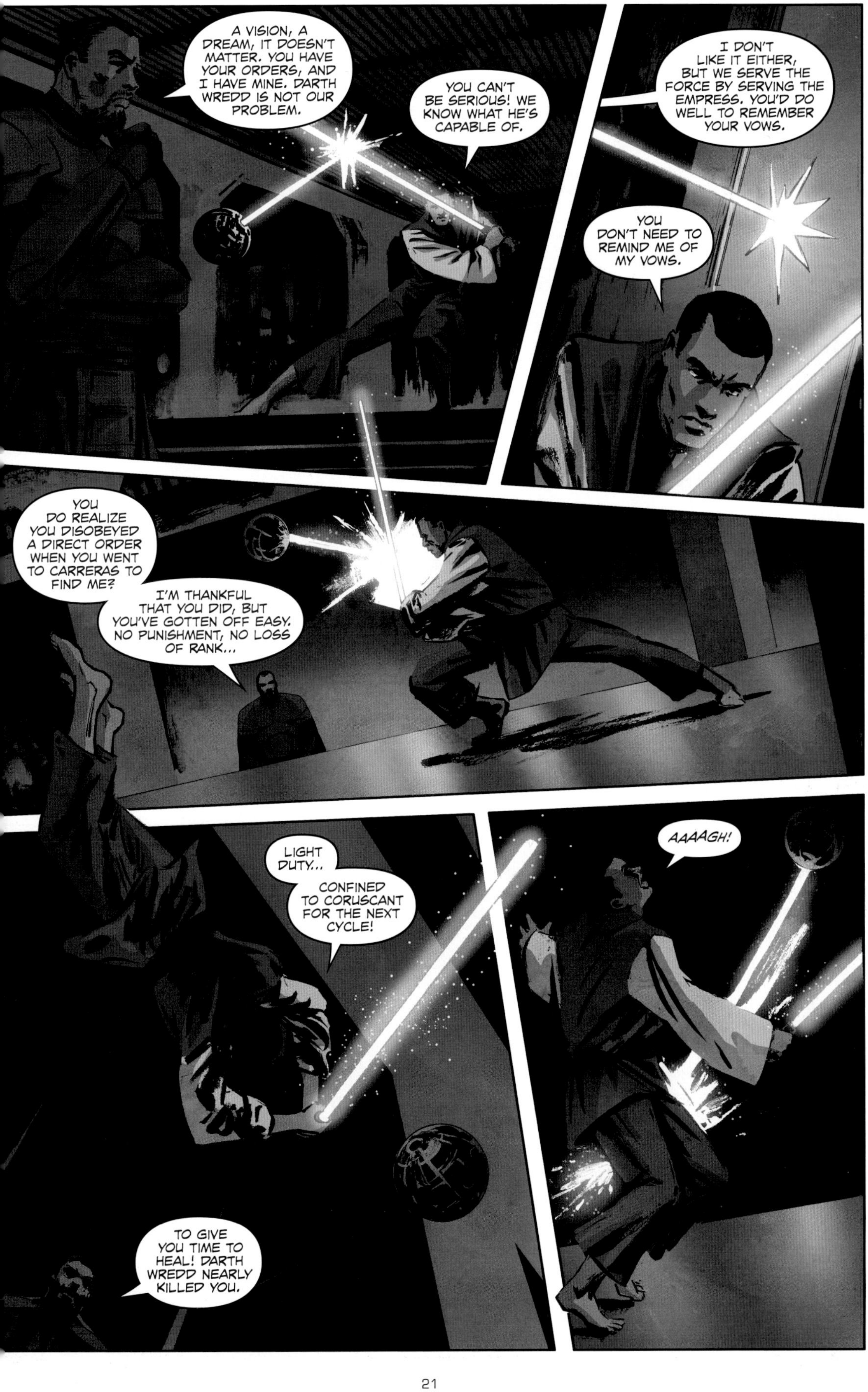

A VISION, A DREAM, IT DOESN'T MATTER. YOU HAVE YOUR ORDERS, AND I HAVE MINE. DARTH WREDD IS NOT OUR PROBLEM.
YOU CAN'T BE SERIOUS! WE KNOW WHAT HE'S CAPABLE OF.
I DON'T LIKE IT EITHER, BUT WE SERVE THE FORCE BY SERVING THE EMPRESS. YOU'D DO WELL TO REMEMBER YOUR VOWS.
YOU DON'T NEED TO REMIND ME OF MY VOWS.
YOU DO REALIZE YOU DISOBEYED A DIRECT ORDER WHEN YOU WENT TO CARRERAS TO FIND ME?
I'M THANKFUL THAT YOU DID, BUT YOU'VE GOTTEN OFF EASY. NO PUNISHMENT, NO LOSS OF RANK...
LIGHT DUTY...
CONFINED TO CORUSCANT FOR THE NEXT CYCLE!
TO GIVE YOU TIME TO HEAL! DARTH WREDD NEARLY KILLED YOU.
AAAAGH!

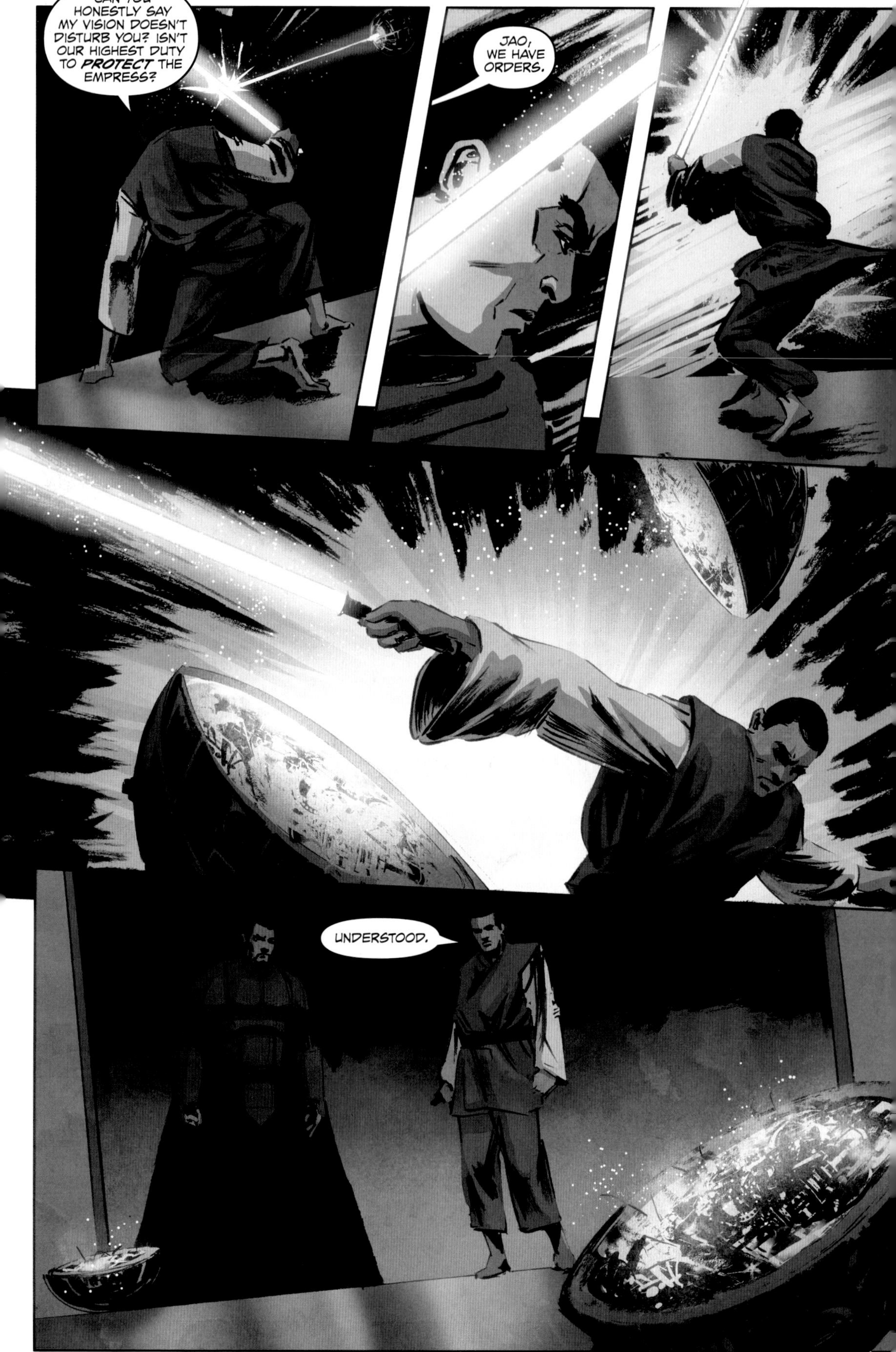
CAN YOU HONESTLY SAY MY VISION DOESN'T DISTURB YOU? ISN'T OUR HIGHEST DUTY TO PROTECT THE EMPRESS?
JAO, WE HAVE ORDERS.
UNDERSTOOD.

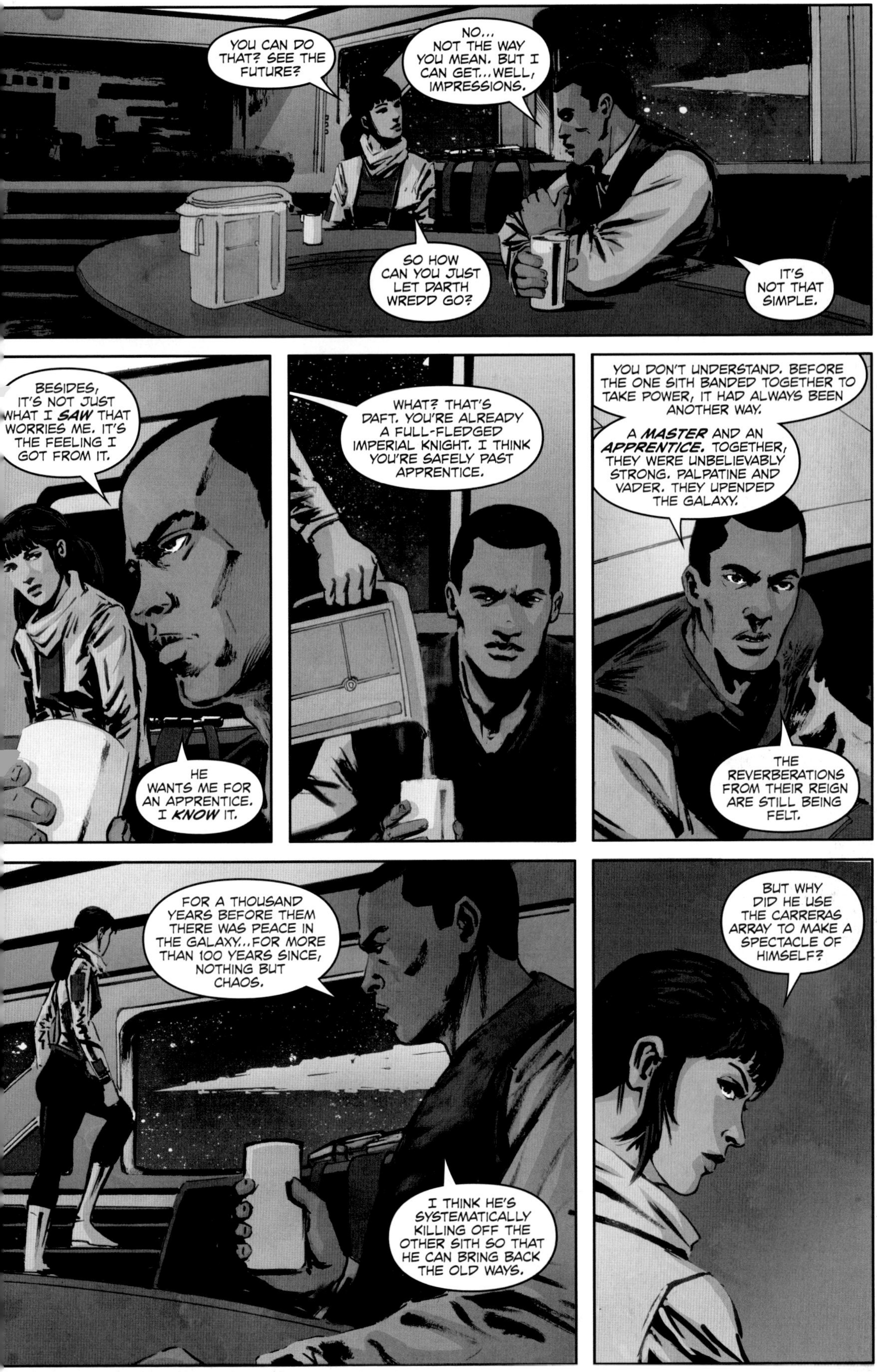
YOU CAN DO THAT? SEE THE FUTURE?
NO... NOT THE WAY YOU MEAN. BUT I CAN GET...WELL, IMPRESSIONS.
SO HOW CAN YOU JUST LET DARTH WREDD GO?
IT'S NOT THAT SIMPLE.
BESIDES, IT'S NOT JUST WHAT I SAW THAT WORRIES ME. IT'S THE FEELING I GOT FROM IT.
HE WANTS ME FOR AN APPRENTICE. I KNOW IT.
WHAT? THAT'S DAFT. YOU'RE ALREADY A FULL-FLEDGED IMPERIAL KNIGHT. I THINK YOU'RE SAFELY PAST APPRENTICE.
YOU DON'T UNDERSTAND. BEFORE THE ONE SITH BANDED TOGETHER TO TAKE POWER, IT HAD ALWAYS BEEN ANOTHER WAY.
A MASTER AND AN APPRENTICE. TOGETHER, THEY WERE UNBELIEVABLY STRONG. PALPATINE AND VADER. THEY UPENDED THE GALAXY.
THE REVERBERATIONS FROM THEIR REIGN ARE STILL BEING FELT.
FOR A THOUSAND YEARS BEFORE THEM THERE WAS PEACE IN THE GALAXY...FOR MORE THAN 100 YEARS SINCE, NOTHING BUT CHAOS.
I THINK HE'S SYSTEMATICALLY KILLING OFF THE OTHER SITH SO THAT HE CAN BRING BACK THE OLD WAYS.
BUT WHY DID HE USE THE CARRERAS ARRAY TO MAKE A SPECTACLE OF HIMSELF?

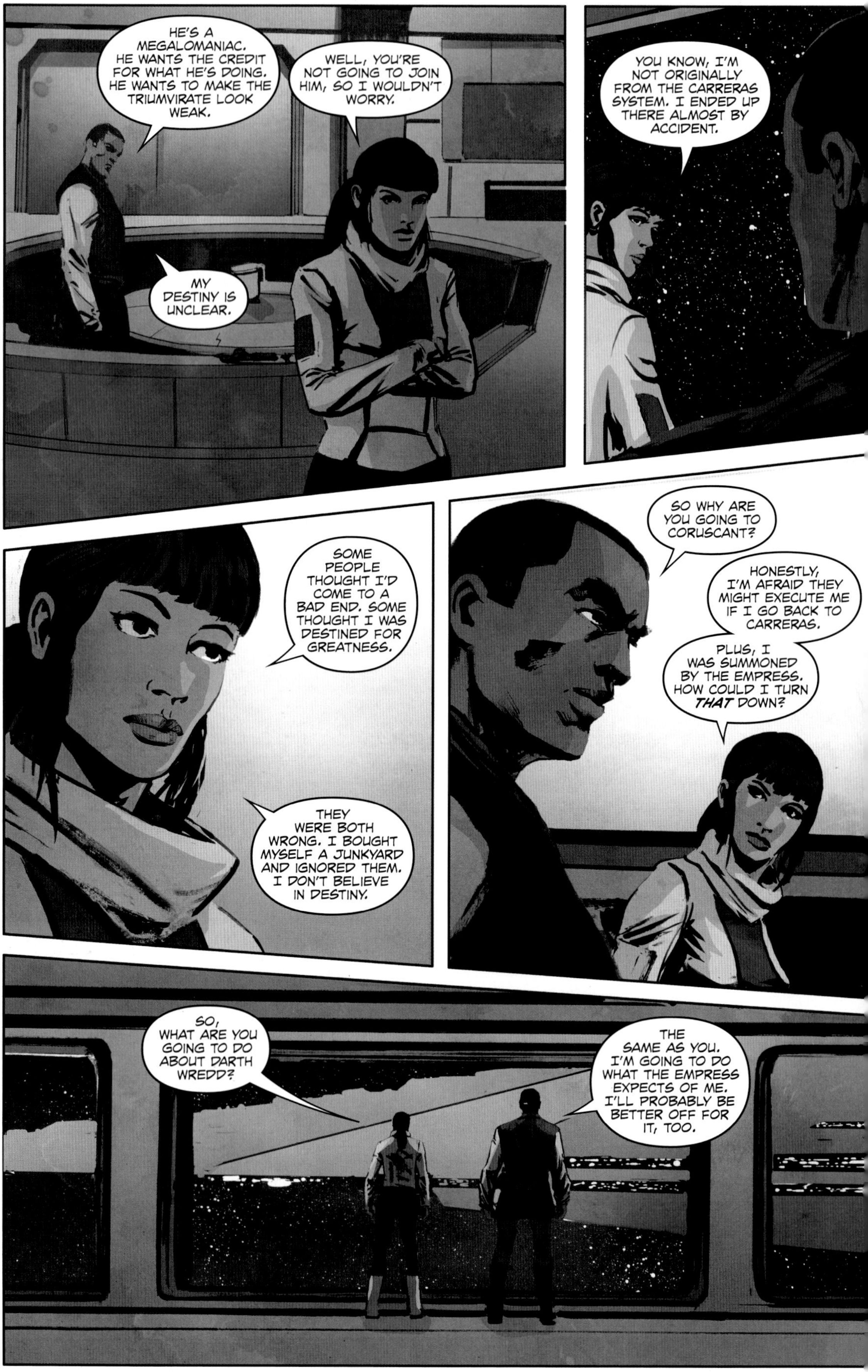
HE'S A MEGALOMANIAC. HE WANTS THE CREDIT FOR WHAT HE'S DOING. HE WANTS TO MAKE THE TRIUMVIRATE LOOK WEAK.
WELL, YOU'RE NOT GOING TO JOIN HIM, SO I WOULDN'T WORRY.
MY DESTINY IS UNCLEAR.
YOU KNOW, I'M NOT ORIGINALLY FROM THE CARRERAS SYSTEM. I ENDED UP THERE ALMOST BY ACCIDENT.
SOME PEOPLE THOUGHT I'D COME TO A BAD END. SOME THOUGHT I WAS DESTINED FOR GREATNESS.
THEY WERE BOTH WRONG. I BOUGHT MYSELF A JUNKYARD AND IGNORED THEM. I DON'T BELIEVE IN DESTINY.
SO WHY ARE YOU GOING TO CORUSCANT?
HONESTLY, I'M AFRAID THEY MIGHT EXECUTE ME IF I GO BACK TO CARRERAS.
PLUS, I WAS SUMMONED BY THE EMPRESS. HOW COULD I TURN *THAT* DOWN?
SO, WHAT ARE YOU GOING TO DO ABOUT DARTH WREDD?
THE SAME AS YOU. I'M GOING TO DO WHAT THE EMPRESS EXPECTS OF ME. I'LL PROBABLY BE BETTER OFF FOR IT, TOO.

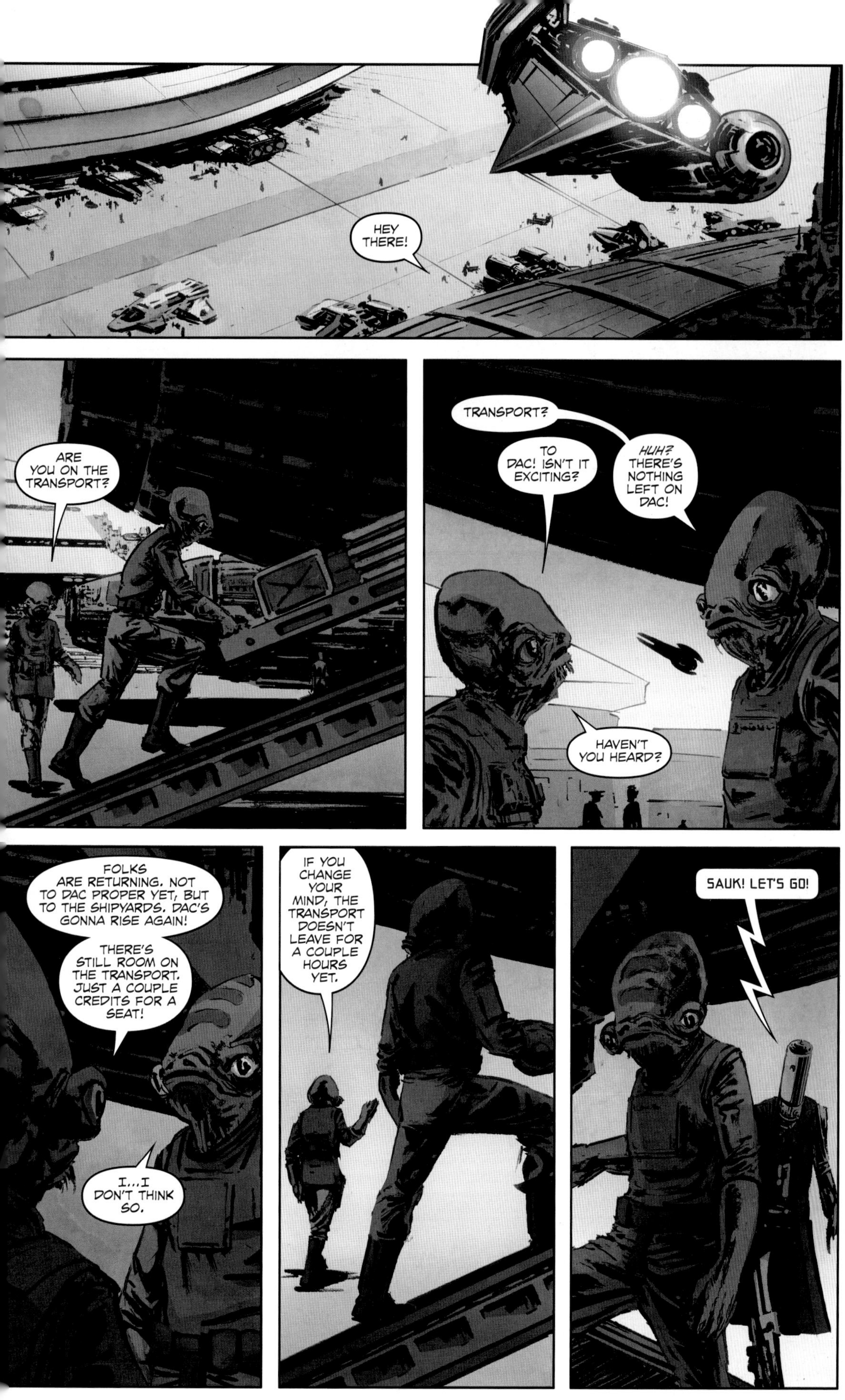
HEY THERE!
ARE YOU ON THE TRANSPORT?
TRANSPORT?
HUH? THERE'S NOTHING LEFT ON DAC!
TO DAC! ISN'T IT EXCITING?
HAVEN'T YOU HEARD?
FOLKS ARE RETURNING. NOT TO DAC PROPER YET, BUT TO THE SHIPYARDS. DAC'S GONNA RISE AGAIN!
THERE'S STILL ROOM ON THE TRANSPORT. JUST A COUPLE CREDITS FOR A SEAT!
I...I DON'T THINK SO.
IF YOU CHANGE YOUR MIND, THE TRANSPORT DOESN'T LEAVE FOR A COUPLE HOURS YET.
SAUK! LET'S GO!

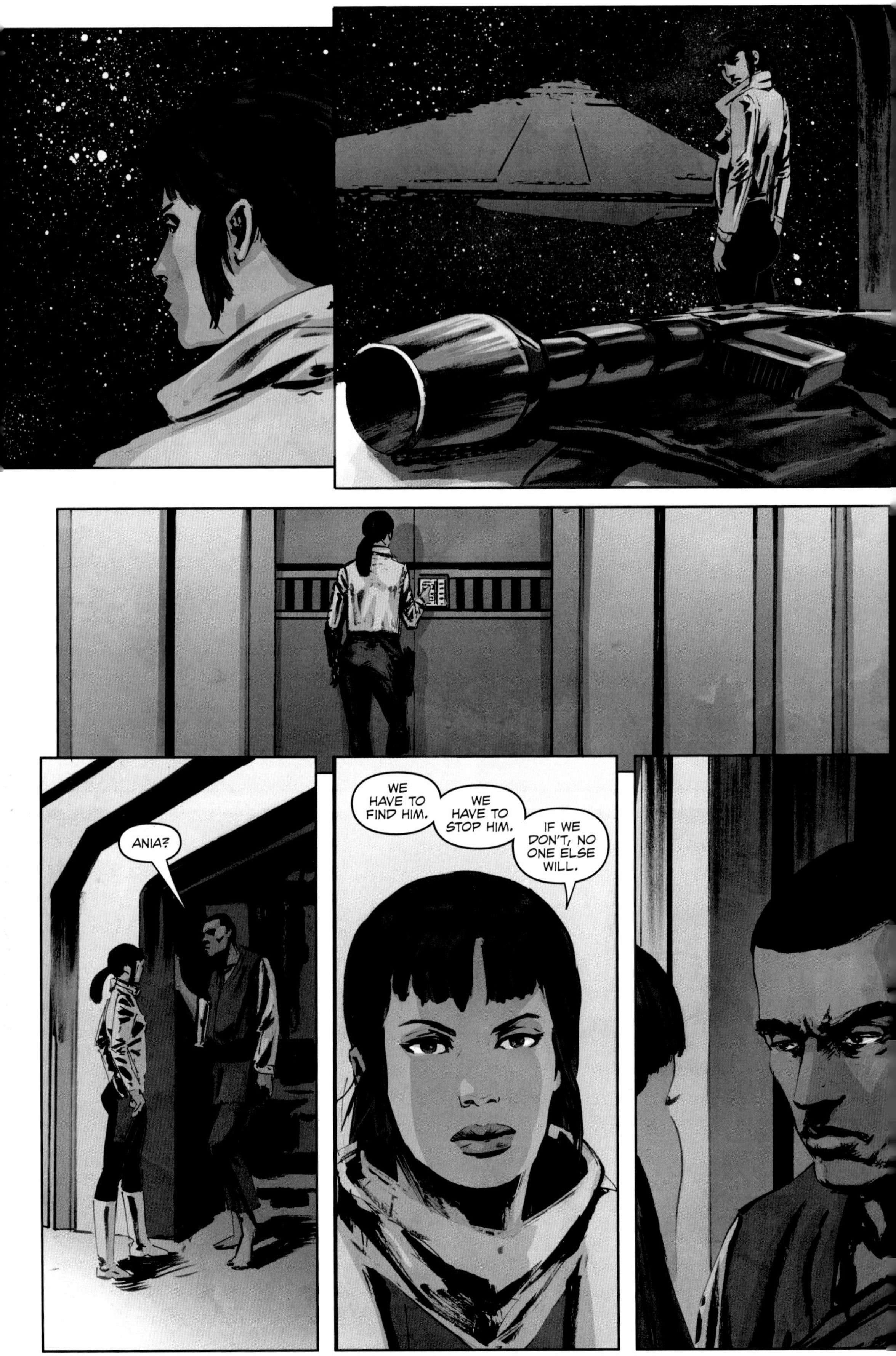
ANIA?
WE HAVE TO FIND HIM.
WE HAVE TO STOP HIM.
IF WE DON'T, NO ONE ELSE WILL.

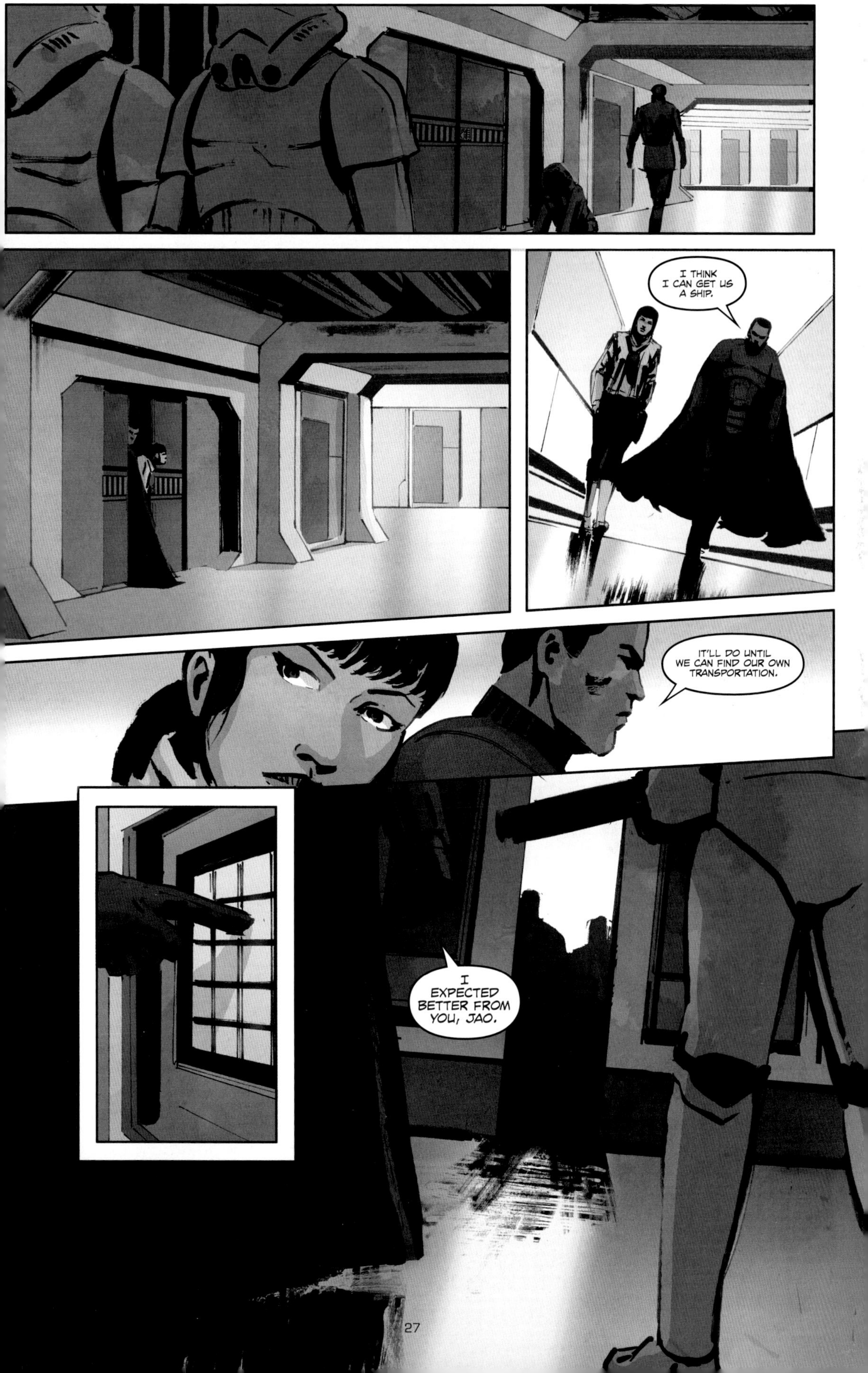
I THINK I CAN GET US A SHIP.
IT'LL DO UNTIL WE CAN FIND OUR OWN TRANSPORTATION.
I EXPECTED BETTER FROM YOU, JAO.

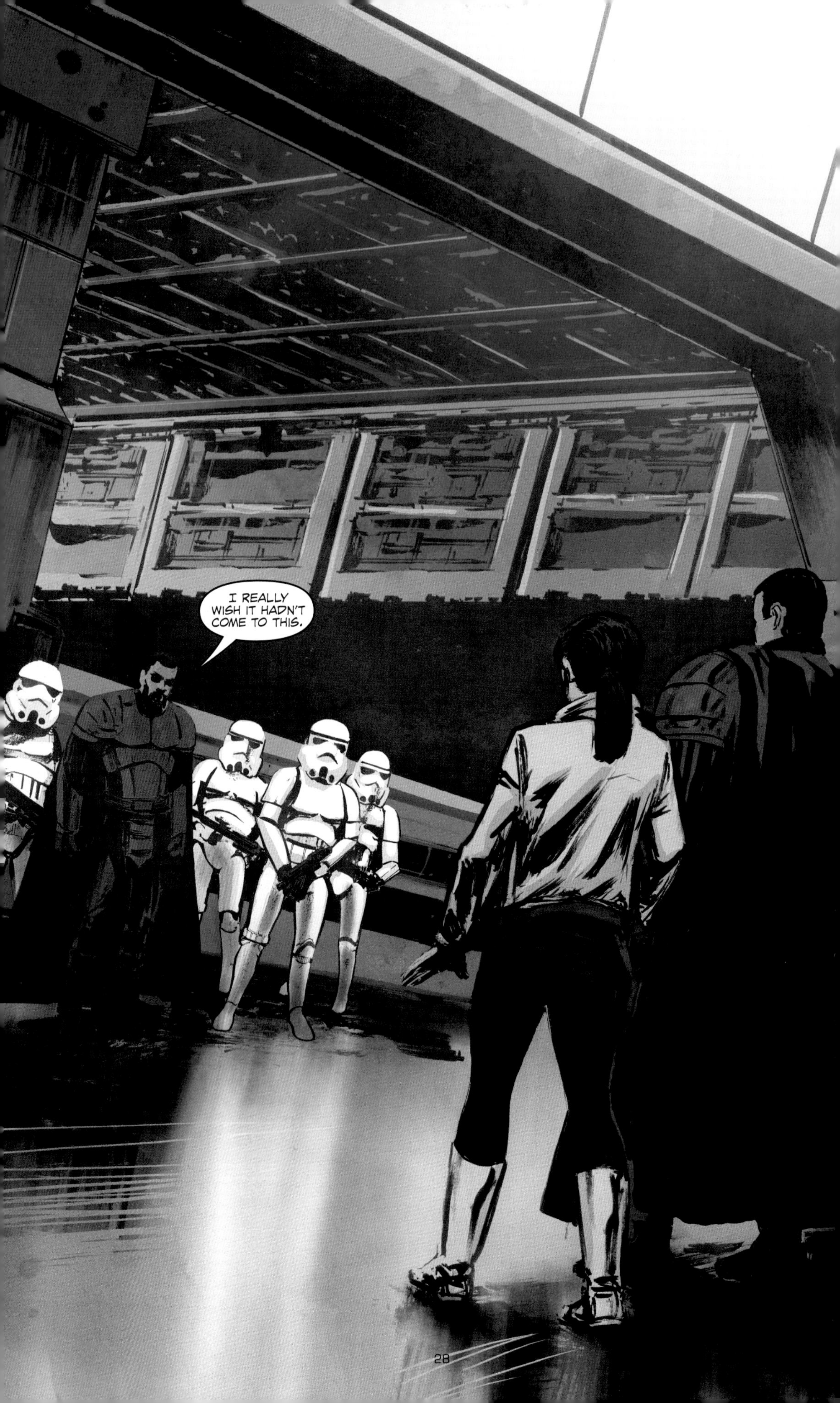
I REALLY WISH IT HADN'T COME TO THIS.

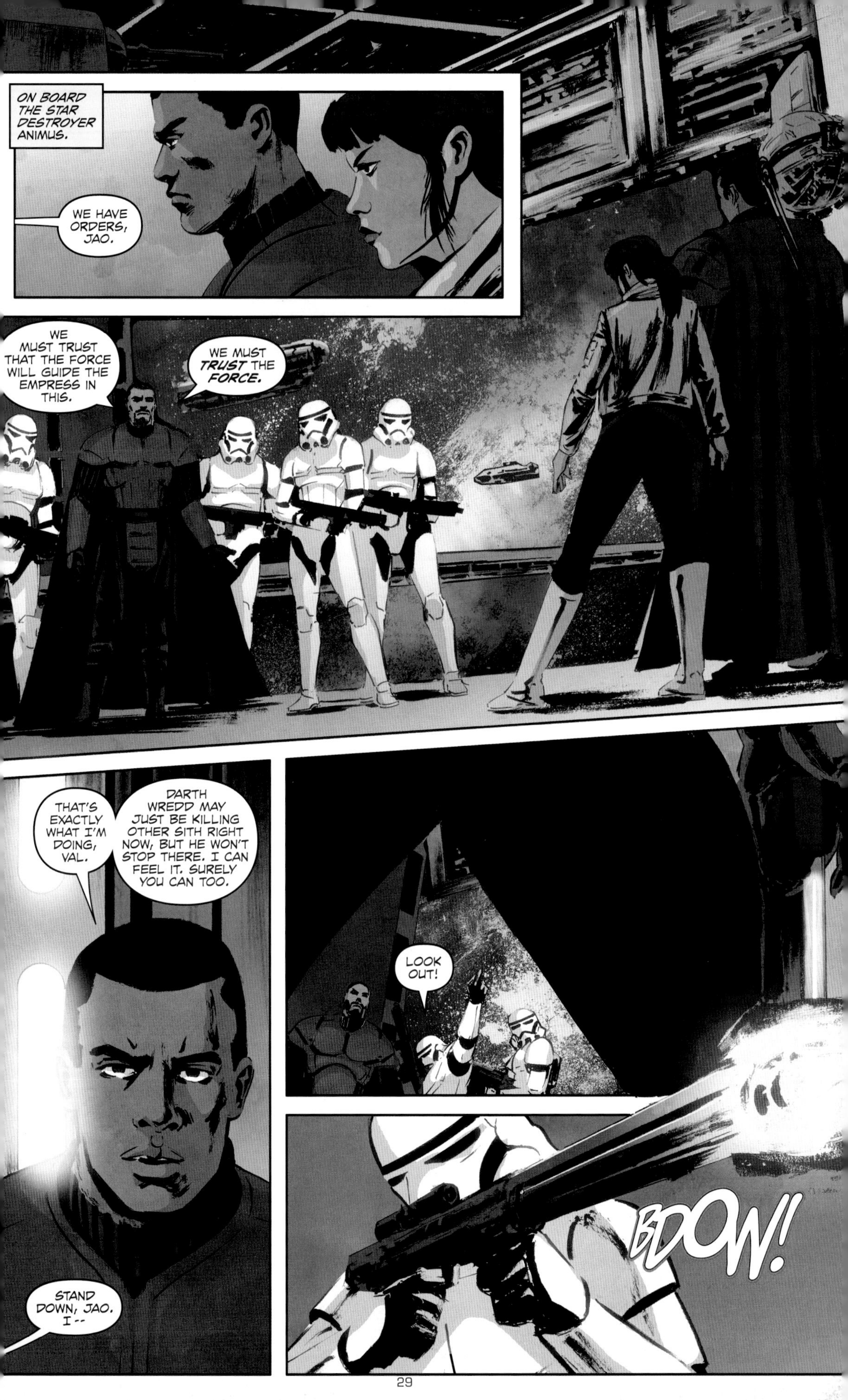
ON BOARD THE STAR DESTROYER ANIMUS.
WE HAVE ORDERS, JAO.
WE MUST TRUST THAT THE FORCE WILL GUIDE THE EMPRESS IN THIS.
WE MUST TRUST THE FORCE.
THAT'S EXACTLY WHAT I'M DOING, VAL.
DARTH WREDD MAY JUST BE KILLING OTHER SITH RIGHT NOW, BUT HE WON'T STOP THERE. I CAN FEEL IT. SURELY YOU CAN TOO.
STAND DOWN, JAO. I--
LOOK OUT!
BDOW!

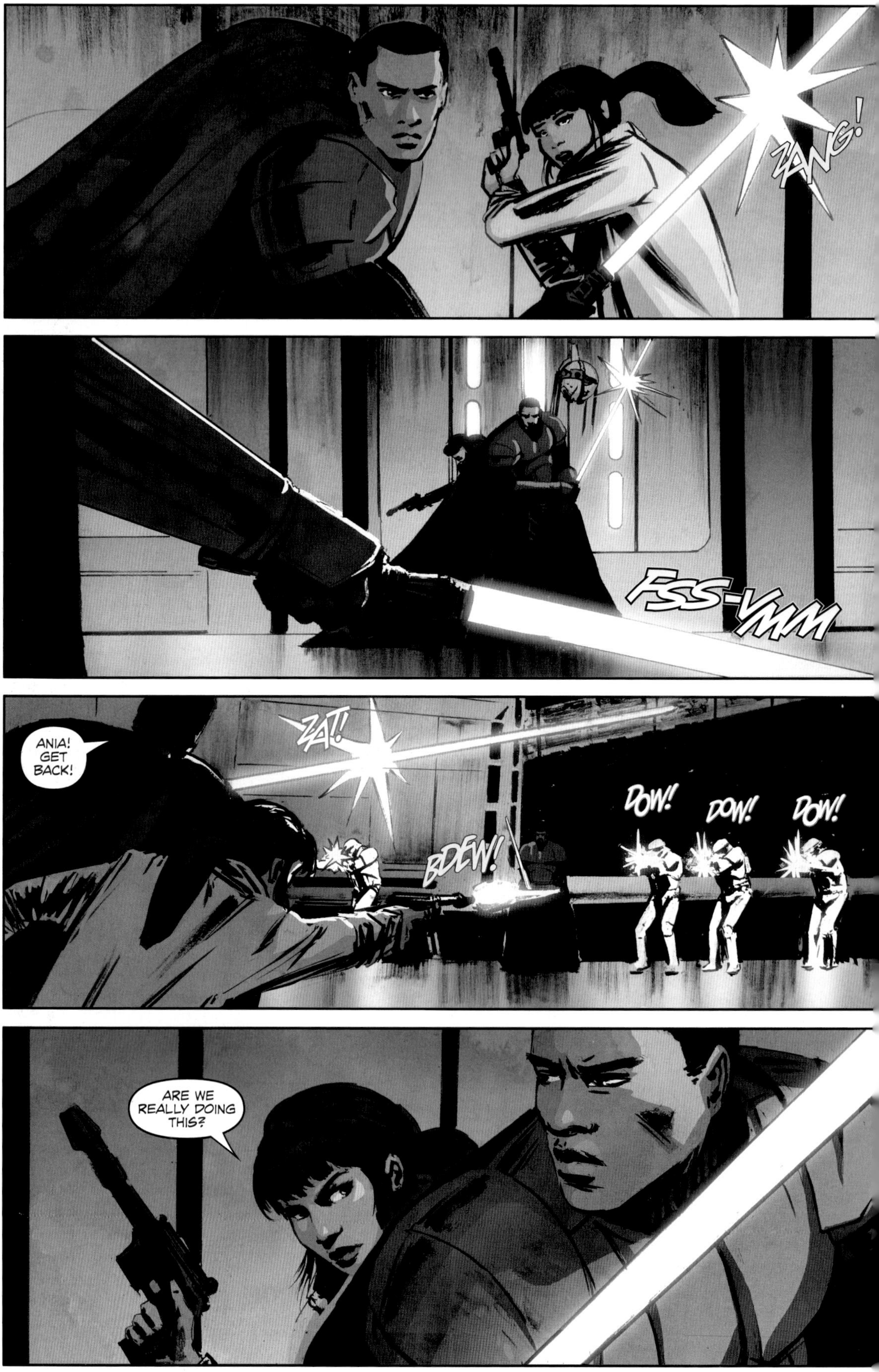
ZANG!
FSS-VMM
ANIA! GET BACK!
ZAT!
BDEW!
DOW!
DOW!
DOW!
ARE WE REALLY DOING THIS?

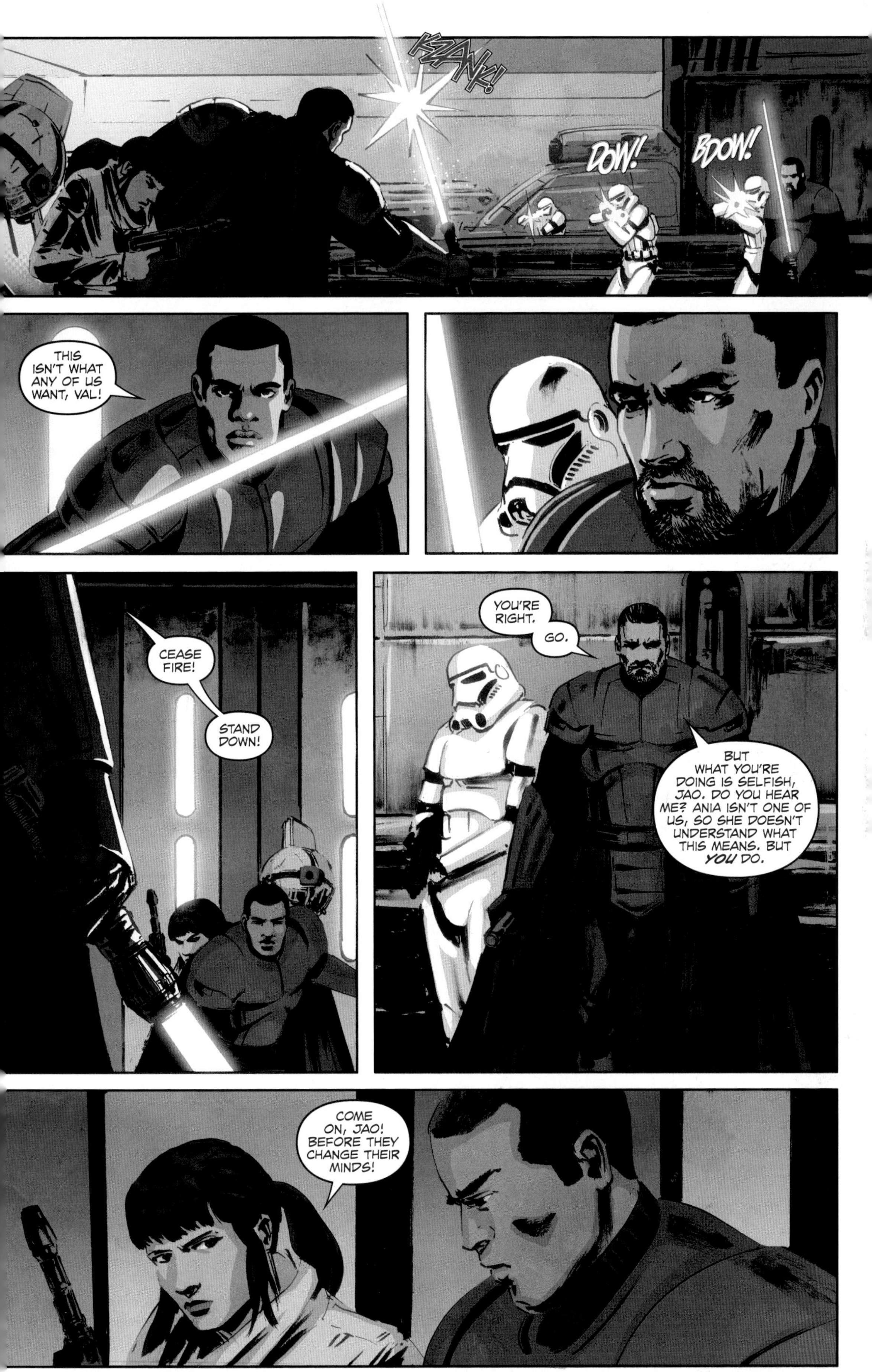
KZANK!
DOW!
BDOW!
THIS ISN'T WHAT ANY OF US WANT, VAL!
CEASE FIRE!
STAND DOWN!
YOU'RE RIGHT. GO.
BUT WHAT YOU'RE DOING IS SELFISH, JAO. DO YOU HEAR ME? ANIA ISN'T ONE OF US, SO SHE DOESN'T UNDERSTAND WHAT THIS MEANS. BUT *YOU* DO.
COME ON, JAO! BEFORE THEY CHANGE THEIR MINDS!

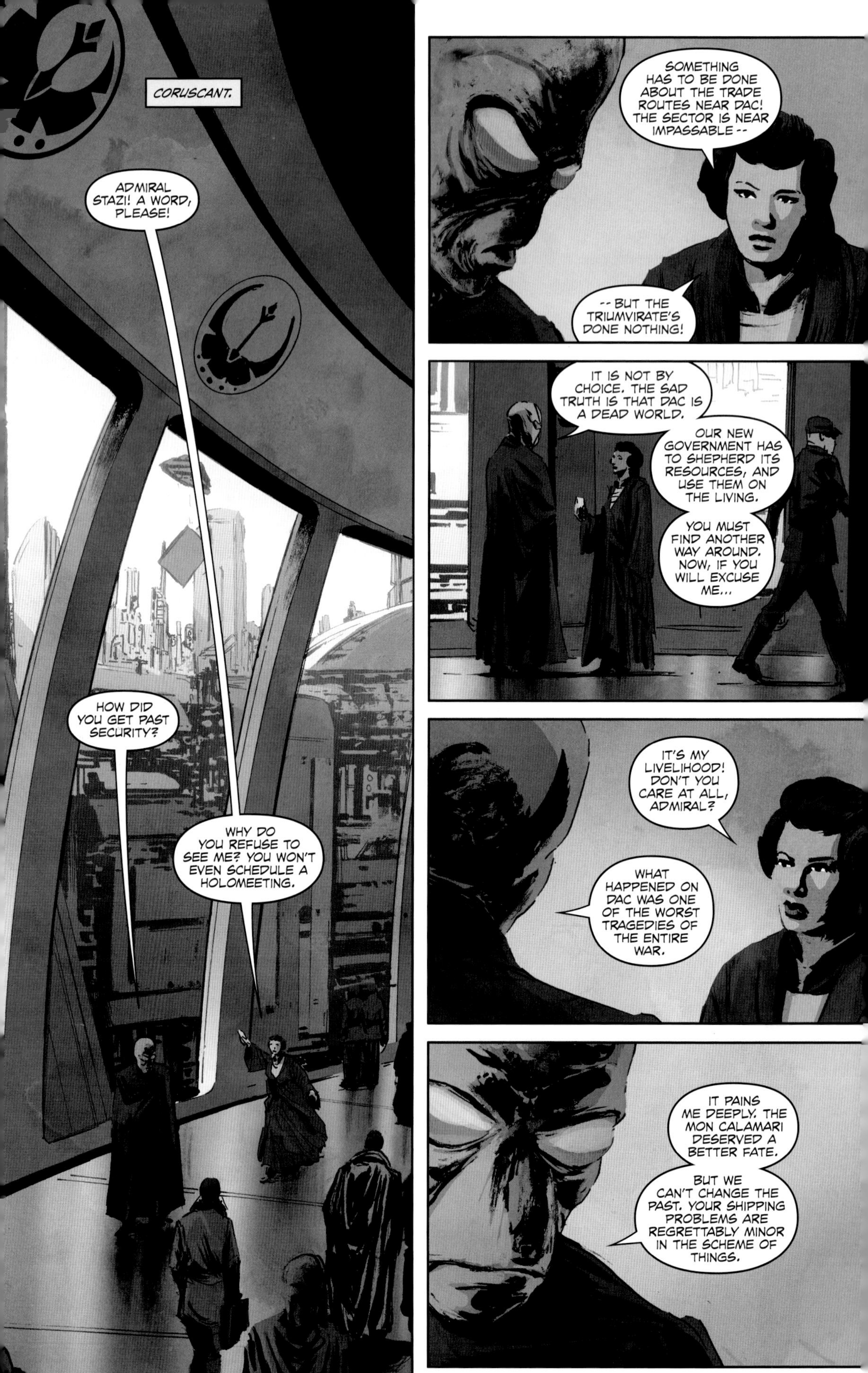
CORUSCANT.
ADMIRAL STAZI! A WORD, PLEASE!
HOW DID YOU GET PAST SECURITY?
WHY DO YOU REFUSE TO SEE ME? YOU WON'T EVEN SCHEDULE A HOLOMEETING.
SOMETHING HAS TO BE DONE ABOUT THE TRADE ROUTES NEAR DAC! THE SECTOR IS NEAR IMPASSABLE --
-- BUT THE TRIUMVIRATE'S DONE NOTHING!
IT IS NOT BY CHOICE. THE SAD TRUTH IS THAT DAC IS A DEAD WORLD.
OUR NEW GOVERNMENT HAS TO SHEPHERD ITS RESOURCES, AND USE THEM ON THE LIVING.
YOU MUST FIND ANOTHER WAY AROUND. NOW, IF YOU WILL EXCUSE ME...
IT'S MY LIVELIHOOD! DON'T YOU CARE AT ALL, ADMIRAL?
WHAT HAPPENED ON DAC WAS ONE OF THE WORST TRAGEDIES OF THE ENTIRE WAR.
IT PAINS ME DEEPLY. THE MON CALAMARI DESERVED A BETTER FATE.
BUT WE CAN'T CHANGE THE PAST. YOUR SHIPPING PROBLEMS ARE REGRETTABLY MINOR IN THE SCHEME OF THINGS.

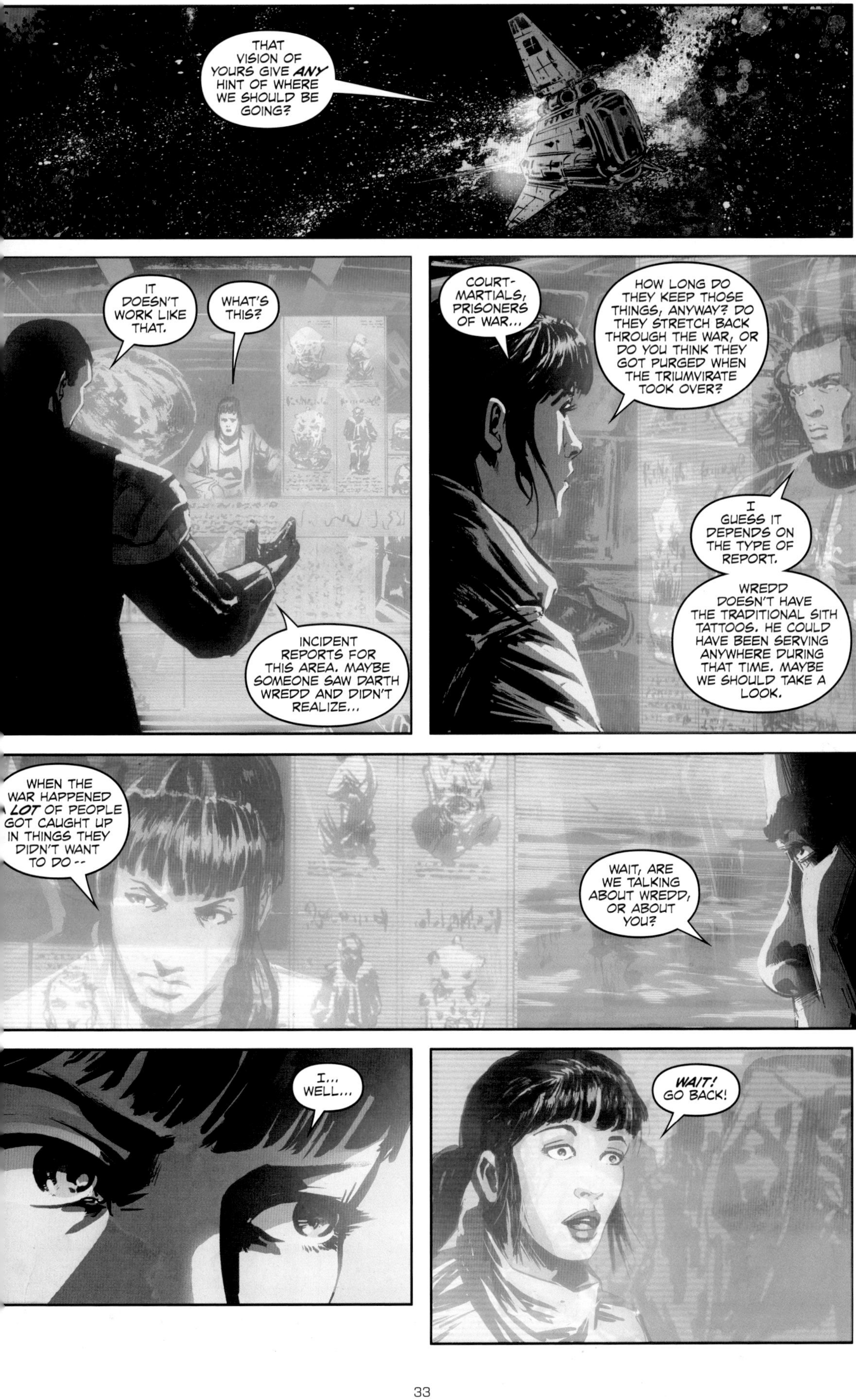
THAT VISION OF YOURS GIVE ANY HINT OF WHERE WE SHOULD BE GOING?
IT DOESN'T WORK LIKE THAT.
WHAT'S THIS?
INCIDENT REPORTS FOR THIS AREA. MAYBE SOMEONE SAW DARTH WREDD AND DIDN'T REALIZE...
COURT-MARTIALS, PRISONERS OF WAR...
HOW LONG DO THEY KEEP THOSE THINGS, ANYWAY? DO THEY STRETCH BACK THROUGH THE WAR, OR DO YOU THINK THEY GOT PURGED WHEN THE TRIUMVIRATE TOOK OVER?
I GUESS IT DEPENDS ON THE TYPE OF REPORT.
WREDD DOESN'T HAVE THE TRADITIONAL SITH TATTOOS. HE COULD HAVE BEEN SERVING ANYWHERE DURING THAT TIME. MAYBE WE SHOULD TAKE A LOOK.
WHEN THE WAR HAPPENED LOT OF PEOPLE GOT CAUGHT UP IN THINGS THEY DIDN'T WANT TO DO --
WAIT, ARE WE TALKING ABOUT WREDD, OR ABOUT YOU?
I... WELL...
WAIT! GO BACK!

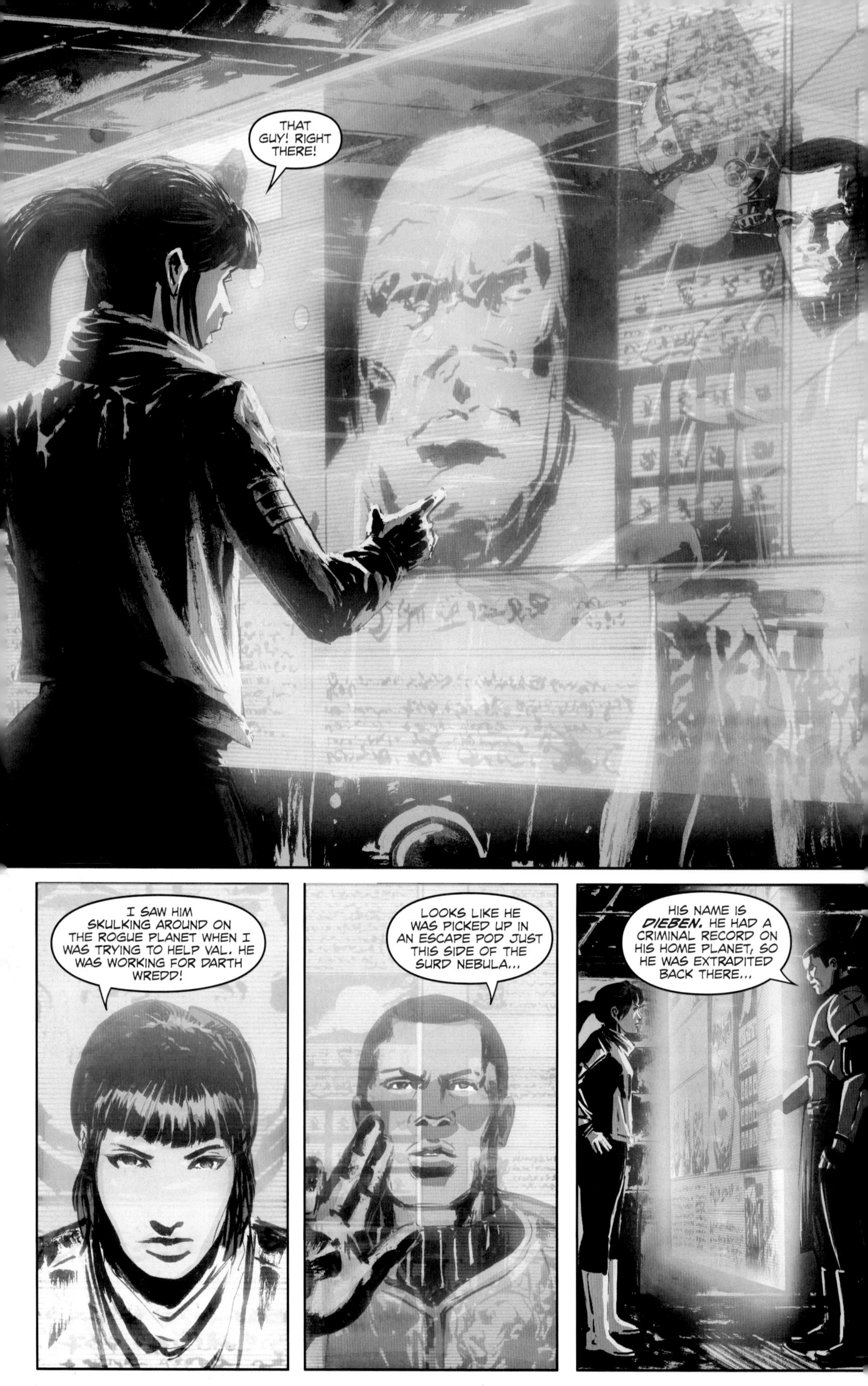
THAT GUY! RIGHT THERE!
I SAW HIM SKULKING AROUND ON THE ROGUE PLANET WHEN I WAS TRYING TO HELP VAL. HE WAS WORKING FOR DARTH WREDD!
LOOKS LIKE HE WAS PICKED UP IN AN ESCAPE POD JUST THIS SIDE OF THE SURD NEBULA...
HIS NAME IS *DIEBEN.* HE HAD A CRIMINAL RECORD ON HIS HOME PLANET, SO HE WAS EXTRADITED BACK THERE...

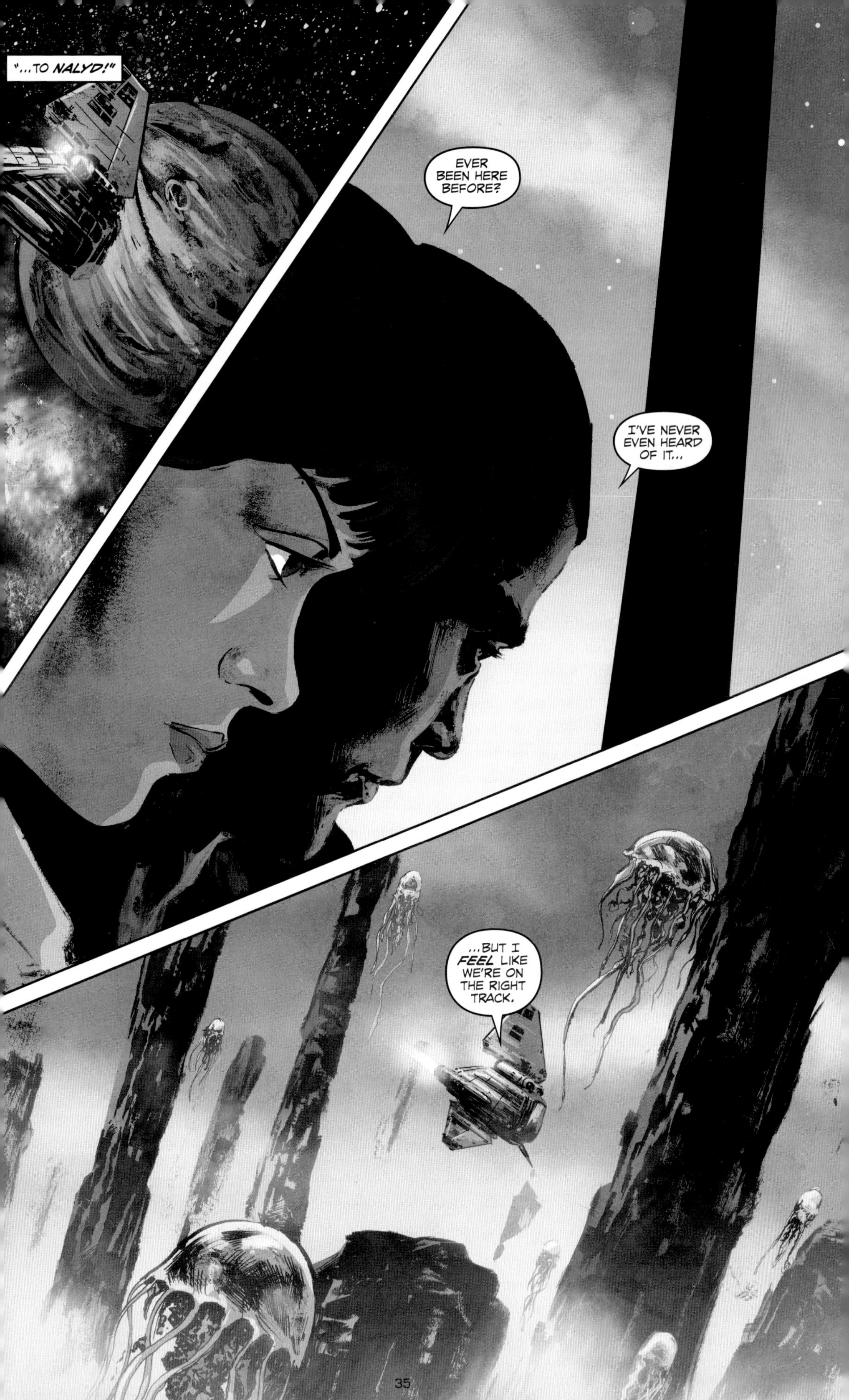
"...TO NALYD!"
EVER BEEN HERE BEFORE?
I'VE NEVER EVEN HEARD OF IT...
...BUT I FEEL LIKE WE'RE ON THE RIGHT TRACK.

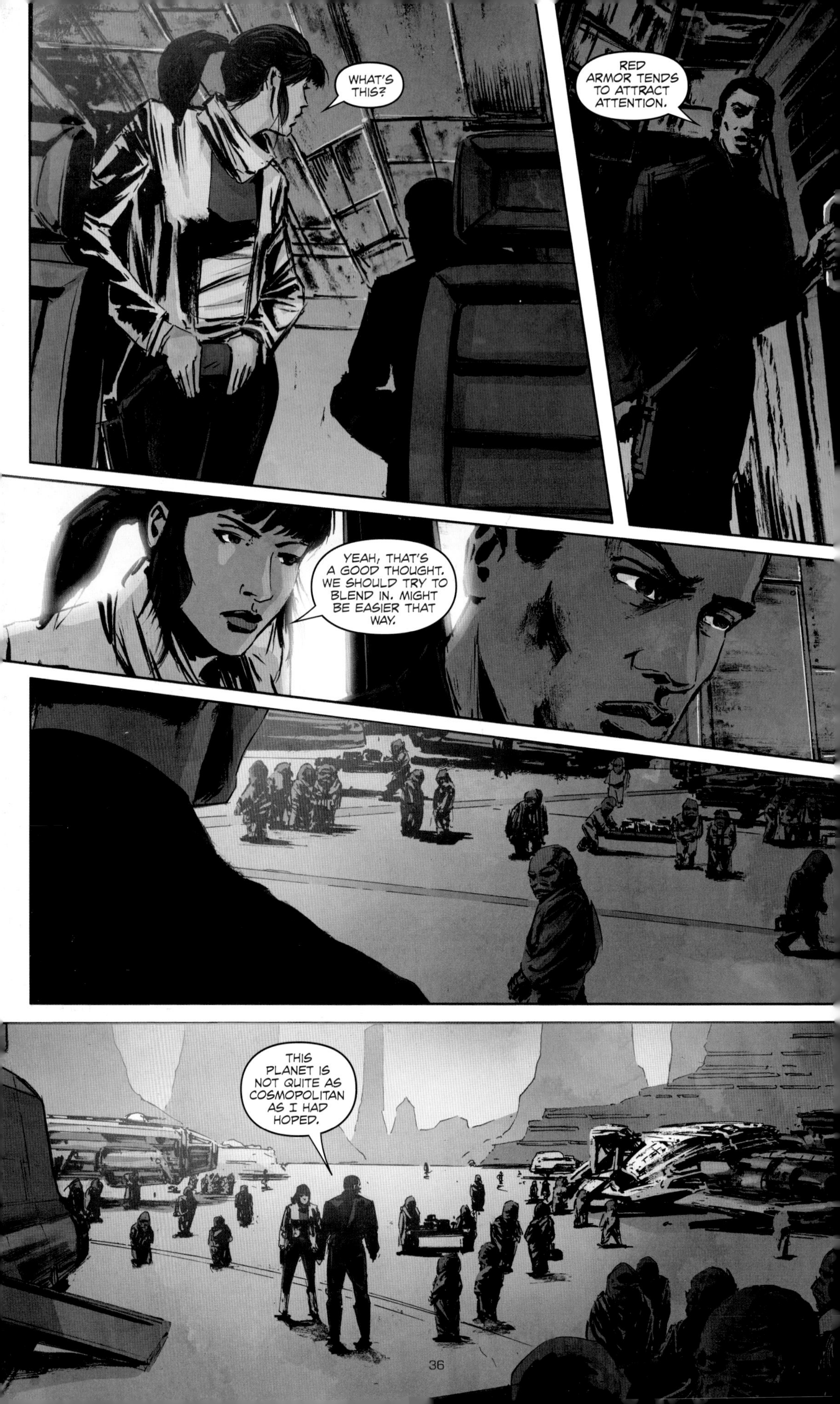

WHAT'S THIS?
RED ARMOR TENDS TO ATTRACT ATTENTION.
YEAH, THAT'S A GOOD THOUGHT. WE SHOULD TRY TO BLEND IN. MIGHT BE EASIER THAT WAY.
THIS PLANET IS NOT QUITE AS COSMOPOLITAN AS I HAD HOPED.

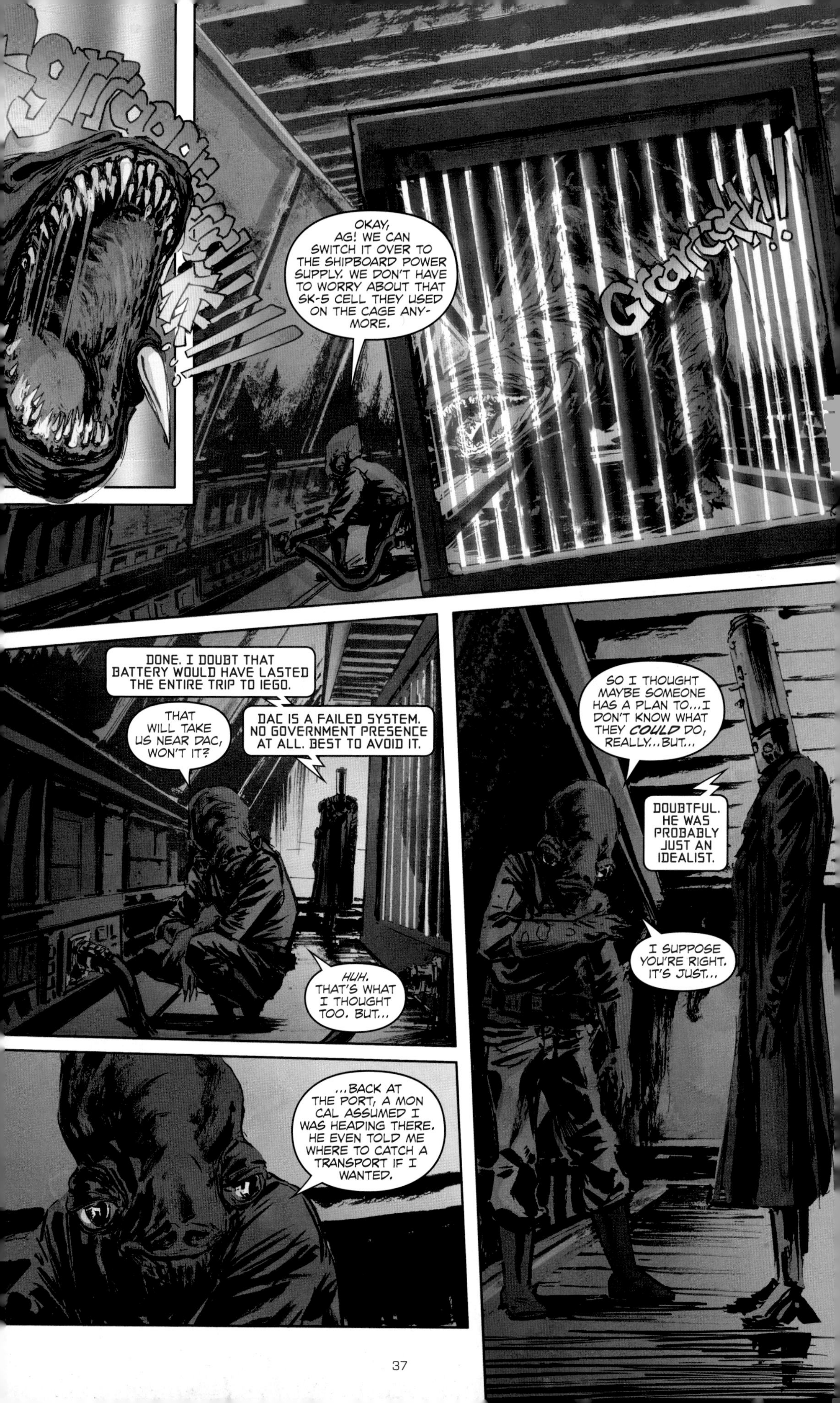
GRRAAARRR
OKAY, AG! WE CAN SWITCH IT OVER TO THE SHIPBOARD POWER SUPPLY. WE DON'T HAVE TO WORRY ABOUT THAT SK-5 CELL THEY USED ON THE CAGE ANYMORE.
GKRRKK!!
DONE. I DOUBT THAT BATTERY WOULD HAVE LASTED THE ENTIRE TRIP TO IEGO.
THAT WILL TAKE US NEAR DAC, WON'T IT?
DAC IS A FAILED SYSTEM. NO GOVERNMENT PRESENCE AT ALL. BEST TO AVOID IT.
HUH. THAT'S WHAT I THOUGHT TOO. BUT...
...BACK AT THE PORT, A MON CAL ASSUMED I WAS HEADING THERE. HE EVEN TOLD ME WHERE TO CATCH A TRANSPORT IF I WANTED.
SO I THOUGHT MAYBE SOMEONE HAS A PLAN TO...I DON'T KNOW WHAT THEY *COULD* DO, REALLY...BUT...
DOUBTFUL. HE WAS PROBABLY JUST AN IDEALIST.
I SUPPOSE YOU'RE RIGHT. IT'S JUST...

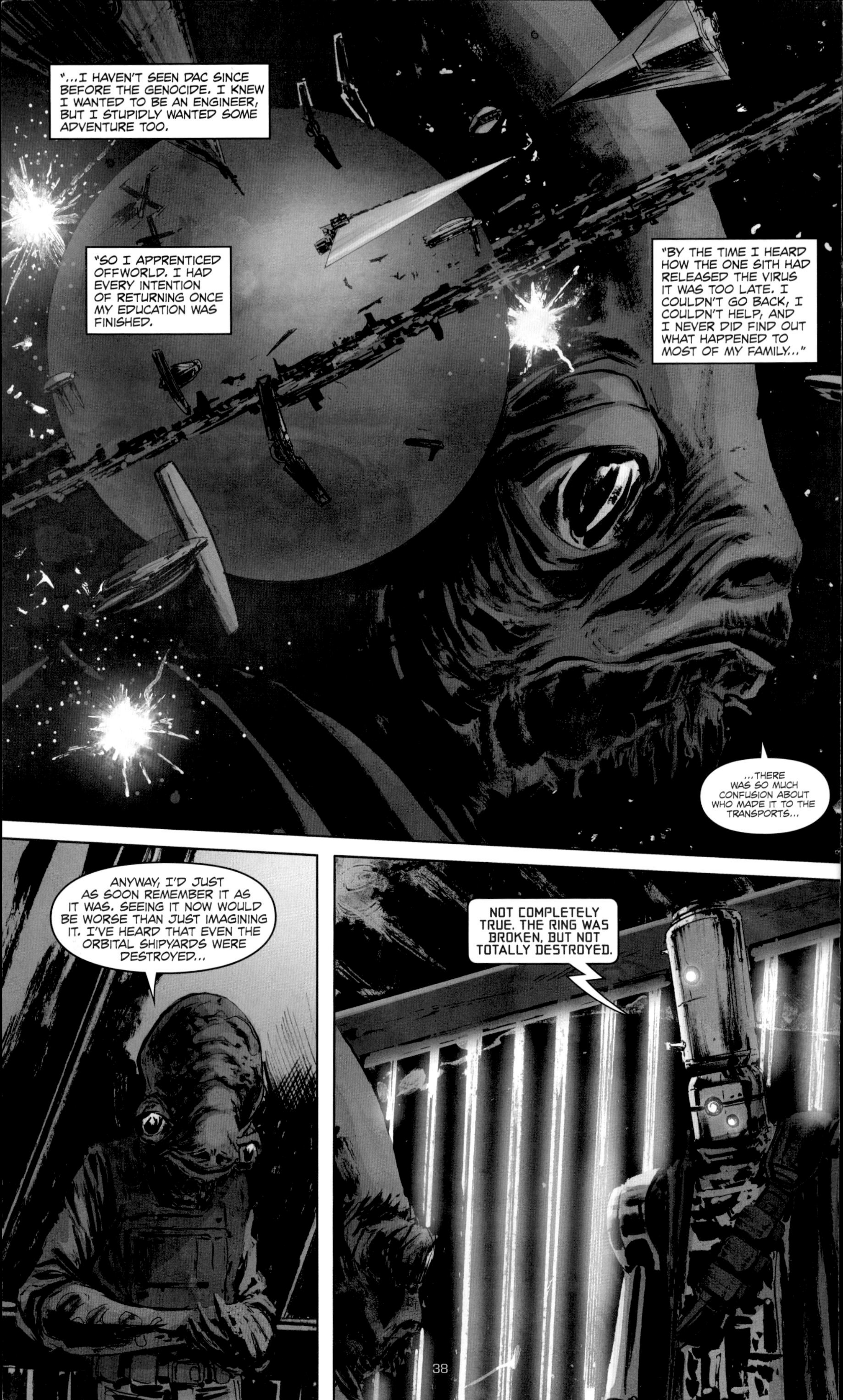
"...I HAVEN'T SEEN DAC SINCE BEFORE THE GENOCIDE. I KNEW I WANTED TO BE AN ENGINEER, BUT I STUPIDLY WANTED SOME ADVENTURE TOO.
"SO I APPRENTICED OFFWORLD. I HAD EVERY INTENTION OF RETURNING ONCE MY EDUCATION WAS FINISHED.
"BY THE TIME I HEARD HOW THE ONE SITH HAD RELEASED THE VIRUS IT WAS TOO LATE. I COULDN'T GO BACK, I COULDN'T HELP, AND I NEVER DID FIND OUT WHAT HAPPENED TO MOST OF MY FAMILY..."
...THERE WAS SO MUCH CONFUSION ABOUT WHO MADE IT TO THE TRANSPORTS...
ANYWAY, I'D JUST AS SOON REMEMBER IT AS IT WAS. SEEING IT NOW WOULD BE WORSE THAN JUST IMAGINING IT. I'VE HEARD THAT EVEN THE ORBITAL SHIPYARDS WERE DESTROYED...
NOT COMPLETELY TRUE. THE RING WAS BROKEN, BUT NOT TOTALLY DESTROYED.

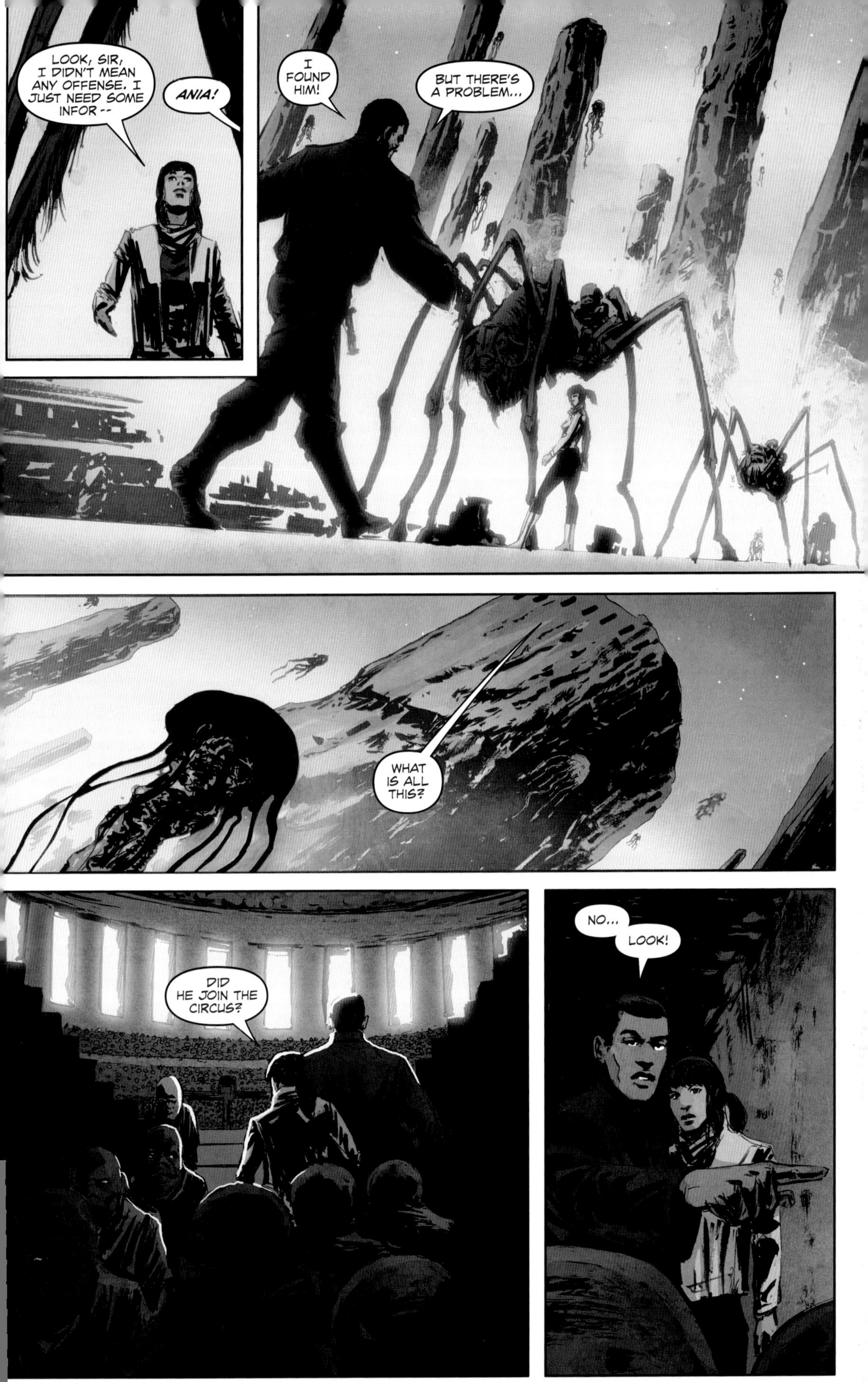

LOOK, SIR, I DIDN'T MEAN ANY OFFENSE. I JUST NEED SOME INFOR --
ANIA!
I FOUND HIM!
BUT THERE'S A PROBLEM...
WHAT IS ALL THIS?
DID HE JOIN THE CIRCUS?
NO...
LOOK!

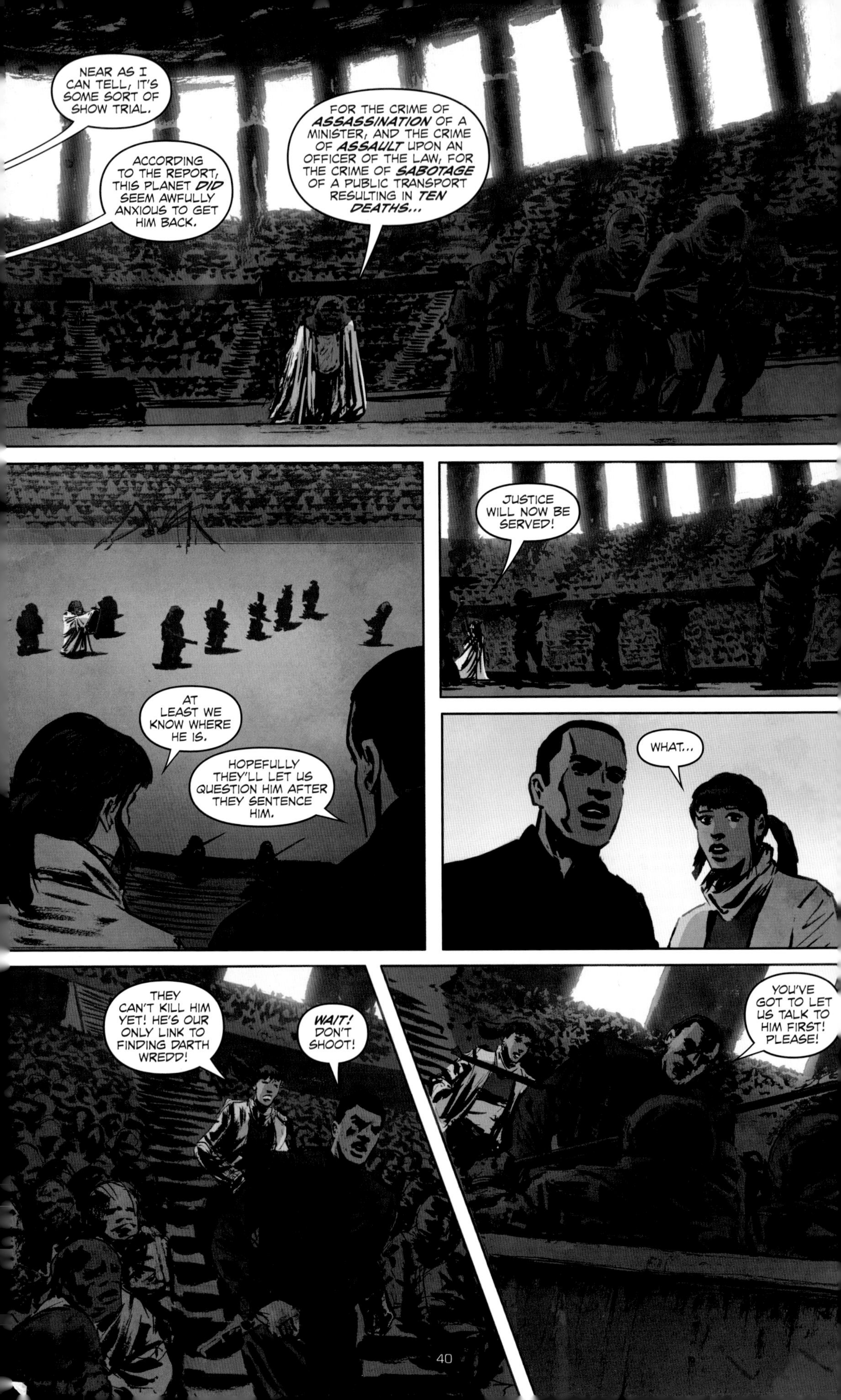
NEAR AS I CAN TELL, IT'S SOME SORT OF SHOW TRIAL.
ACCORDING TO THE REPORT, THIS PLANET DID SEEM AWFULLY ANXIOUS TO GET HIM BACK.
FOR THE CRIME OF ASSASSINATION OF A MINISTER, AND THE CRIME OF ASSAULT UPON AN OFFICER OF THE LAW, FOR THE CRIME OF SABOTAGE OF A PUBLIC TRANSPORT RESULTING IN TEN DEATHS...
AT LEAST WE KNOW WHERE HE IS.
HOPEFULLY THEY'LL LET US QUESTION HIM AFTER THEY SENTENCE HIM.
JUSTICE WILL NOW BE SERVED!
WHAT...
THEY CAN'T KILL HIM YET! HE'S OUR ONLY LINK TO FINDING DARTH WREDD!
WAIT! DON'T SHOOT!
YOU'VE GOT TO LET US TALK TO HIM FIRST! PLEASE!

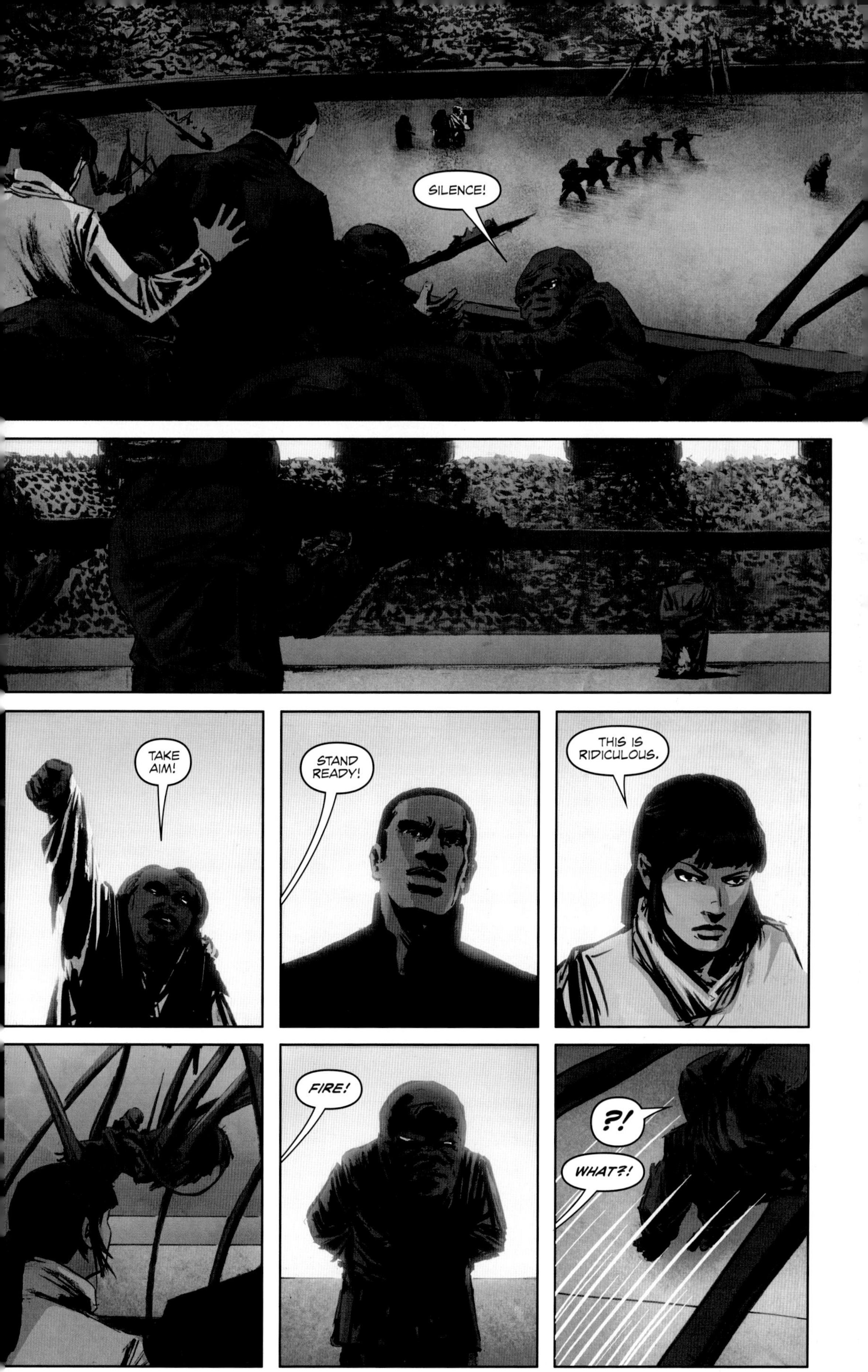
SILENCE!
TAKE AIM!
STAND READY!
THIS IS RIDICULOUS.
FIRE!
?!
WHAT?!

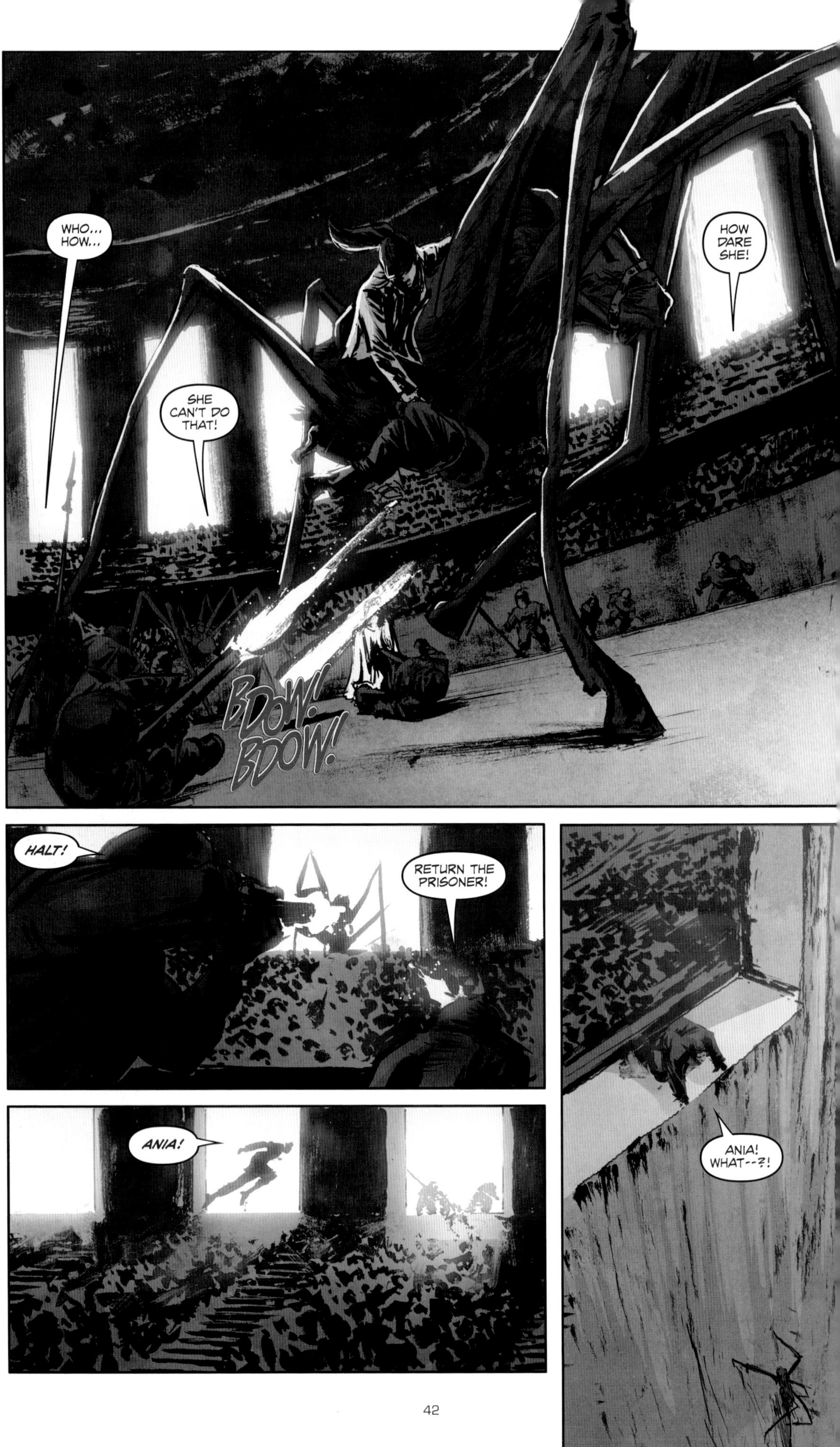
WHO... HOW...
HOW DARE SHE!
SHE CAN'T DO THAT!
BDOW! BDOW!
HALT!
RETURN THE PRISONER!
ANIA! WHAT--?!
ANIA!

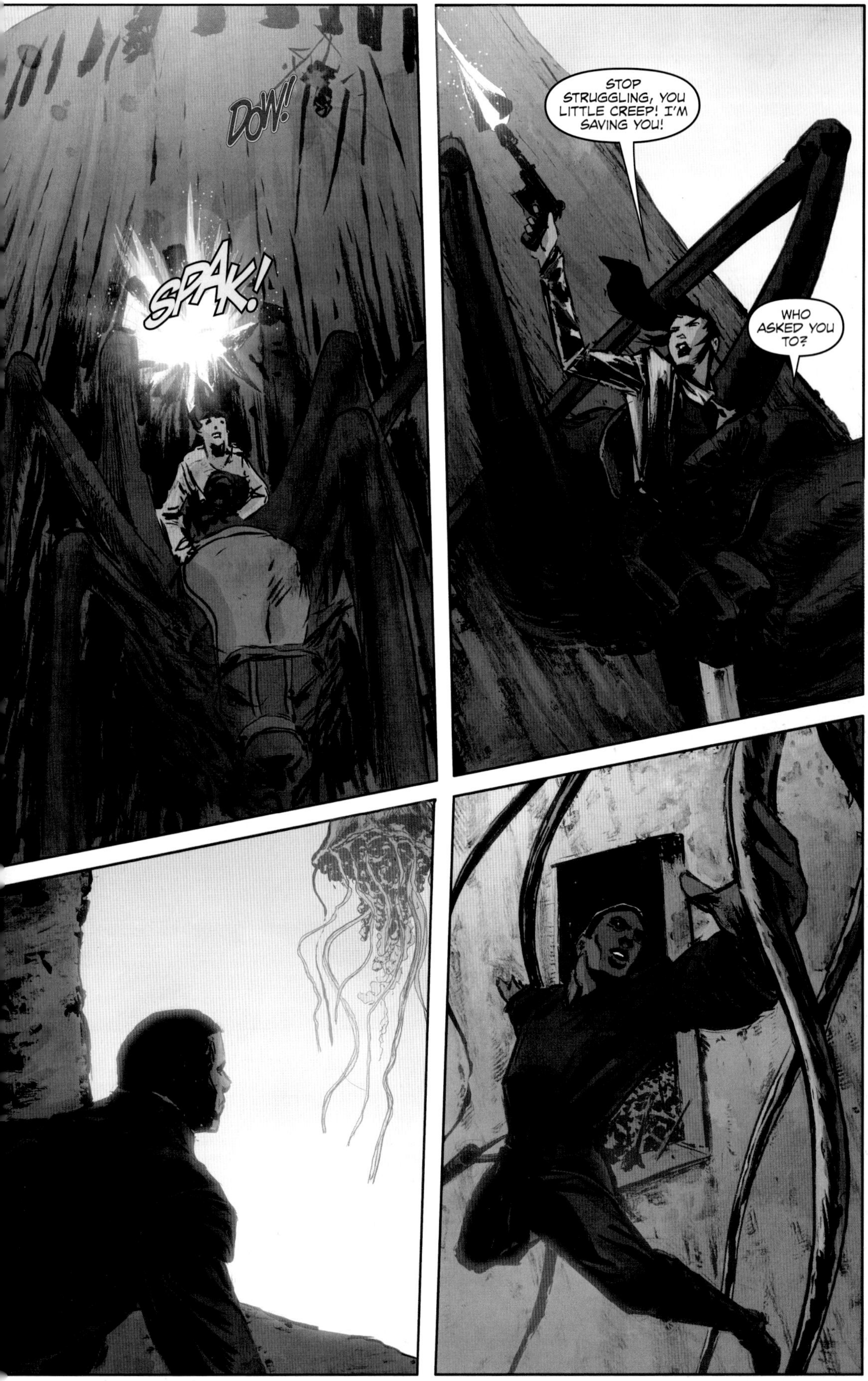
DOW!
SPAK!
STOP STRUGGLING, YOU LITTLE CREEP! I'M SAVING YOU!
WHO ASKED YOU TO?

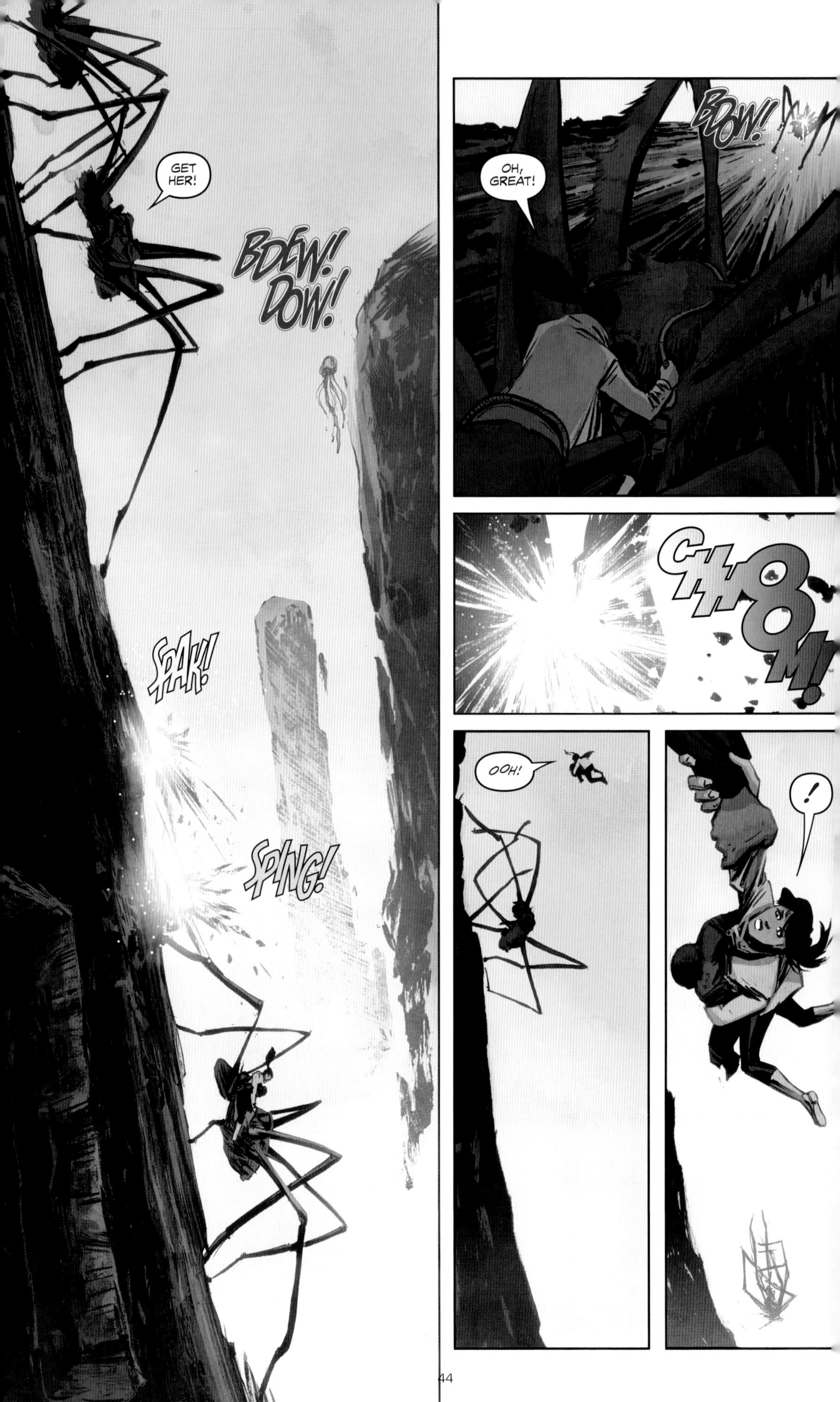
GET HER!
BDEW! DOW!
SPAK!
SPING!
OH, GREAT!
BDOW!
CHOOOM!
OOH!
!

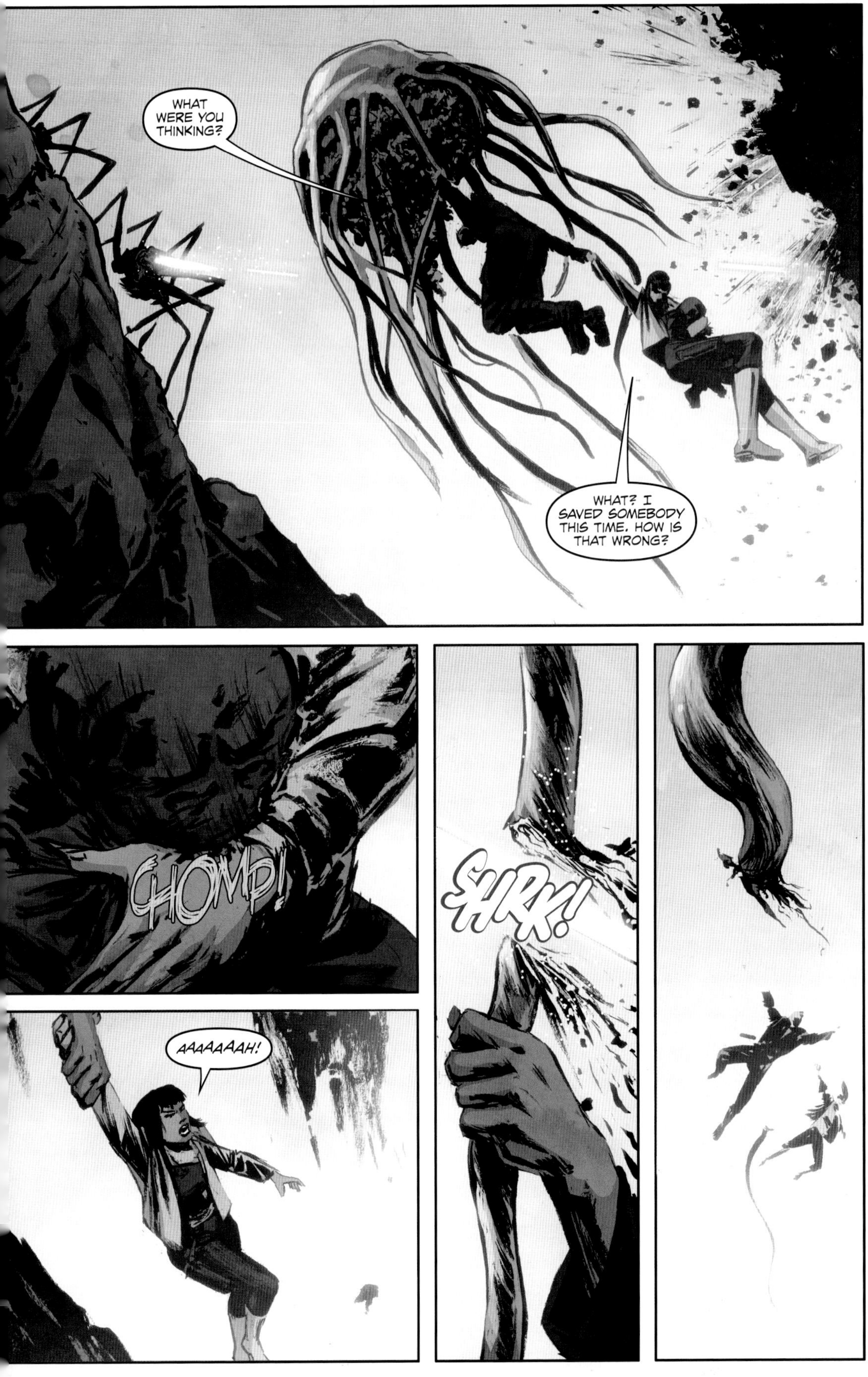
WHAT WERE YOU THINKING?
WHAT? I SAVED SOMEBODY THIS TIME. HOW IS THAT WRONG?
CHOMP!
AAAAAAAH!
SHRK!

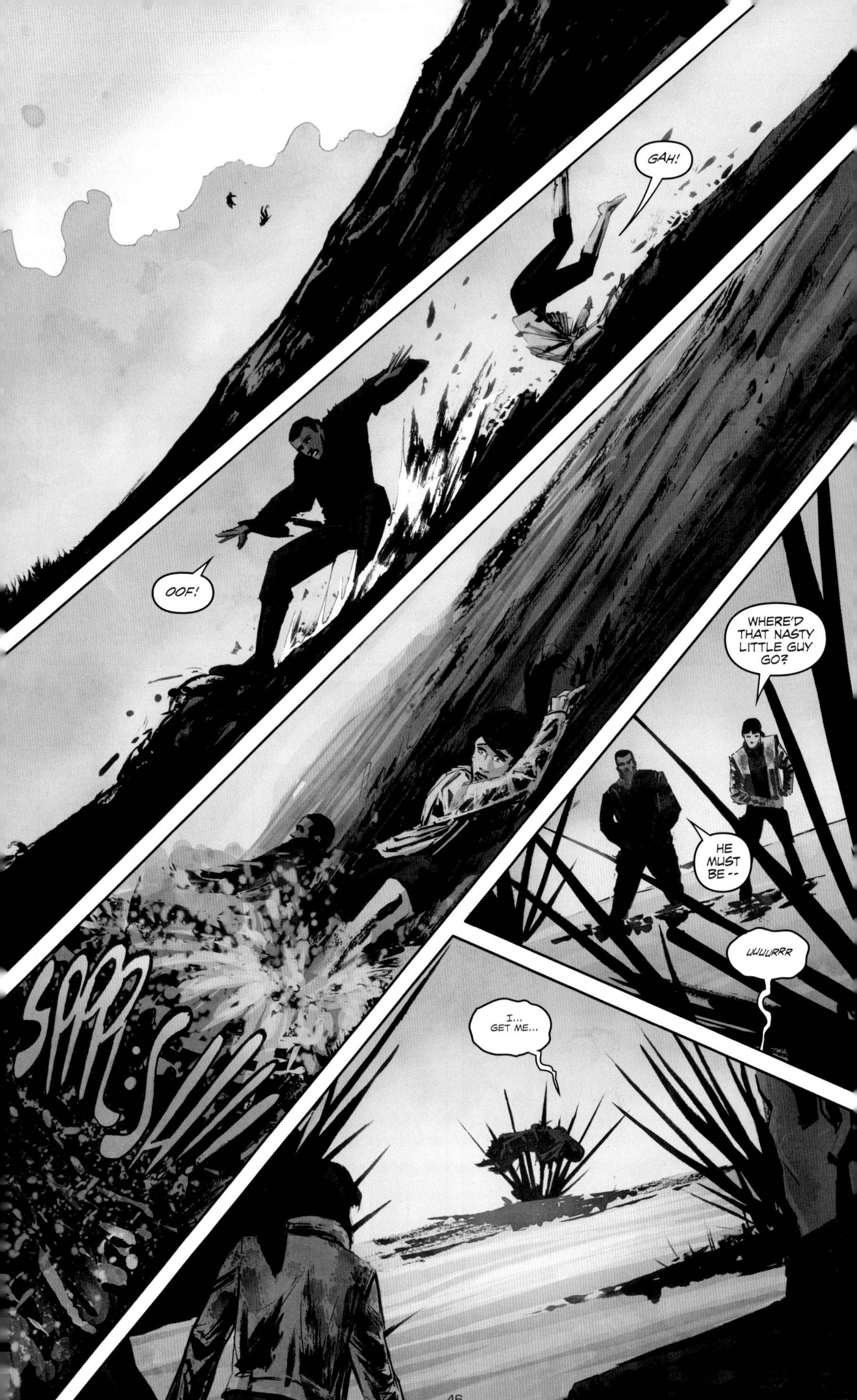
GAH!
OOF!
SPPPLSHHH
WHERE'D THAT NASTY LITTLE GUY GO?
HE MUST BE --
UUUURRR
I... GET ME...

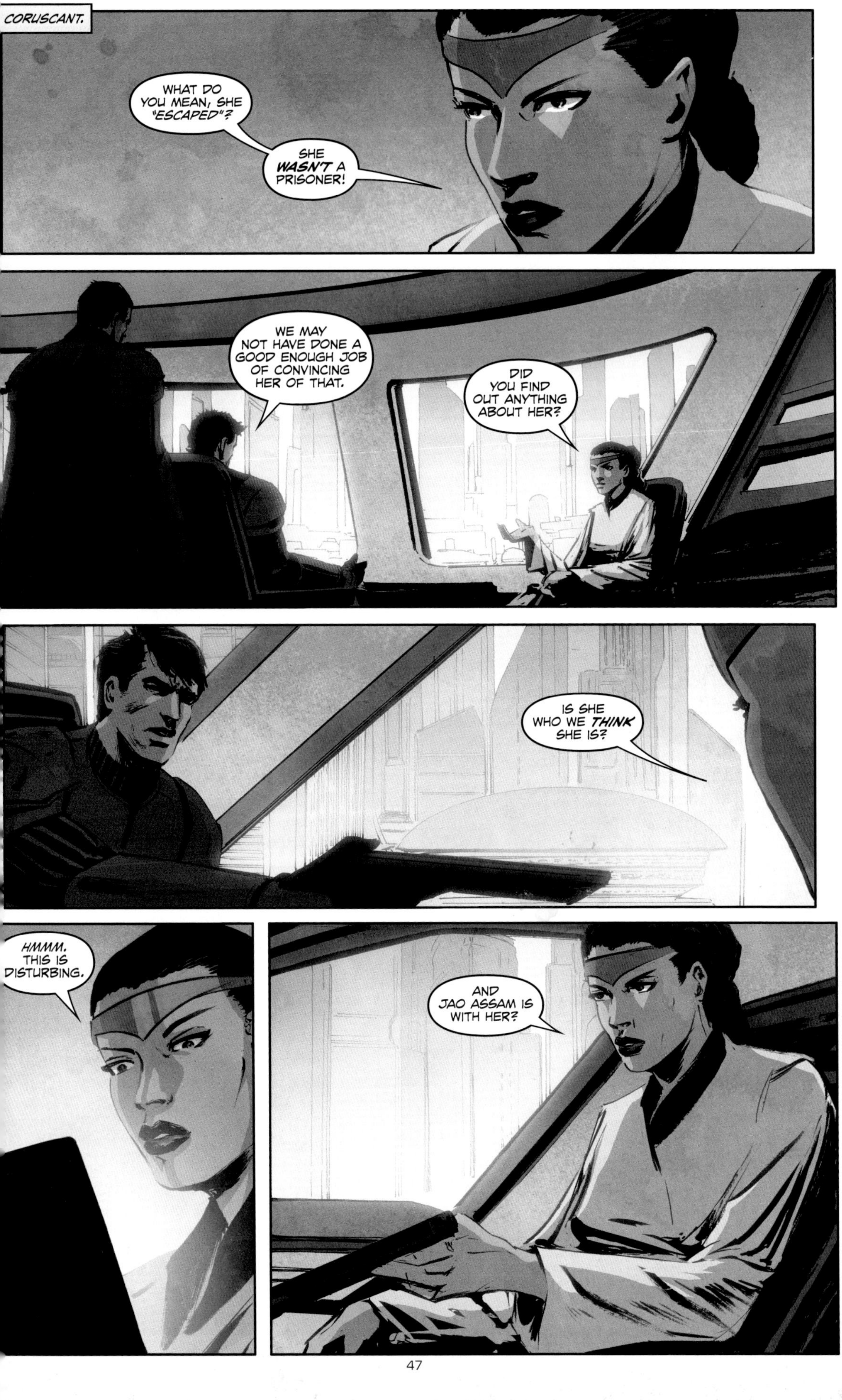
CORUSCANT.
WHAT DO YOU MEAN, SHE "ESCAPED"?
SHE WASN'T A PRISONER!
WE MAY NOT HAVE DONE A GOOD ENOUGH JOB OF CONVINCING HER OF THAT.
DID YOU FIND OUT ANYTHING ABOUT HER?
IS SHE WHO WE THINK SHE IS?
HMMM. THIS IS DISTURBING.
AND JAO ASSAM IS WITH HER?

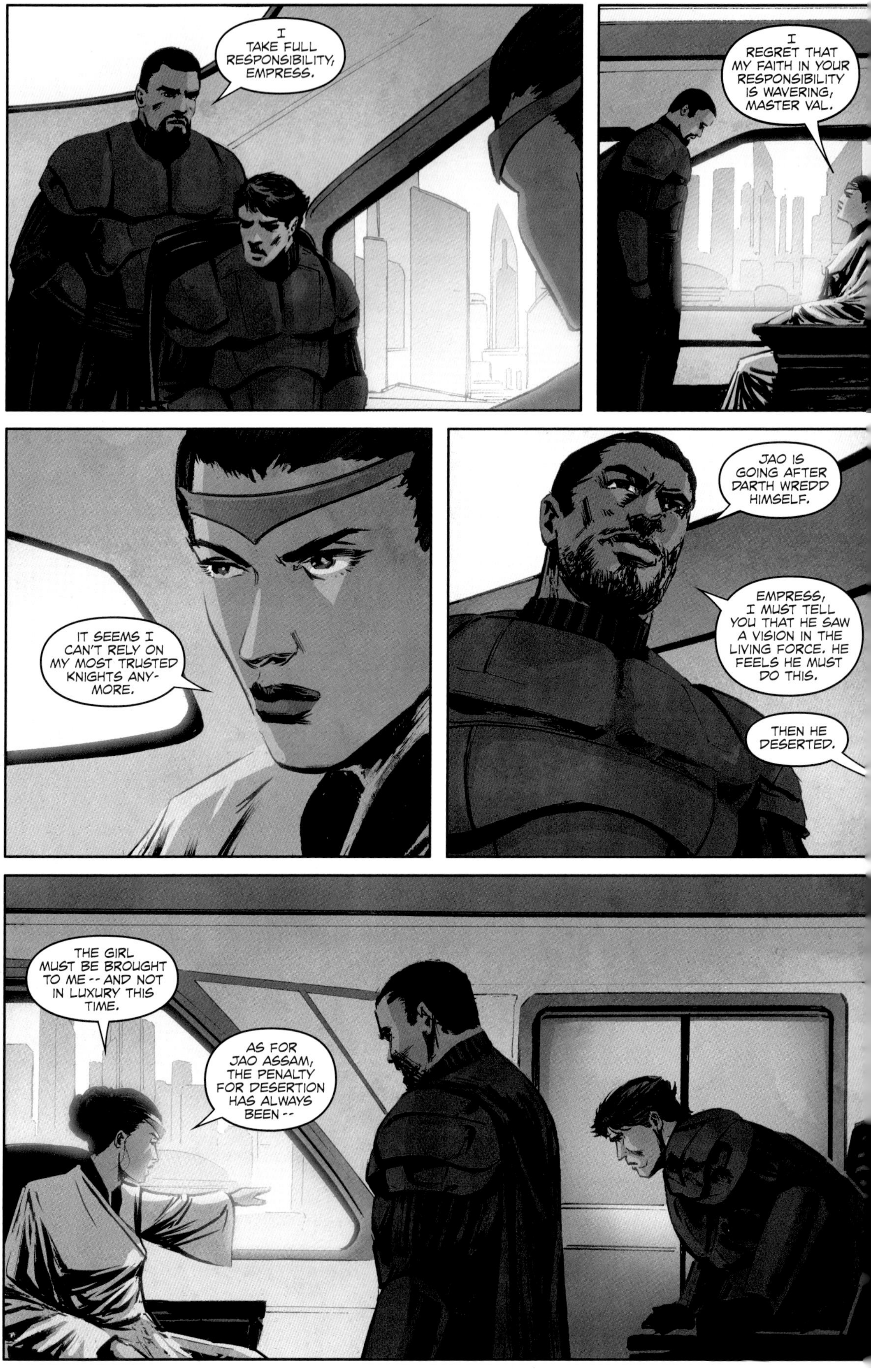
I TAKE FULL RESPONSIBILITY, EMPRESS.
I REGRET THAT MY FAITH IN YOUR RESPONSIBILITY IS WAVERING, MASTER VAL.
IT SEEMS I CAN'T RELY ON MY MOST TRUSTED KNIGHTS ANY-MORE.
JAO IS GOING AFTER DARTH WREDD HIMSELF.
EMPRESS, I MUST TELL YOU THAT HE SAW A VISION IN THE LIVING FORCE. HE FEELS HE MUST DO THIS.
THEN HE DESERTED.
THE GIRL MUST BE BROUGHT TO ME -- AND NOT IN LUXURY THIS TIME.
AS FOR JAO ASSAM, THE PENALTY FOR DESERTION HAS ALWAYS BEEN --

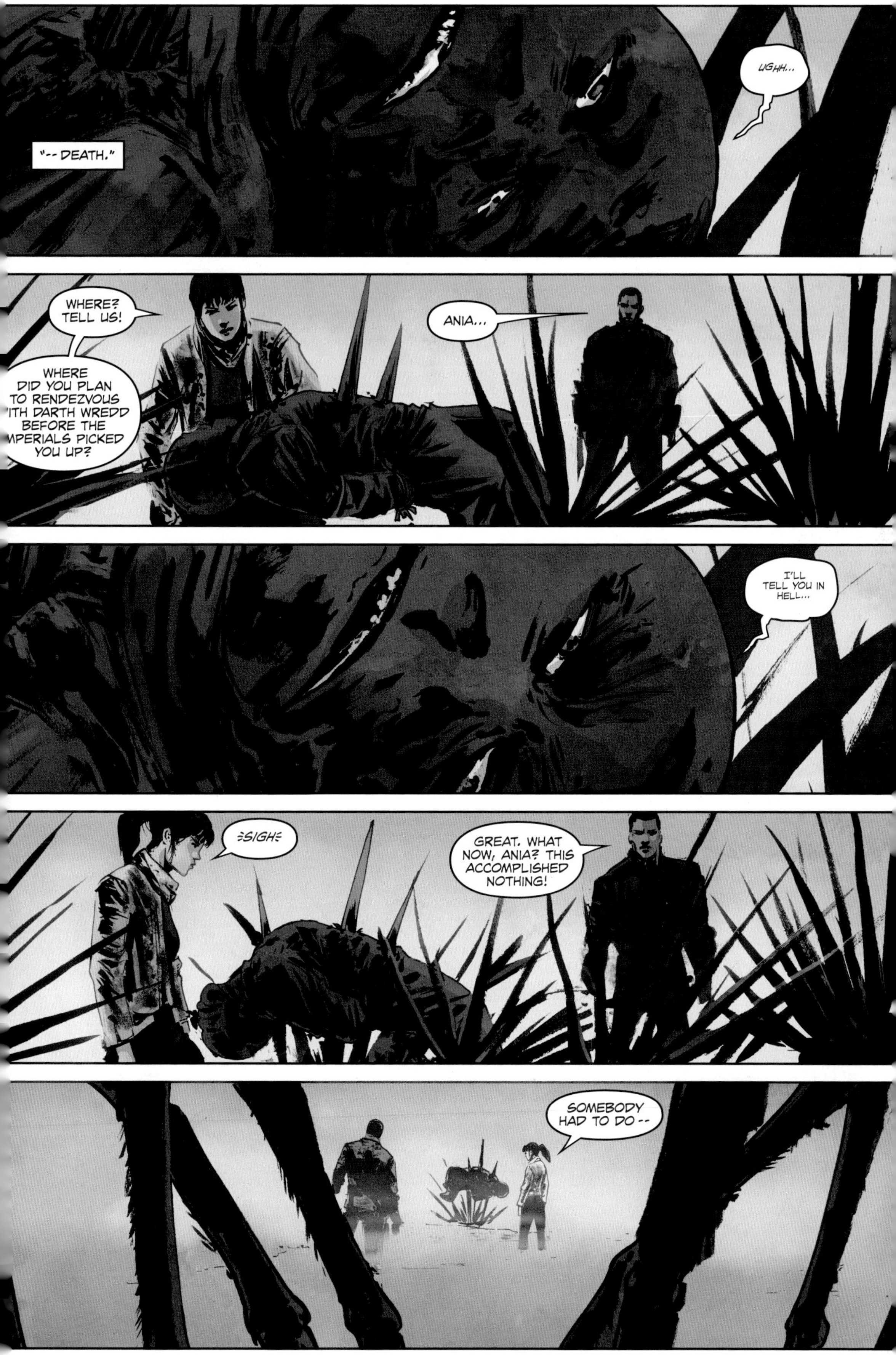
"-- DEATH."
UGHH...
WHERE? TELL US!
WHERE DID YOU PLAN TO RENDEZVOUS WITH DARTH WREDD BEFORE THE IMPERIALS PICKED YOU UP?
ANIA...
I'LL TELL YOU IN HELL...
SIGH
GREAT. WHAT NOW, ANIA? THIS ACCOMPLISHED NOTHING!
SOMEBODY HAD TO DO --

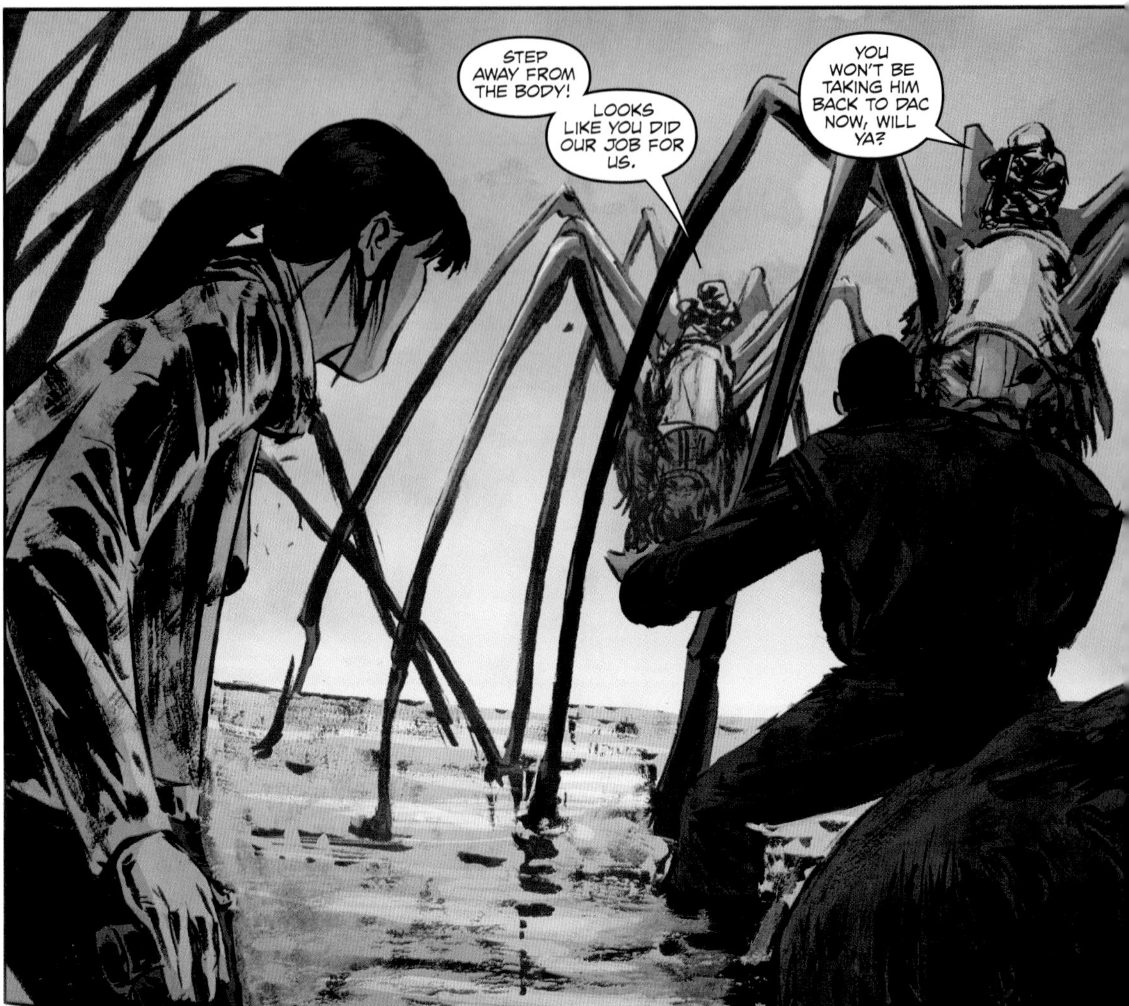
STEP AWAY FROM THE BODY!
LOOKS LIKE YOU DID OUR JOB FOR US.
YOU WON'T BE TAKING HIM BACK TO DAC NOW, WILL YA?

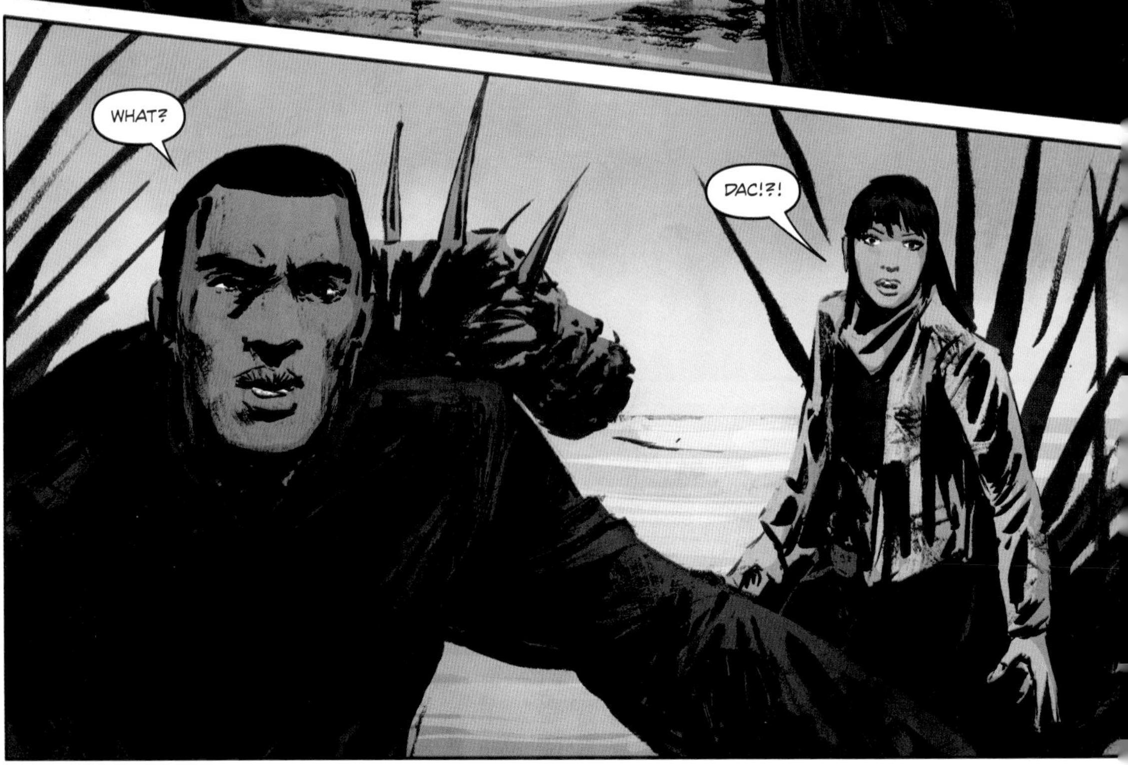
WHAT?
DAC!?!

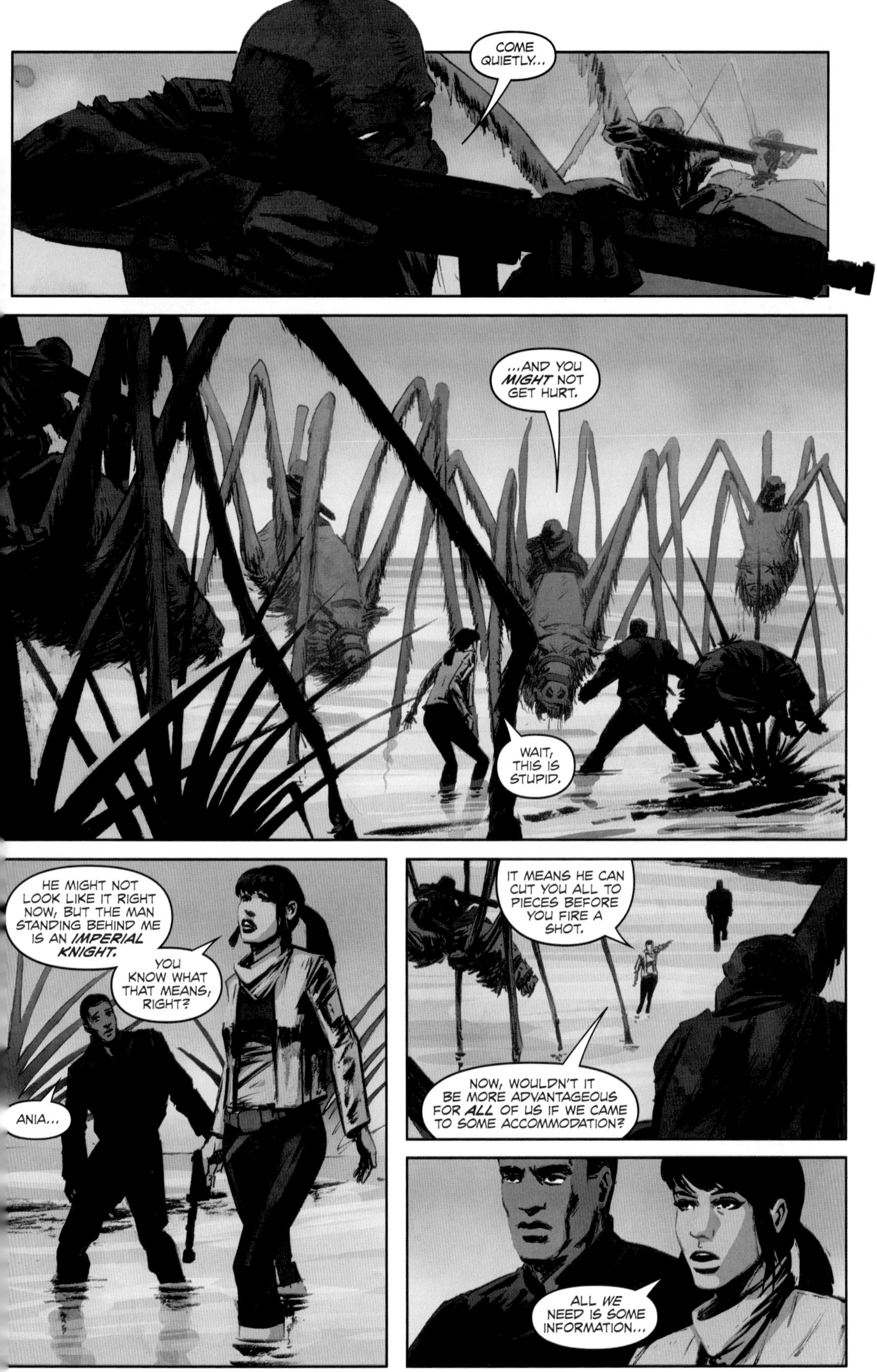
COME QUIETLY...
...AND YOU MIGHT NOT GET HURT.
WAIT, THIS IS STUPID.
HE MIGHT NOT LOOK LIKE IT RIGHT NOW, BUT THE MAN STANDING BEHIND ME IS AN IMPERIAL KNIGHT.
YOU KNOW WHAT THAT MEANS, RIGHT?
ANIA...
IT MEANS HE CAN CUT YOU ALL TO PIECES BEFORE YOU FIRE A SHOT.
NOW, WOULDN'T IT BE MORE ADVANTAGEOUS FOR ALL OF US IF WE CAME TO SOME ACCOMMODATION?
ALL WE NEED IS SOME INFORMATION...

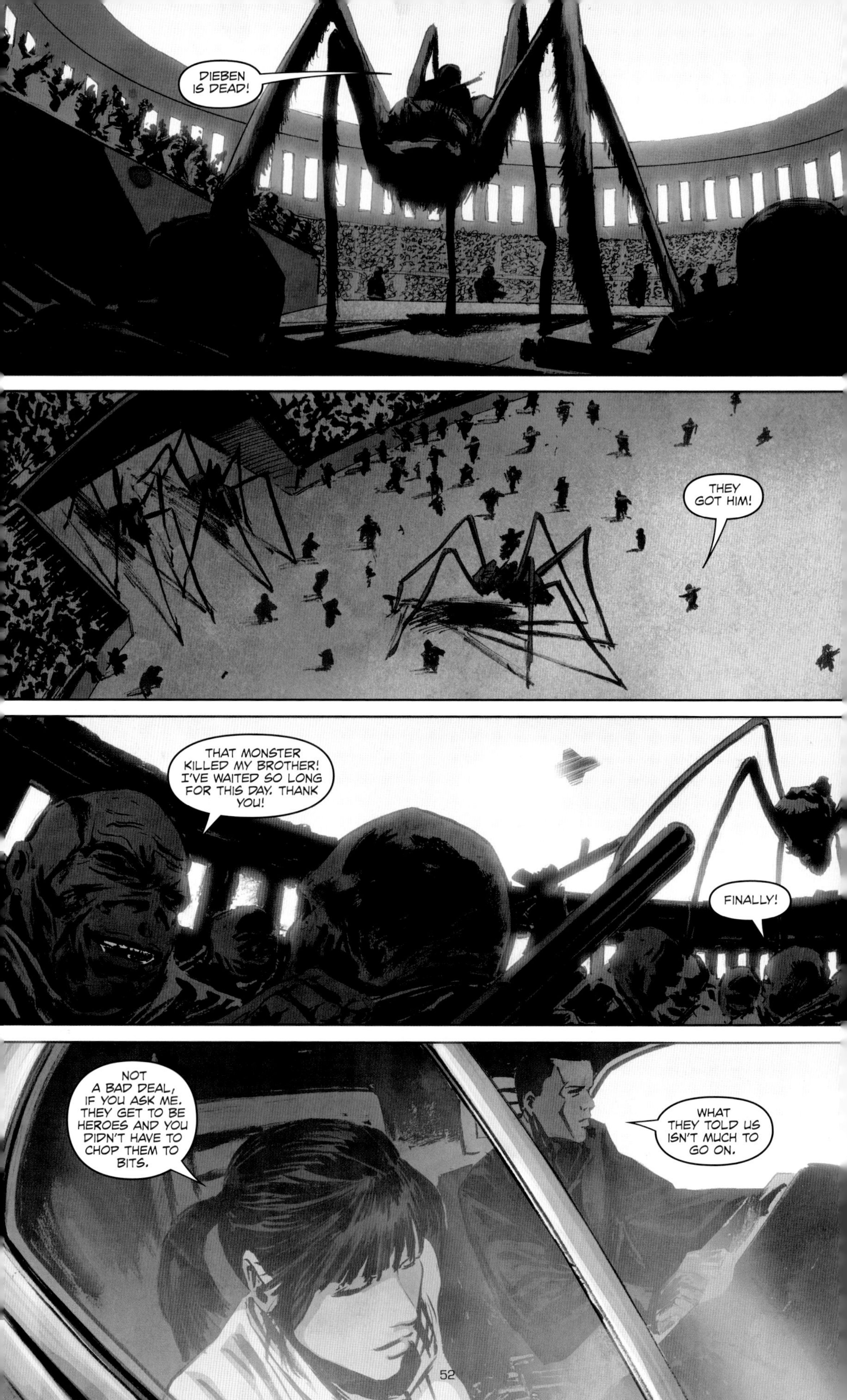
DIEBEN IS DEAD!
THEY GOT HIM!
THAT MONSTER KILLED MY BROTHER! I'VE WAITED SO LONG FOR THIS DAY. THANK YOU!
FINALLY!
NOT A BAD DEAL, IF YOU ASK ME. THEY GET TO BE HEROES AND YOU DIDN'T HAVE TO CHOP THEM TO BITS.
WHAT THEY TOLD US ISN'T MUCH TO GO ON.

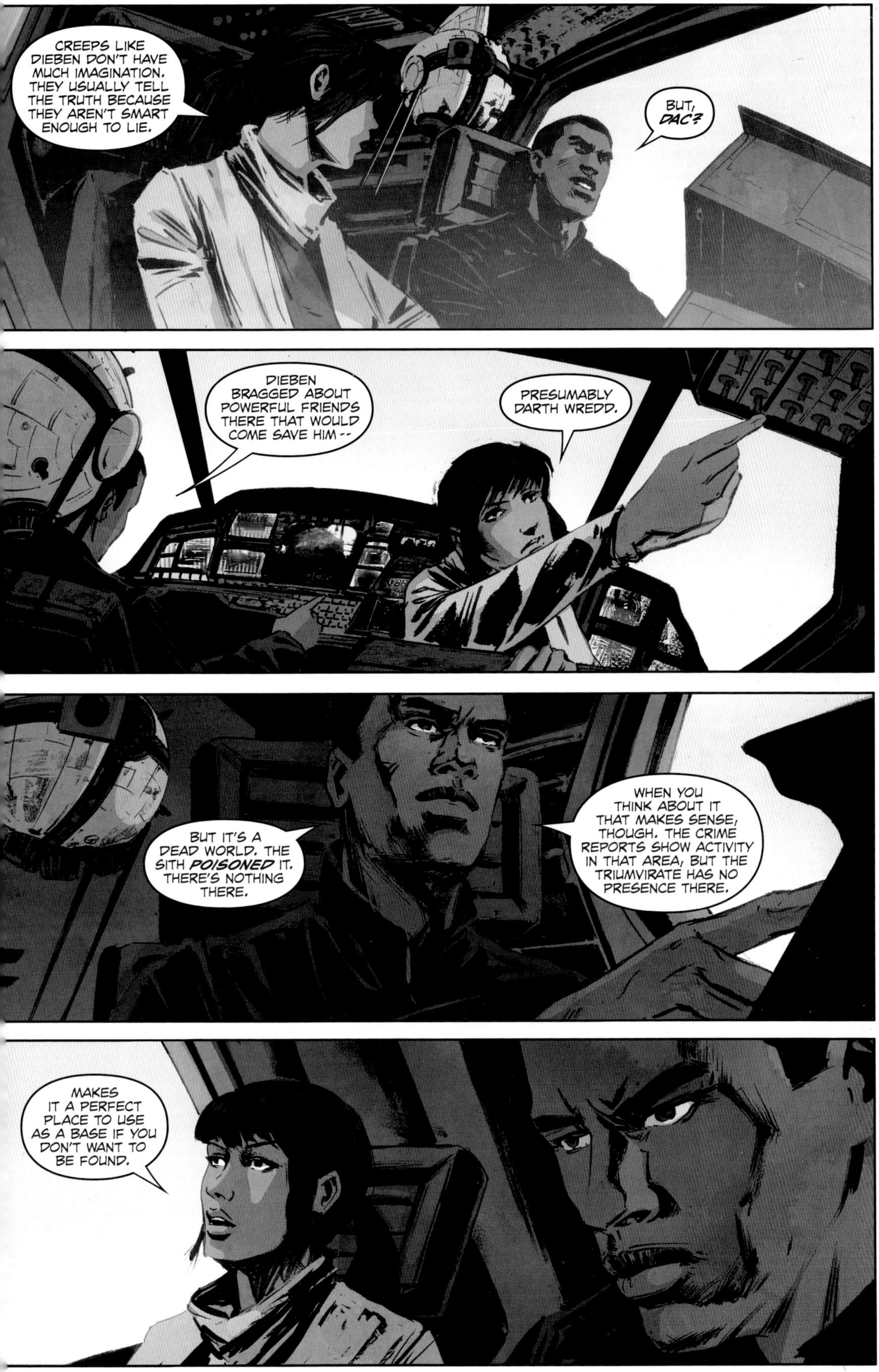
CREEPS LIKE DIEBEN DON'T HAVE MUCH IMAGINATION. THEY USUALLY TELL THE TRUTH BECAUSE THEY AREN'T SMART ENOUGH TO LIE.
BUT, *DAC?*
DIEBEN BRAGGED ABOUT POWERFUL FRIENDS THERE THAT WOULD COME SAVE HIM --
PRESUMABLY DARTH WREDD.
BUT IT'S A DEAD WORLD. THE SITH *POISONED* IT. THERE'S NOTHING THERE.
WHEN YOU THINK ABOUT IT THAT MAKES SENSE, THOUGH. THE CRIME REPORTS SHOW ACTIVITY IN THAT AREA, BUT THE TRIUMVIRATE HAS NO PRESENCE THERE.
MAKES IT A PERFECT PLACE TO USE AS A BASE IF YOU DON'T WANT TO BE FOUND.

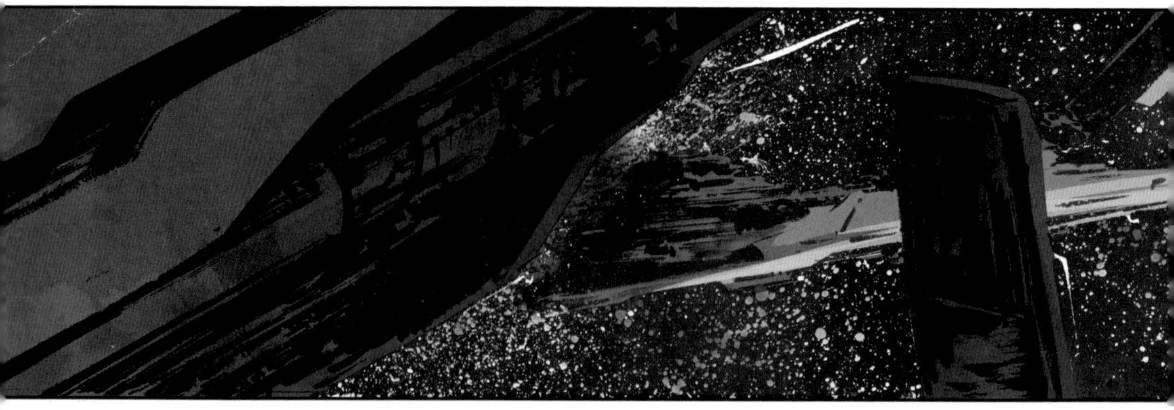

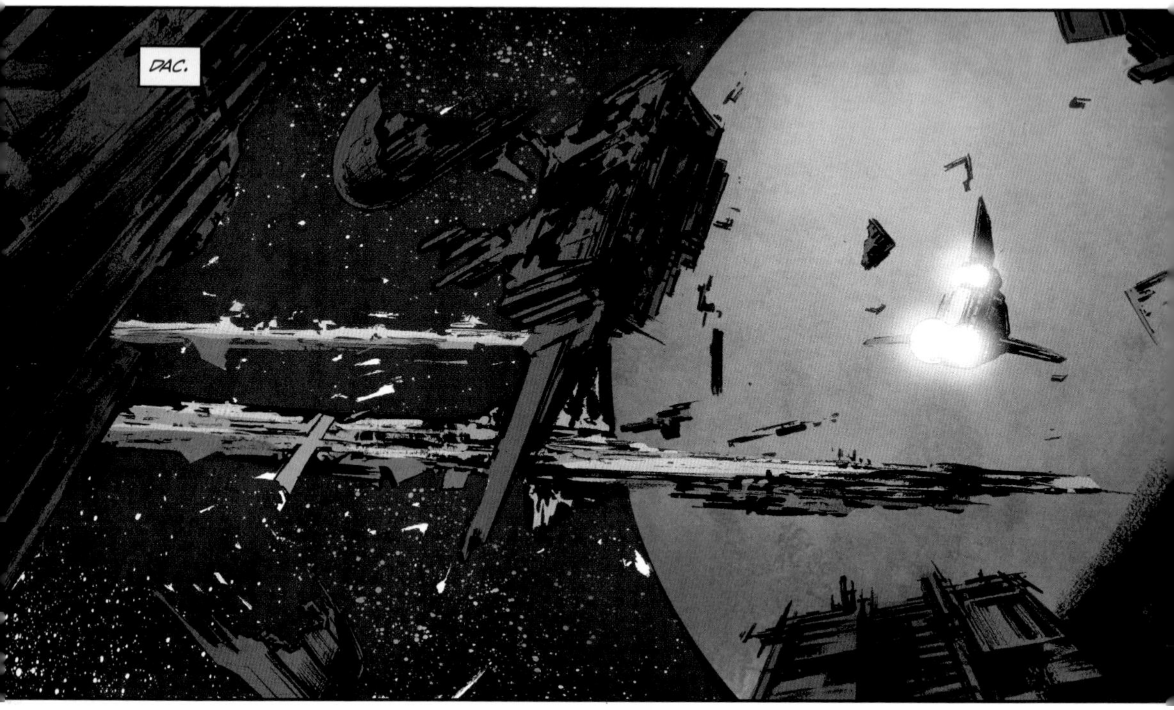
DAC.

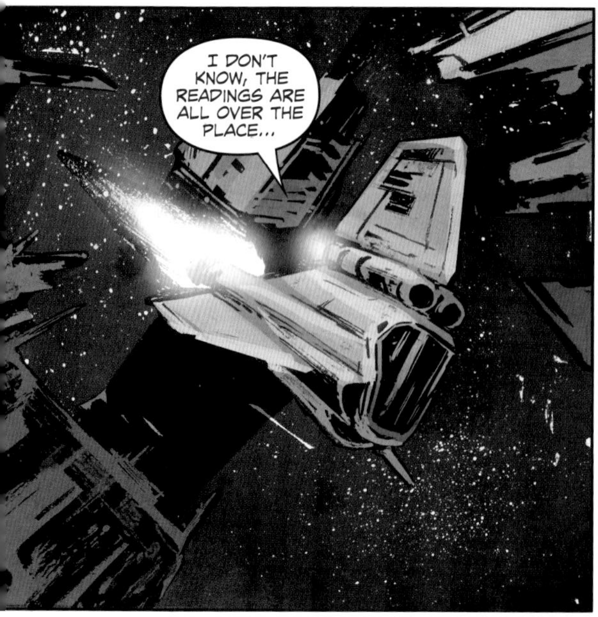
I DON'T KNOW, THE READINGS ARE ALL OVER THE PLACE...

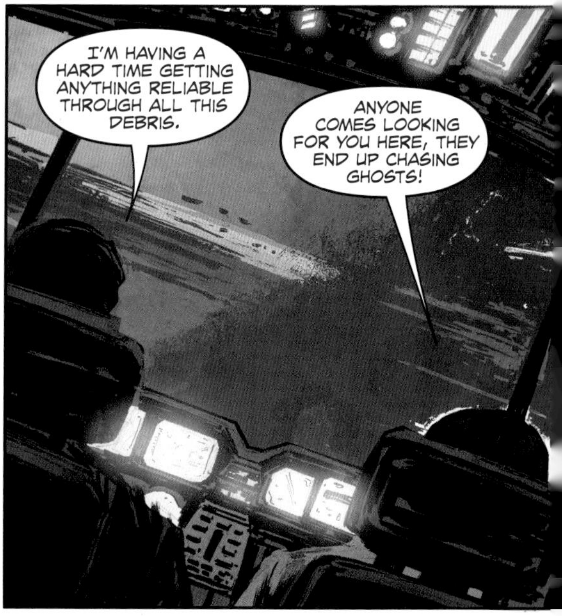
I'M HAVING A HARD TIME GETTING ANYTHING RELIABLE THROUGH ALL THIS DEBRIS.
ANYONE COMES LOOKING FOR YOU HERE, THEY END UP CHASING GHOSTS!

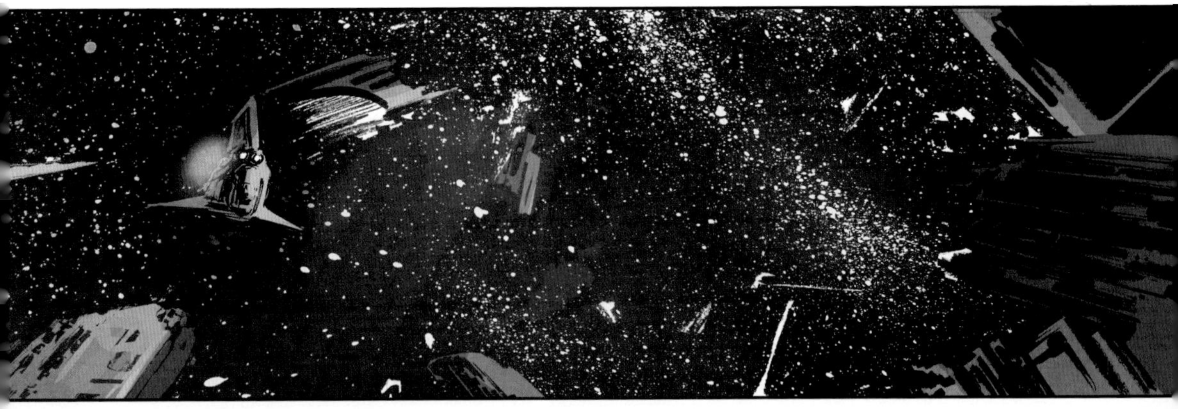

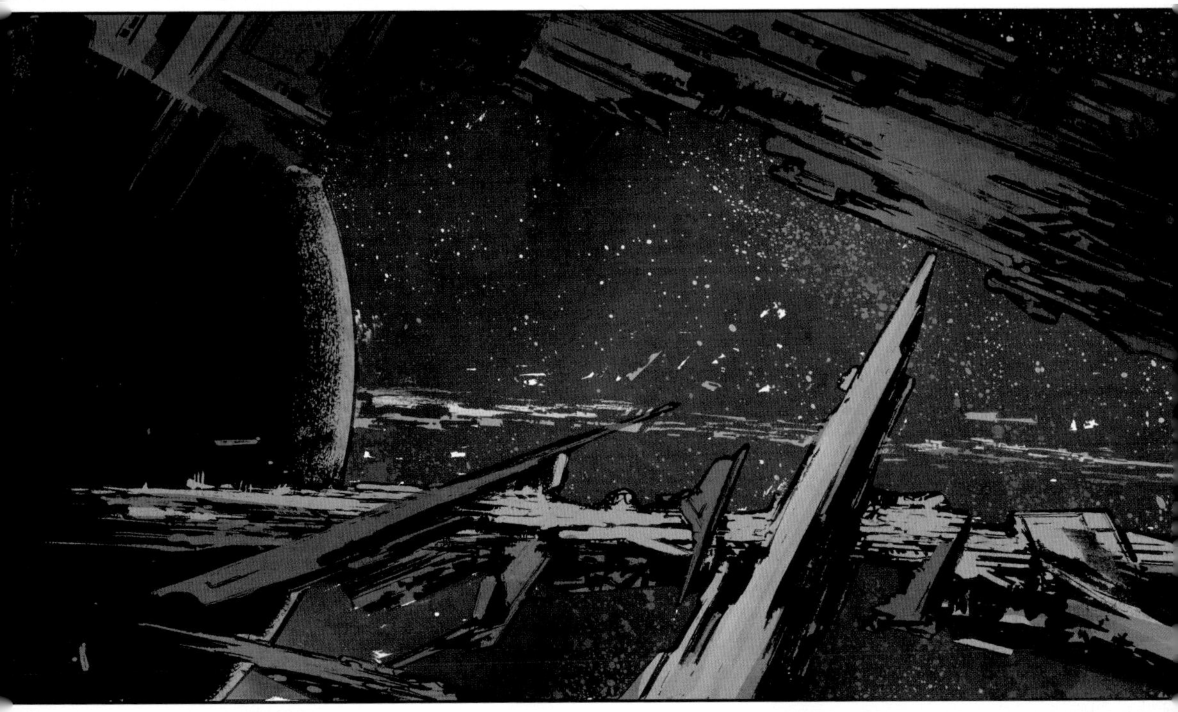

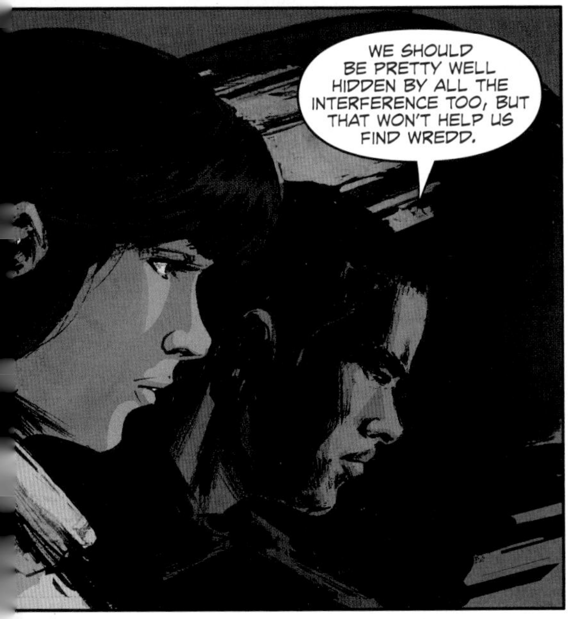
WE SHOULD BE PRETTY WELL HIDDEN BY ALL THE INTERFERENCE TOO, BUT THAT WON'T HELP US FIND WREDD.

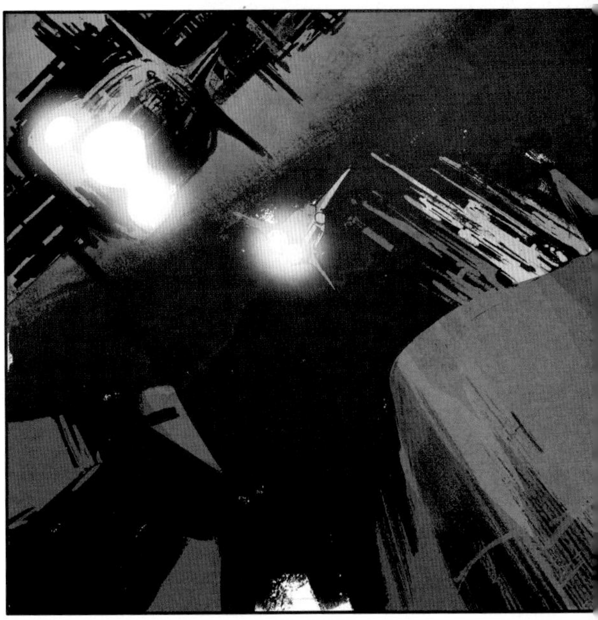

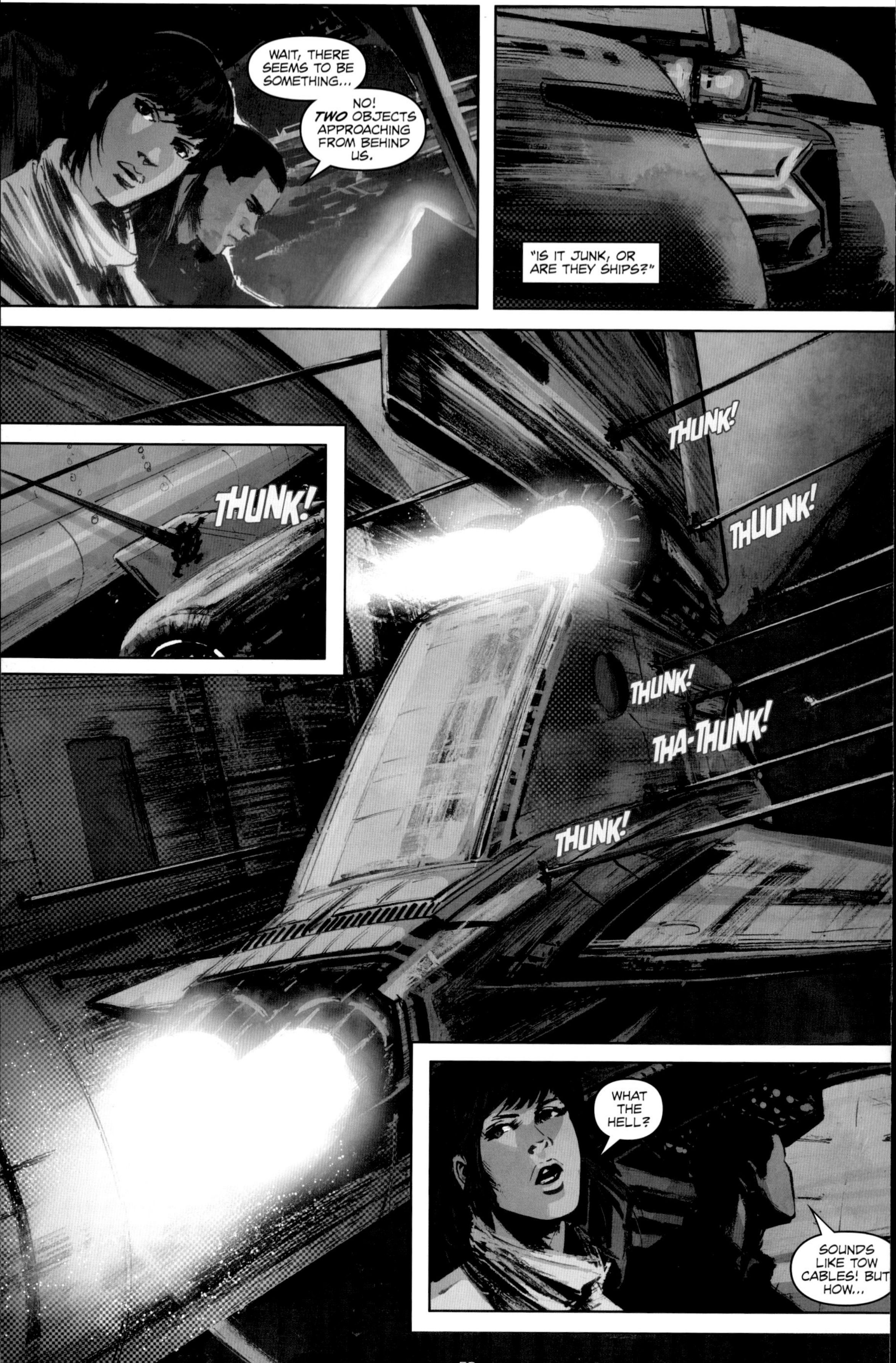
WAIT, THERE SEEMS TO BE SOMETHING...
NO! *TWO* OBJECTS APPROACHING FROM BEHIND US.
"IS IT JUNK, OR ARE THEY SHIPS?"
THUNK!
THUNK!
THUUNK!
THUNK!
THA-THUNK!
THUNK!
WHAT THE HELL?
SOUNDS LIKE TOW CABLES! BUT HOW...

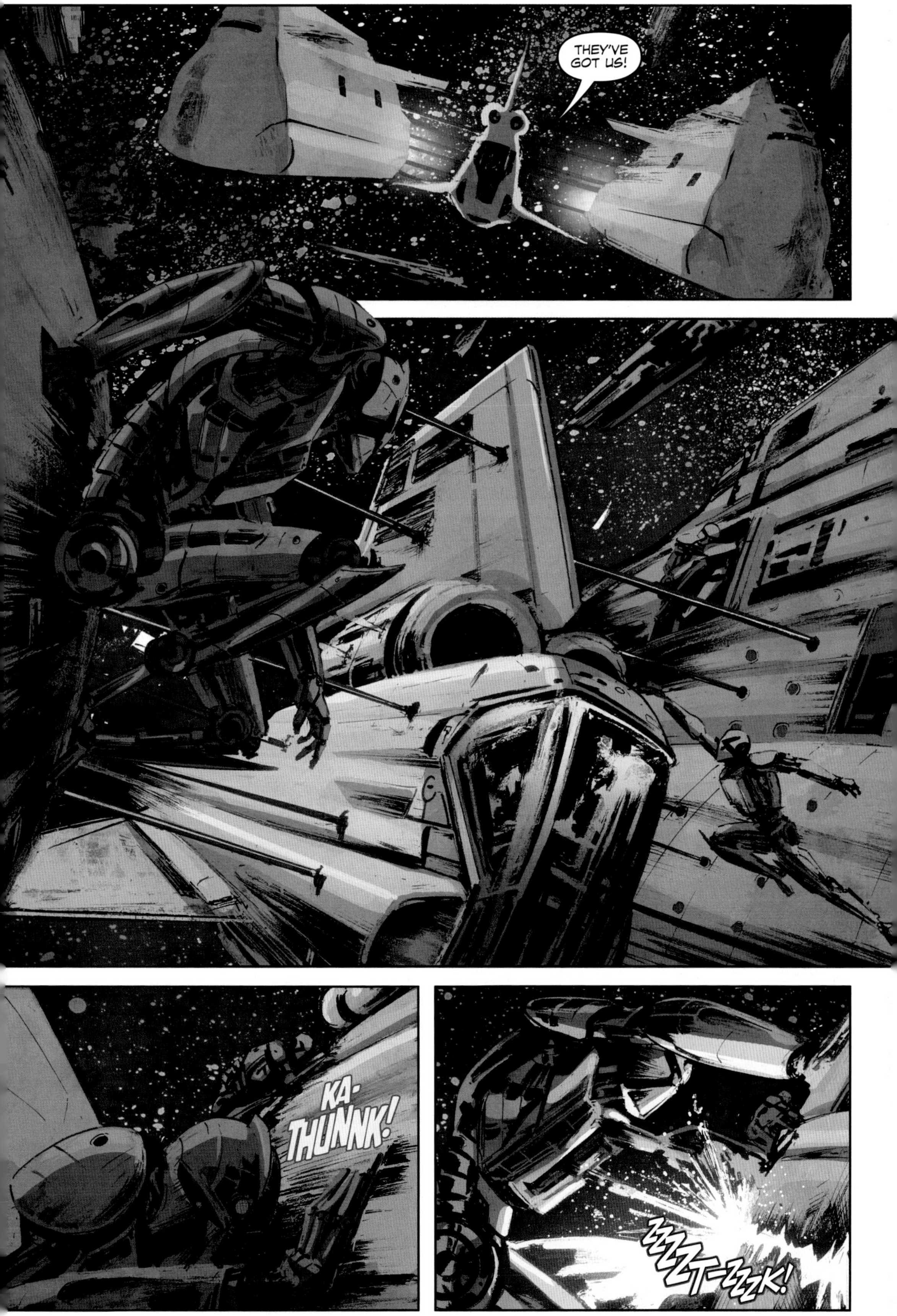
THEY'VE GOT US!
KA-THUNNK!
ZZZZT-ZZZK!

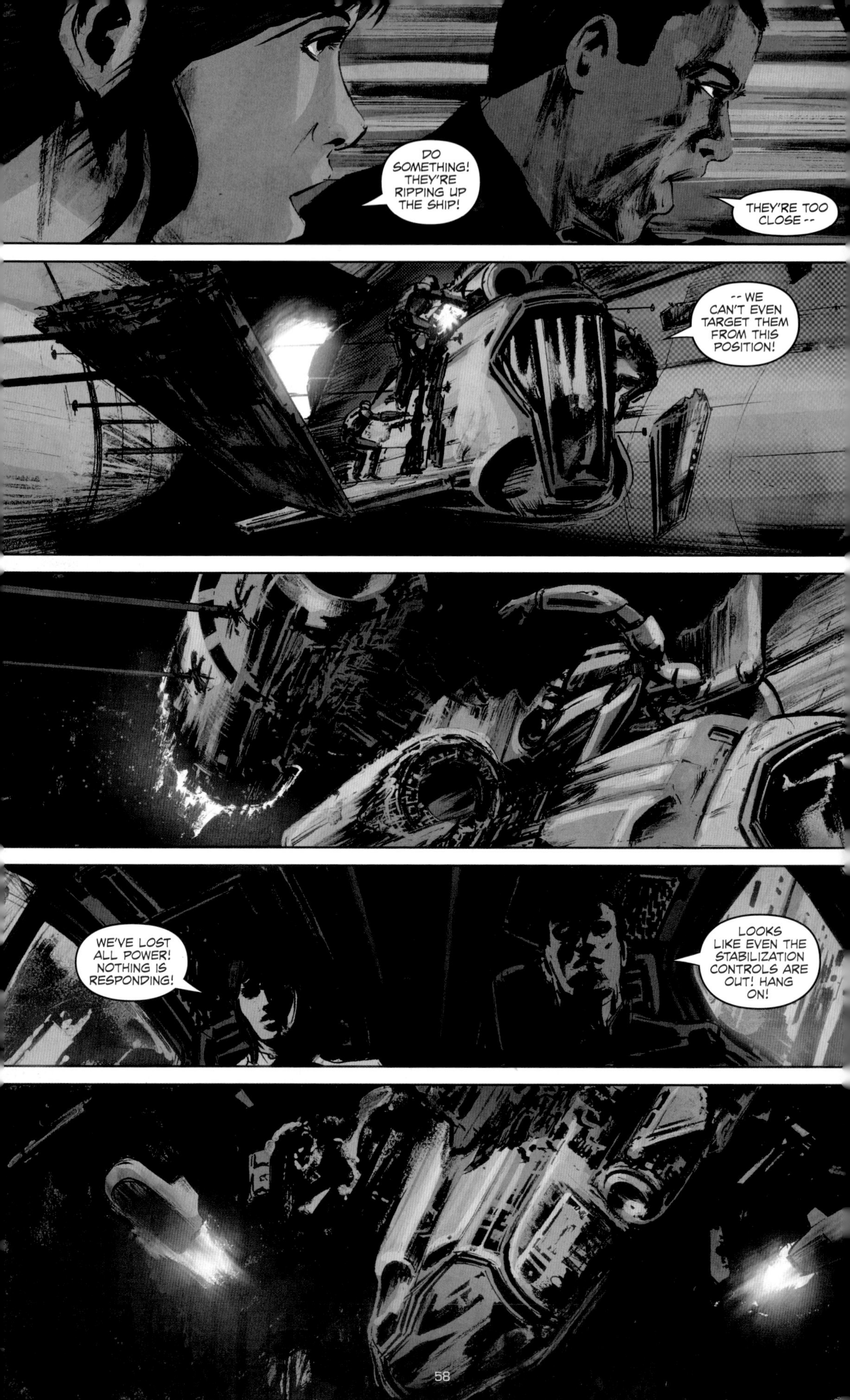
DO SOMETHING! THEY'RE RIPPING UP THE SHIP!
THEY'RE TOO CLOSE --
-- WE CAN'T EVEN TARGET THEM FROM THIS POSITION!
WE'VE LOST ALL POWER! NOTHING IS RESPONDING!
LOOKS LIKE EVEN THE STABILIZATION CONTROLS ARE OUT! HANG ON!

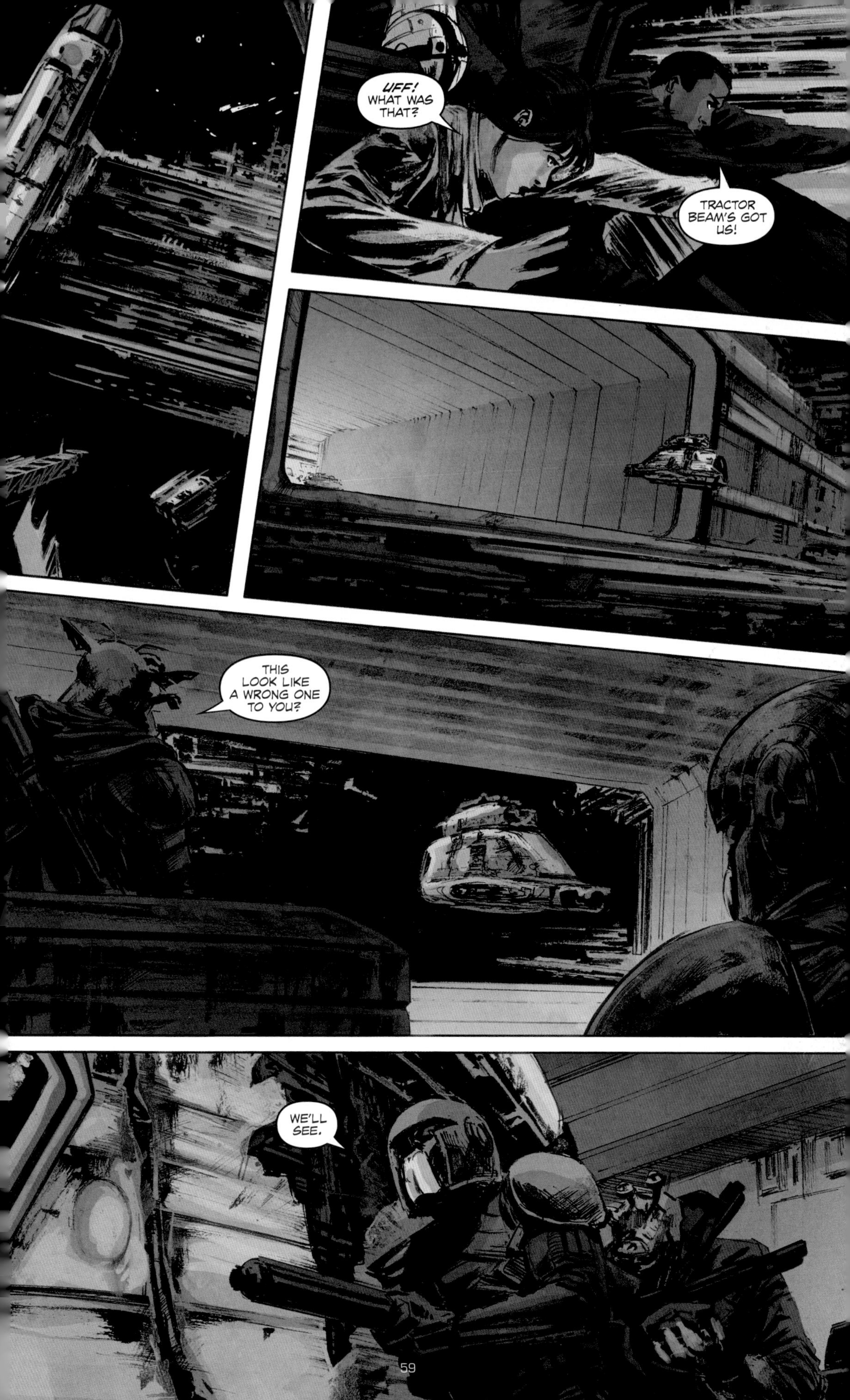
UFF! WHAT WAS THAT?
TRACTOR BEAM'S GOT US!
THIS LOOK LIKE A WRONG ONE TO YOU?
WE'LL SEE.

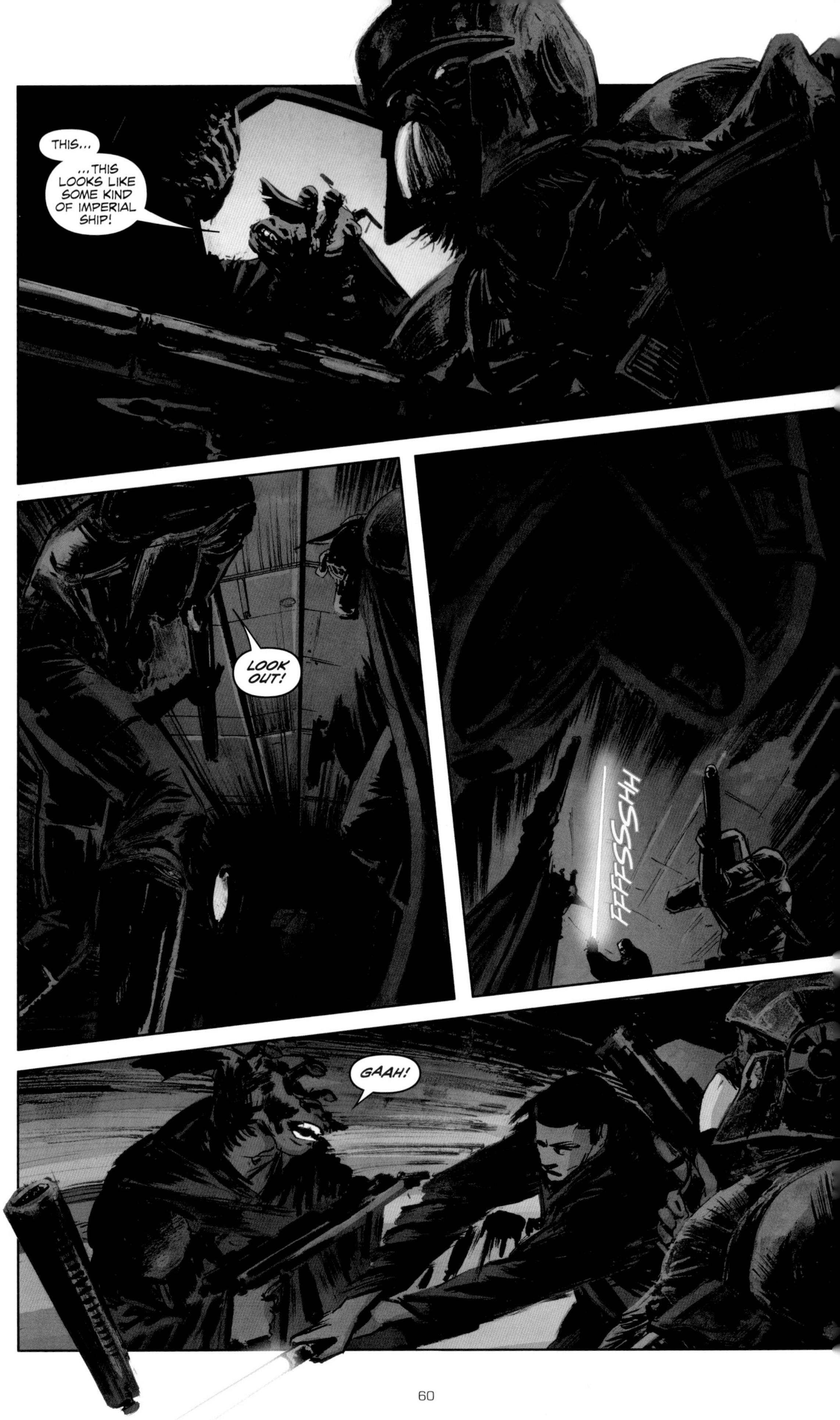
THIS...
...THIS LOOKS LIKE SOME KIND OF IMPERIAL SHIP!
LOOK OUT!
FFFFSSSHH
GAAH!

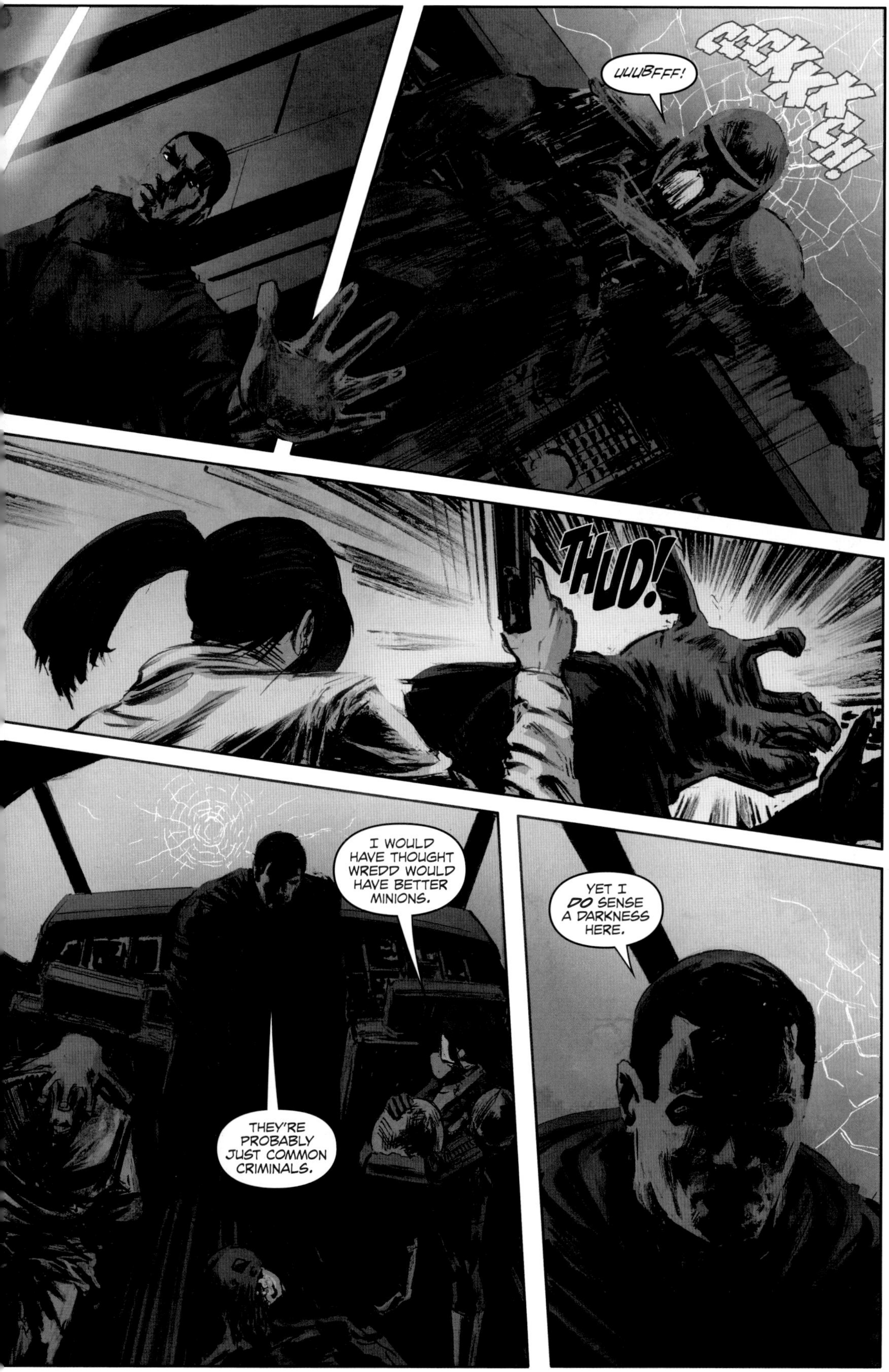

UUUBFFF!
CCCKKKSH!
THUD!
I WOULD HAVE THOUGHT WREDD WOULD HAVE BETTER MINIONS.
THEY'RE PROBABLY JUST COMMON CRIMINALS.
YET I *DO* SENSE A DARKNESS HERE.

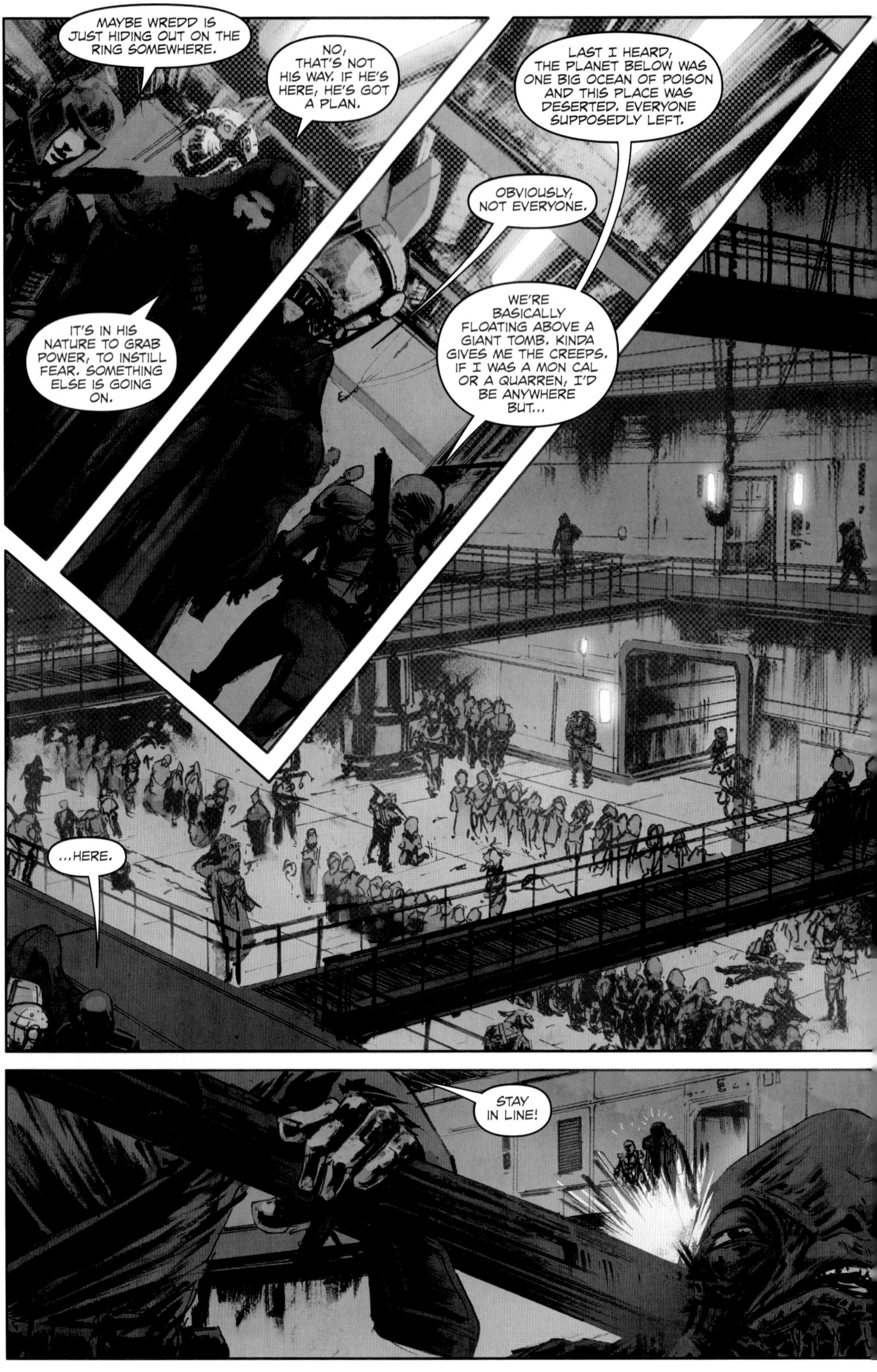

MAYBE WREDD IS JUST HIDING OUT ON THE RING SOMEWHERE.
NO, THAT'S NOT HIS WAY. IF HE'S HERE, HE'S GOT A PLAN.
IT'S IN HIS NATURE TO GRAB POWER, TO INSTILL FEAR. SOMETHING ELSE IS GOING ON.
LAST I HEARD, THE PLANET BELOW WAS ONE BIG OCEAN OF POISON AND THIS PLACE WAS DESERTED. EVERYONE SUPPOSEDLY LEFT.
OBVIOUSLY, NOT EVERYONE.
WE'RE BASICALLY FLOATING ABOVE A GIANT TOMB. KINDA GIVES ME THE CREEPS. IF I WAS A MON CAL OR A QUARREN, I'D BE ANYWHERE BUT...
...HERE.
STAY IN LINE!

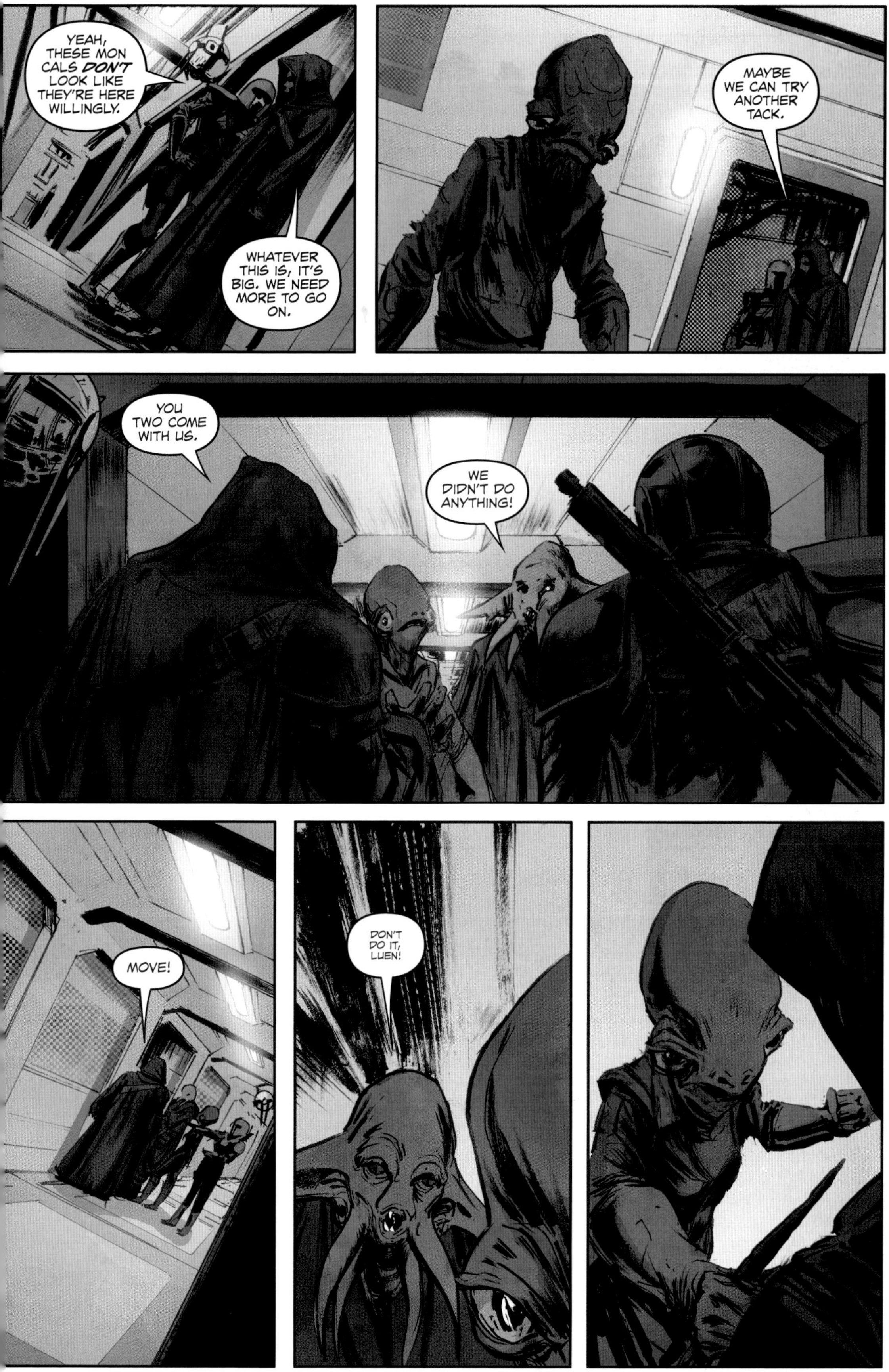
YEAH, THESE MON CALS *DON'T* LOOK LIKE THEY'RE HERE WILLINGLY.
WHATEVER THIS IS, IT'S BIG. WE NEED MORE TO GO ON.
MAYBE WE CAN TRY ANOTHER TACK.
YOU TWO COME WITH US.
WE DIDN'T DO ANYTHING!
MOVE!
DON'T DO IT, LUEN!

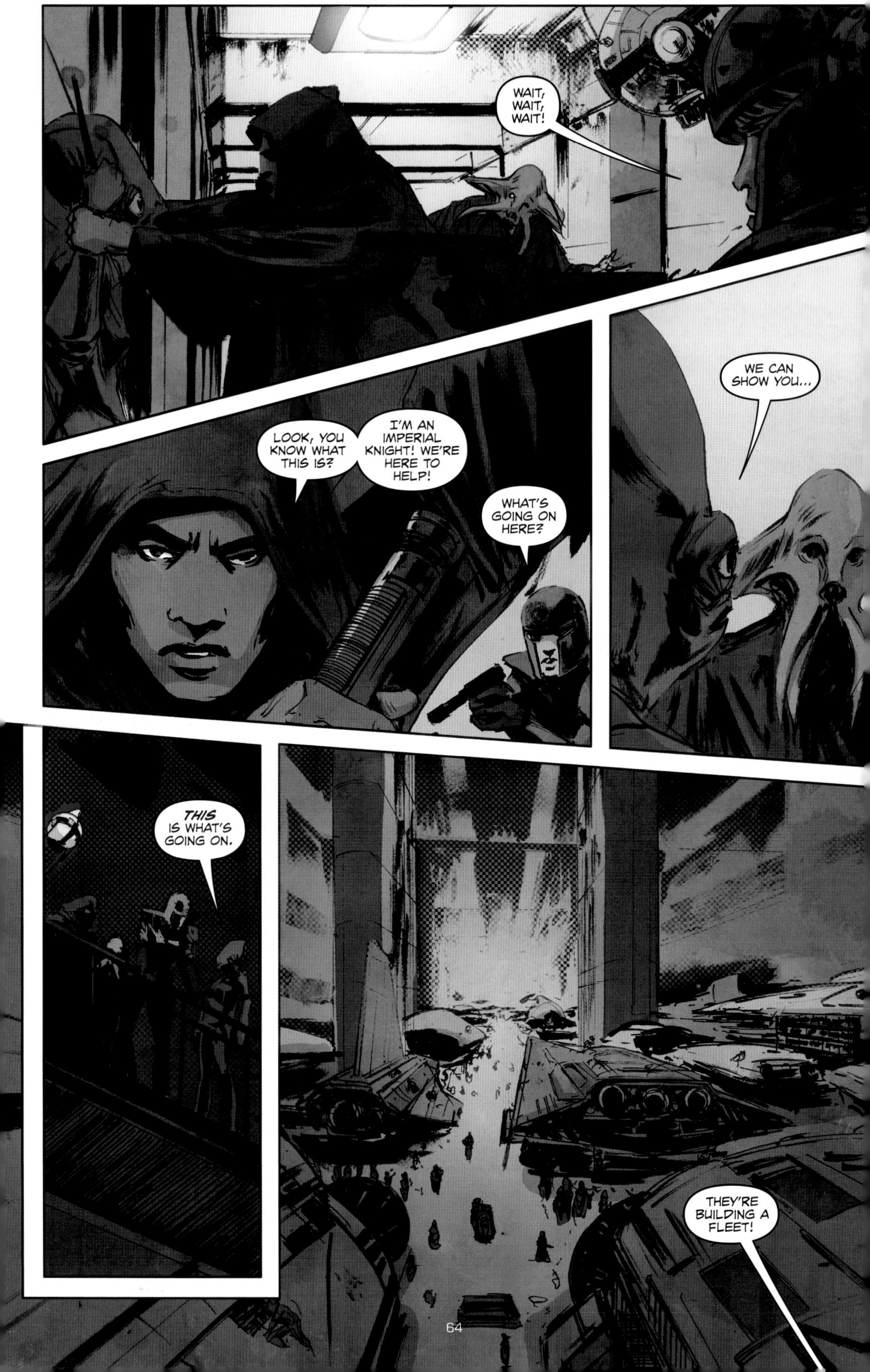
WAIT, WAIT, WAIT!
LOOK, YOU KNOW WHAT THIS IS?
I'M AN IMPERIAL KNIGHT! WE'RE HERE TO HELP!
WHAT'S GOING ON HERE?
WE CAN SHOW YOU...
THIS IS WHAT'S GOING ON.
THEY'RE BUILDING A FLEET!

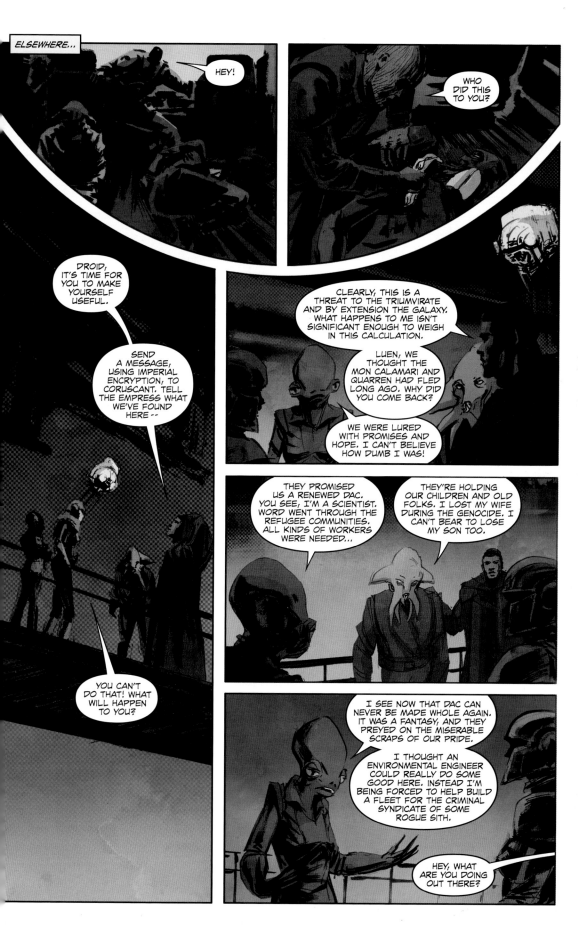

ELSEWHERE...

HEY!

WHO DID THIS TO YOU?

DROID, IT'S TIME FOR YOU TO MAKE YOURSELF USEFUL.

SEND A MESSAGE, USING IMPERIAL ENCRYPTION, TO CORUSCANT. TELL THE EMPRESS WHAT WE'VE FOUND HERE --

CLEARLY, THIS IS A THREAT TO THE TRIUMVIRATE AND BY EXTENSION THE GALAXY. WHAT HAPPENS TO ME ISN'T SIGNIFICANT ENOUGH TO WEIGH IN THIS CALCULATION.

LUEN, WE THOUGHT THE MON CALAMARI AND QUARREN HAD FLED LONG AGO. WHY DID YOU COME BACK?

WE WERE LURED WITH PROMISES AND HOPE. I CAN'T BELIEVE HOW DUMB I WAS!

THEY PROMISED US A RENEWED DAC. YOU SEE, I'M A SCIENTIST. WORD WENT THROUGH THE REFUGEE COMMUNITIES. ALL KINDS OF WORKERS WERE NEEDED...

THEY'RE HOLDING OUR CHILDREN AND OLD FOLKS. I LOST MY WIFE DURING THE GENOCIDE. I CAN'T BEAR TO LOSE MY SON TOO.

YOU CAN'T DO THAT! WHAT WILL HAPPEN TO YOU?

I SEE NOW THAT DAC CAN NEVER BE MADE WHOLE AGAIN. IT WAS A FANTASY, AND THEY PREYED ON THE MISERABLE SCRAPS OF OUR PRIDE.

I THOUGHT AN ENVIRONMENTAL ENGINEER COULD REALLY DO SOME GOOD HERE. INSTEAD I'M BEING FORCED TO HELP BUILD A FLEET FOR THE CRIMINAL SYNDICATE OF SOME ROGUE SITH.

HEY, WHAT ARE YOU DOING OUT THERE?

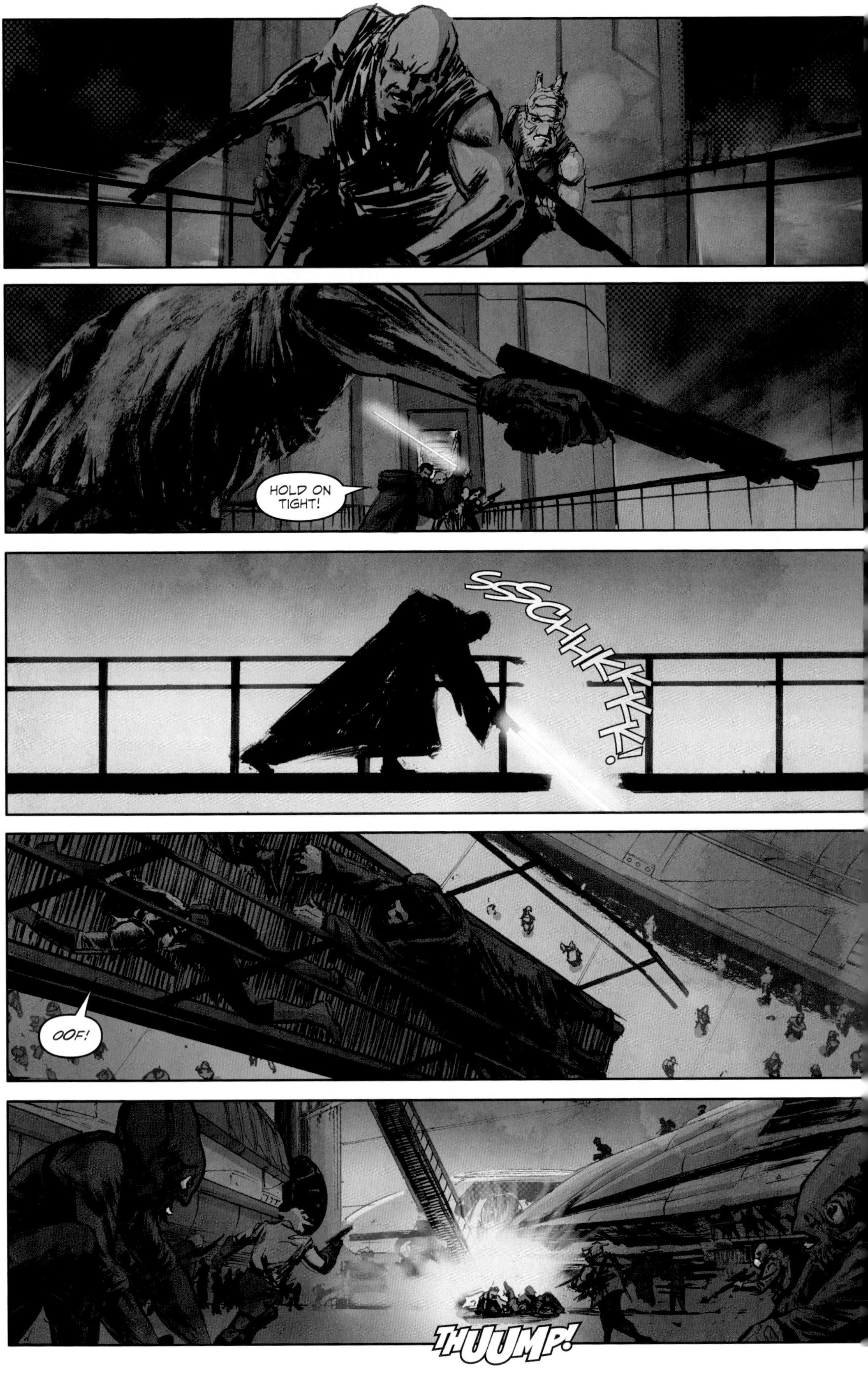
HOLD ON TIGHT!
SSSCHHKKKK!
OOF!
THUUMP!

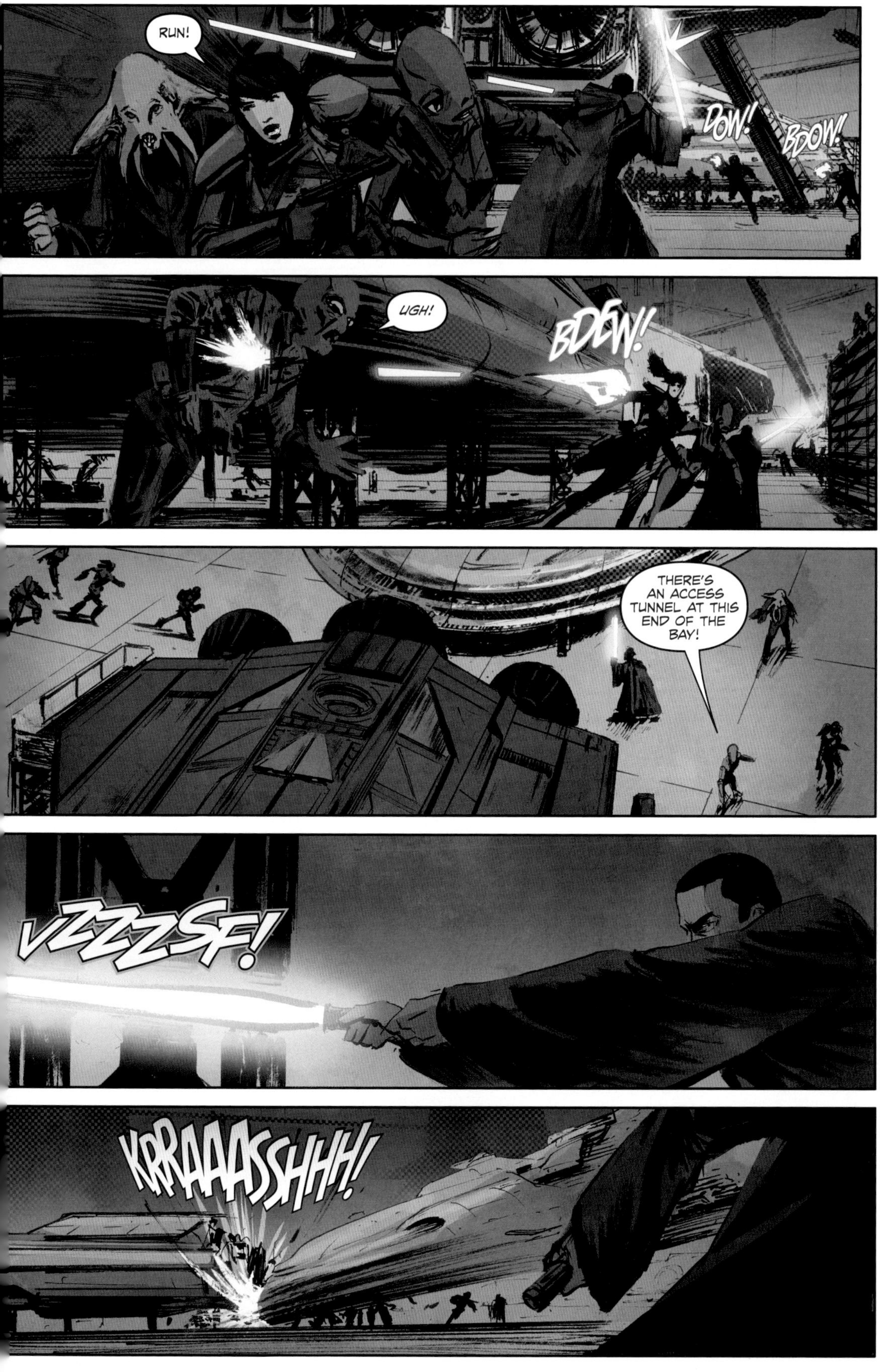
RUN!
DOW!
BDOW!
UGH!
BDEW!
THERE'S AN ACCESS TUNNEL AT THIS END OF THE BAY!
VZZZSF!
KRRAAASSHHH!

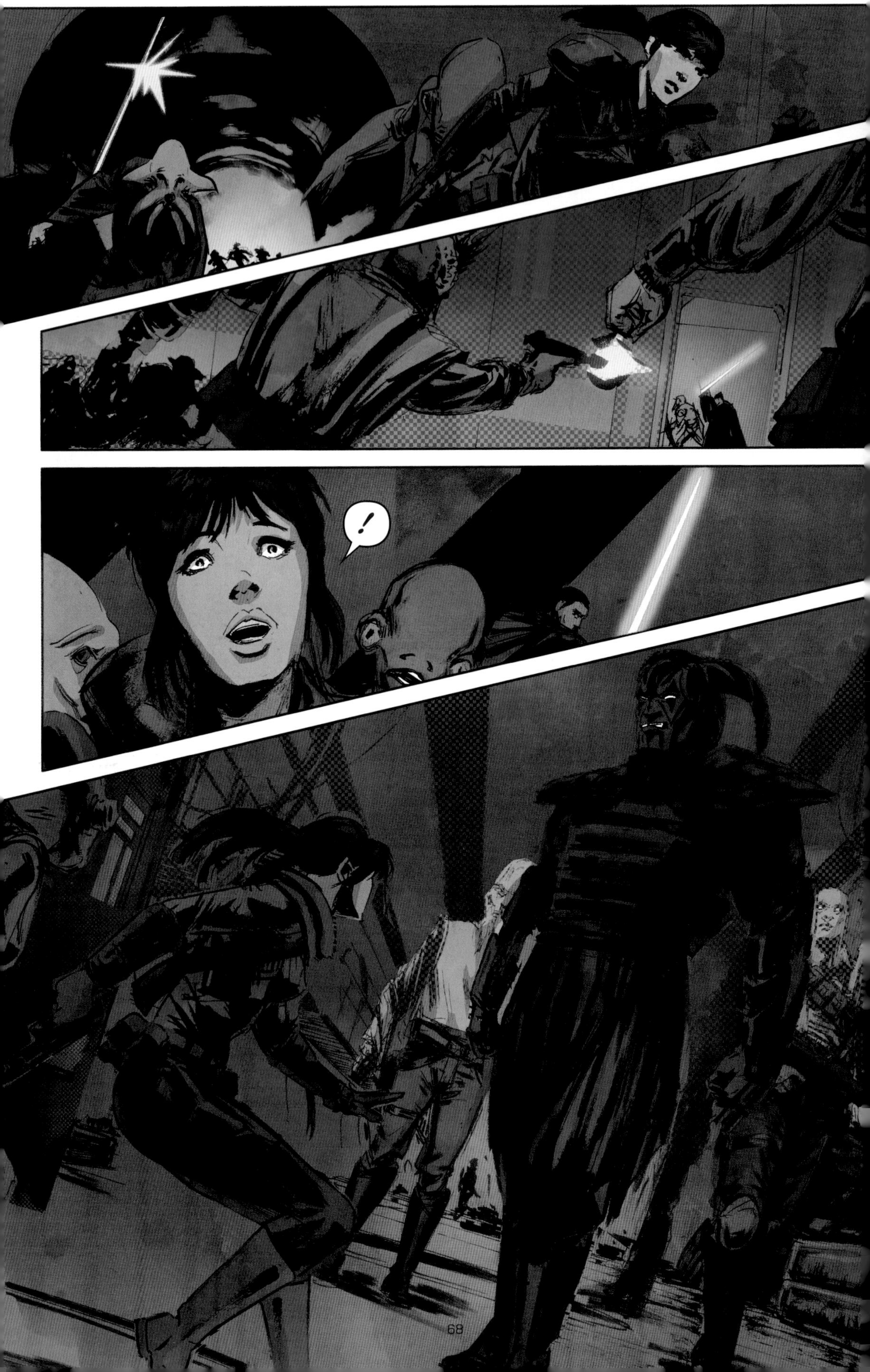
!

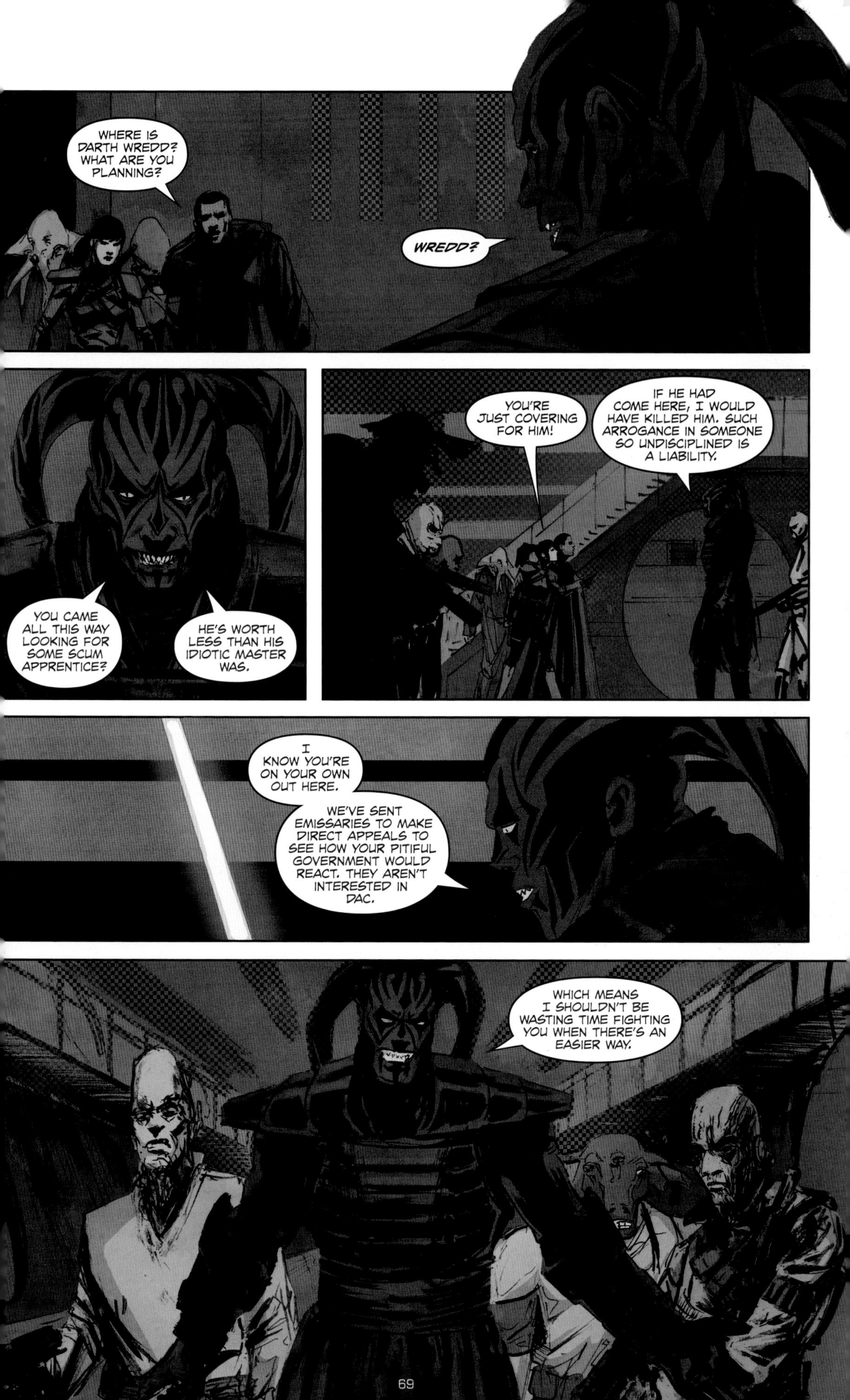
WHERE IS DARTH WREDD? WHAT ARE YOU PLANNING?
WREDD?
YOU CAME ALL THIS WAY LOOKING FOR SOME SCUM APPRENTICE?
HE'S WORTH LESS THAN HIS IDIOTIC MASTER WAS.
YOU'RE JUST COVERING FOR HIM!
IF HE HAD COME HERE, I WOULD HAVE KILLED HIM. SUCH ARROGANCE IN SOMEONE SO UNDISCIPLINED IS A LIABILITY.
I KNOW YOU'RE ON YOUR OWN OUT HERE.
WE'VE SENT EMISSARIES TO MAKE DIRECT APPEALS TO SEE HOW YOUR PITIFUL GOVERNMENT WOULD REACT. THEY AREN'T INTERESTED IN DAC.
WHICH MEANS I SHOULDN'T BE WASTING TIME FIGHTING YOU WHEN THERE'S AN EASIER WAY.

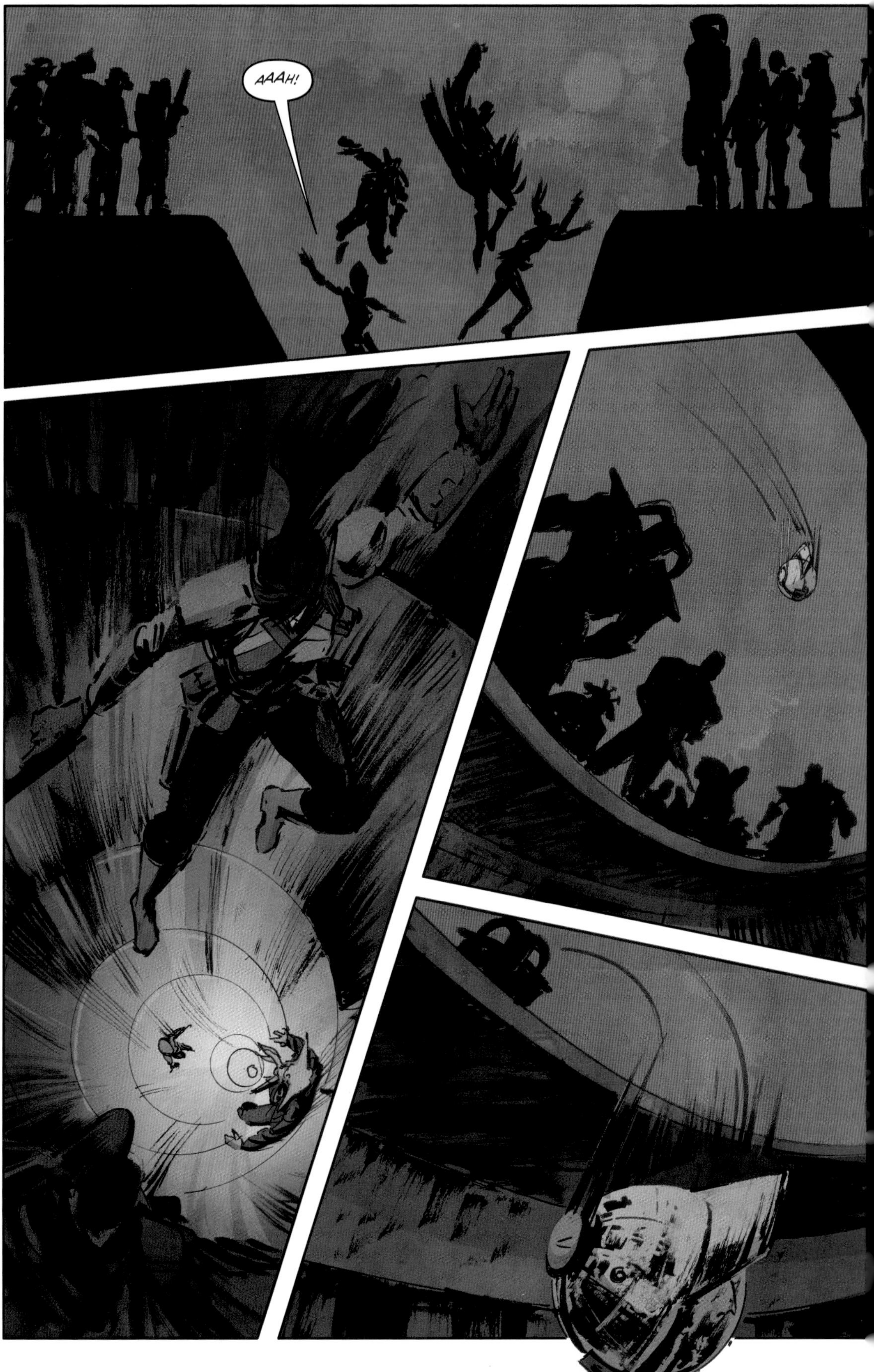
AAAH!

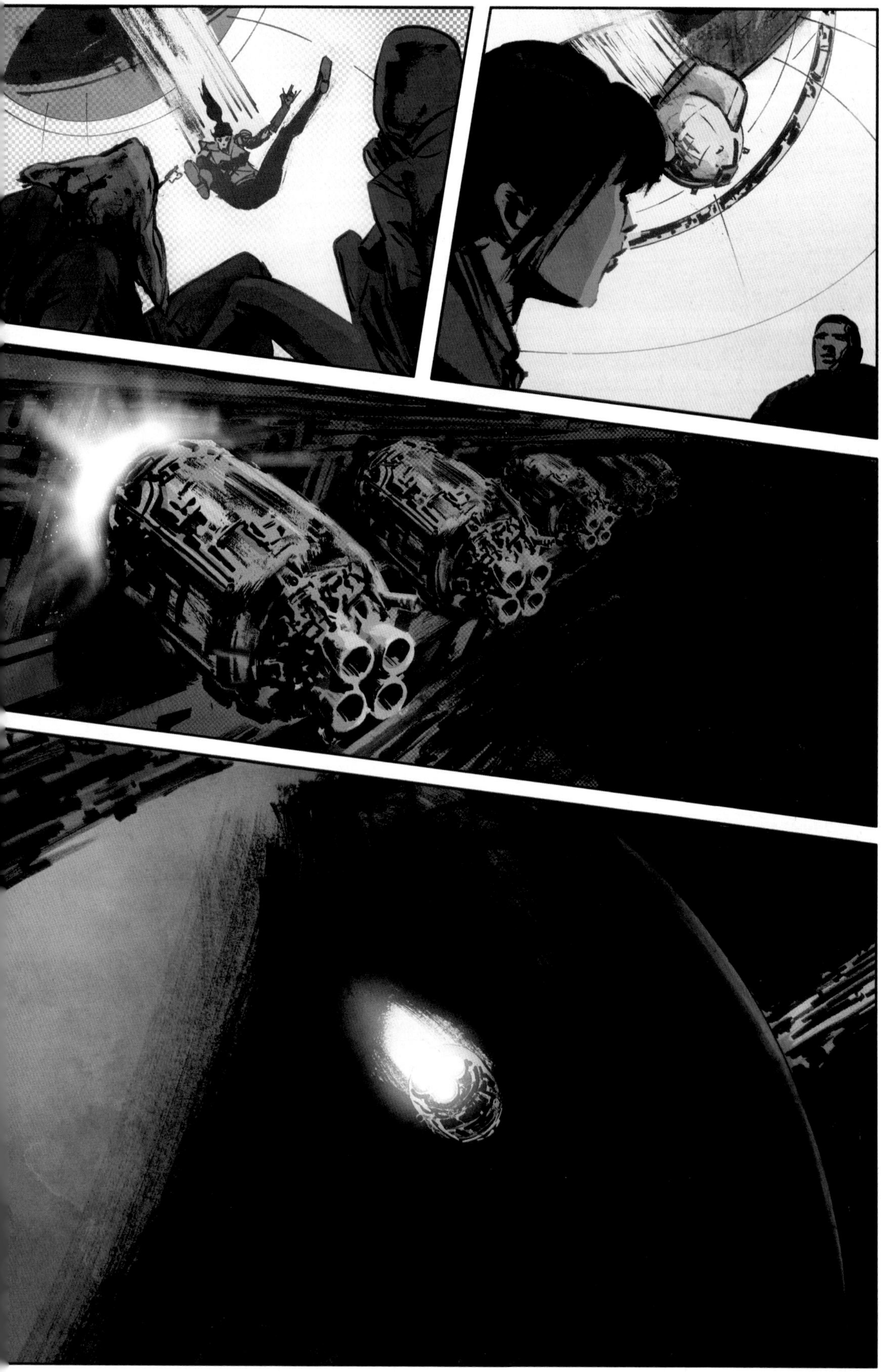

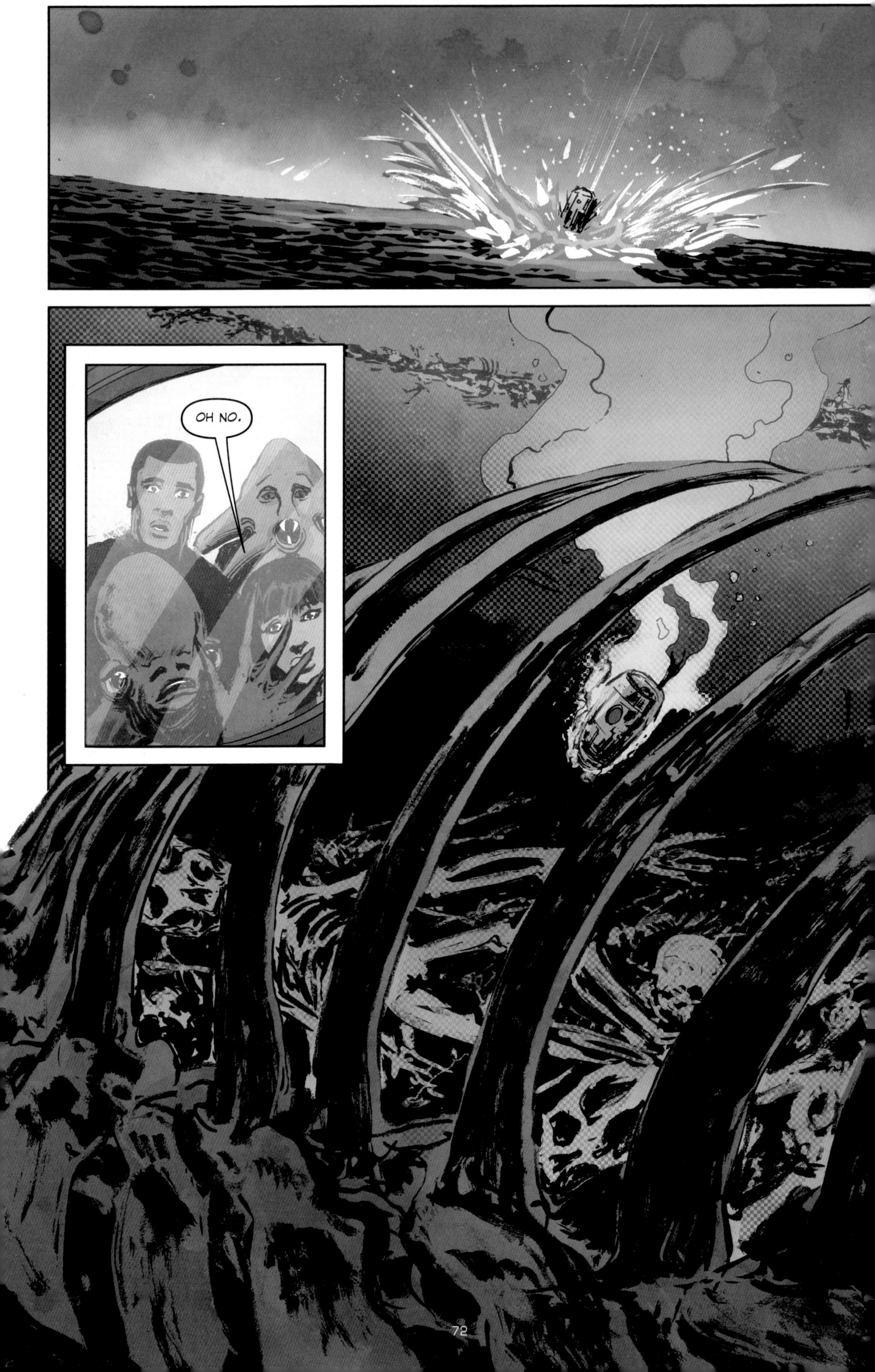
OH NO.

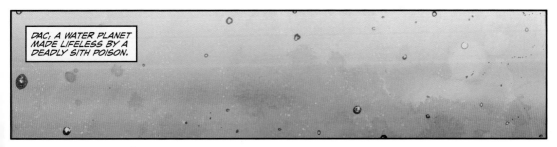

DAC, A WATER PLANET MADE LIFELESS BY A DEADLY SITH POISON.

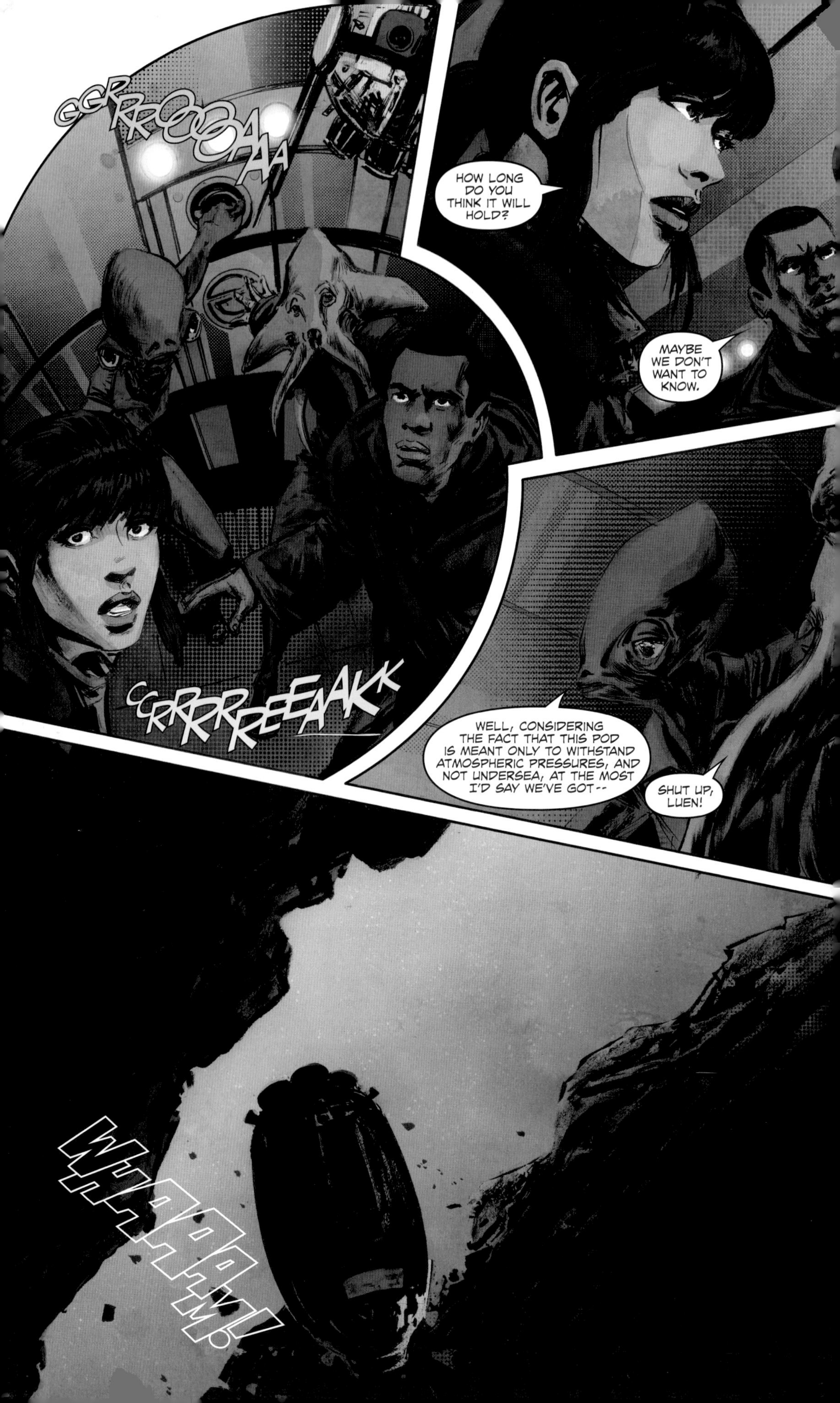
GGRRROOOOAAAA
CCRRRRREEEAAKK
HOW LONG DO YOU THINK IT WILL HOLD?
MAYBE WE DON'T WANT TO KNOW.
WELL, CONSIDERING THE FACT THAT THIS POD IS MEANT ONLY TO WITHSTAND ATMOSPHERIC PRESSURES, AND NOT UNDERSEA, AT THE MOST I'D SAY WE'VE GOT--
SHUT UP, LUEN!
WHAAM!

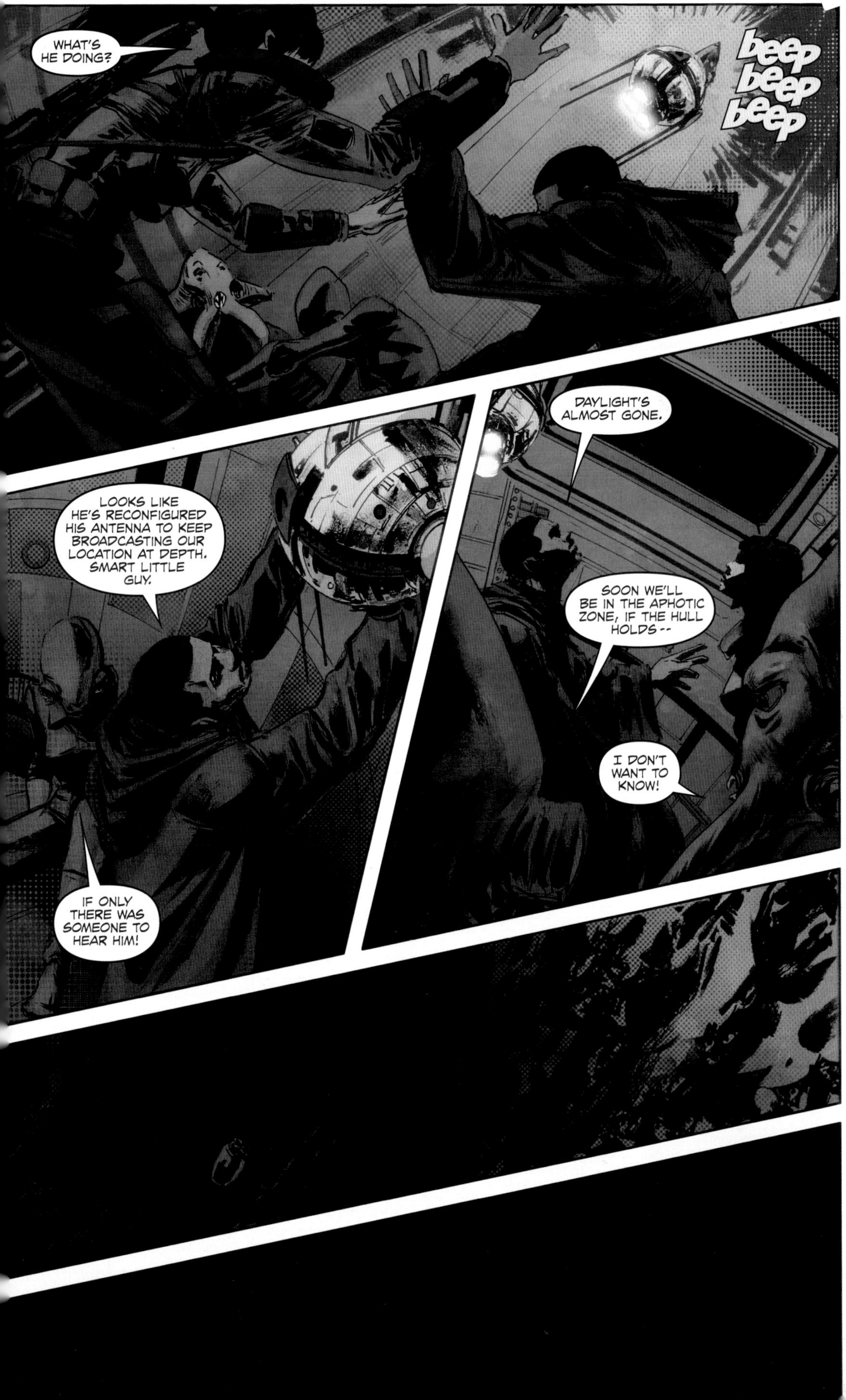
WHAT'S HE DOING?
beep beep beep
LOOKS LIKE HE'S RECONFIGURED HIS ANTENNA TO KEEP BROADCASTING OUR LOCATION AT DEPTH. SMART LITTLE GUY.
IF ONLY THERE WAS SOMEONE TO HEAR HIM!
DAYLIGHT'S ALMOST GONE.
SOON WE'LL BE IN THE APHOTIC ZONE, IF THE HULL HOLDS--
I DON'T WANT TO KNOW!

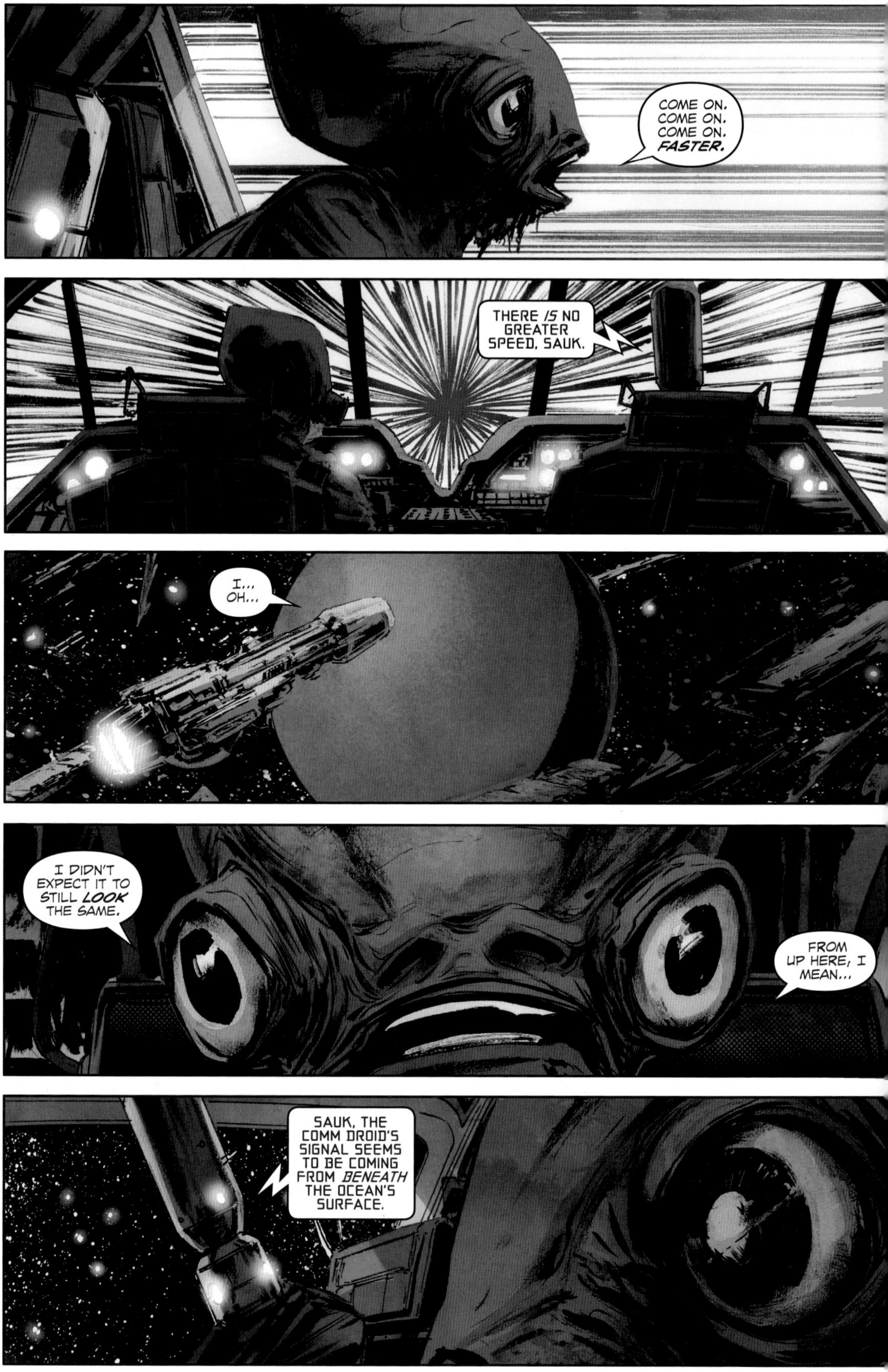

COME ON. COME ON. COME ON. FASTER.
THERE IS NO GREATER SPEED, SAUK.
I... OH...
I DIDN'T EXPECT IT TO STILL LOOK THE SAME.
FROM UP HERE, I MEAN...
SAUK, THE COMM DROID'S SIGNAL SEEMS TO BE COMING FROM BENEATH THE OCEAN'S SURFACE.

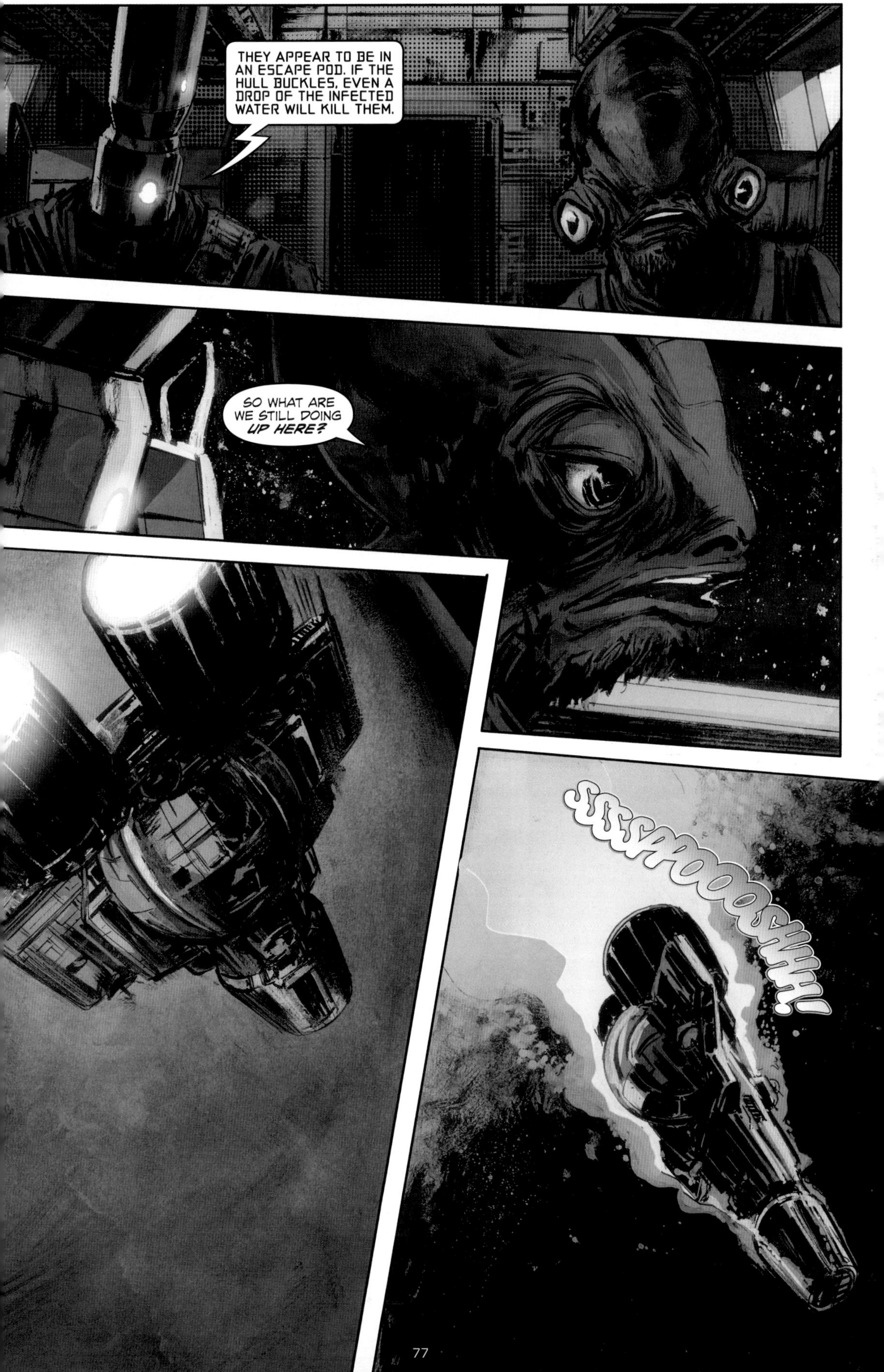

THEY APPEAR TO BE IN AN ESCAPE POD. IF THE HULL BUCKLES, EVEN A DROP OF THE INFECTED WATER WILL KILL THEM.
SO WHAT ARE WE STILL DOING UP HERE?
SSSPOOOSHH!

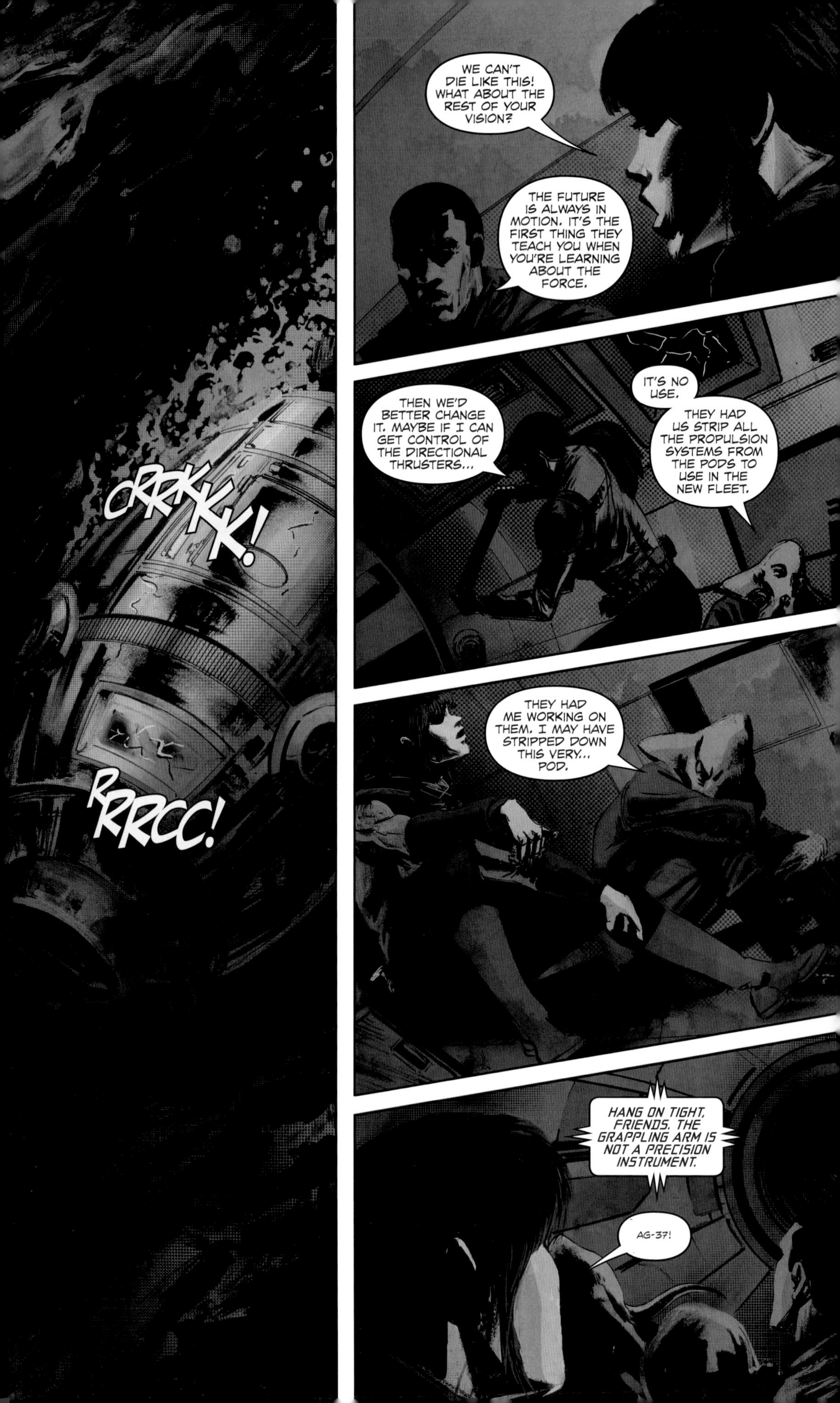
CRRKKK!
RRRCC!
WE CAN'T DIE LIKE THIS! WHAT ABOUT THE REST OF YOUR VISION?
THE FUTURE IS ALWAYS IN MOTION. IT'S THE FIRST THING THEY TEACH YOU WHEN YOU'RE LEARNING ABOUT THE FORCE.
THEN WE'D BETTER CHANGE IT. MAYBE IF I CAN GET CONTROL OF THE DIRECTIONAL THRUSTERS...
IT'S NO USE.
THEY HAD US STRIP ALL THE PROPULSION SYSTEMS FROM THE PODS TO USE IN THE NEW FLEET.
THEY HAD ME WORKING ON THEM. I MAY HAVE STRIPPED DOWN THIS VERY... POD.
HANG ON TIGHT, FRIENDS. THE GRAPPLING ARM IS NOT A PRECISION INSTRUMENT.
AG-37!

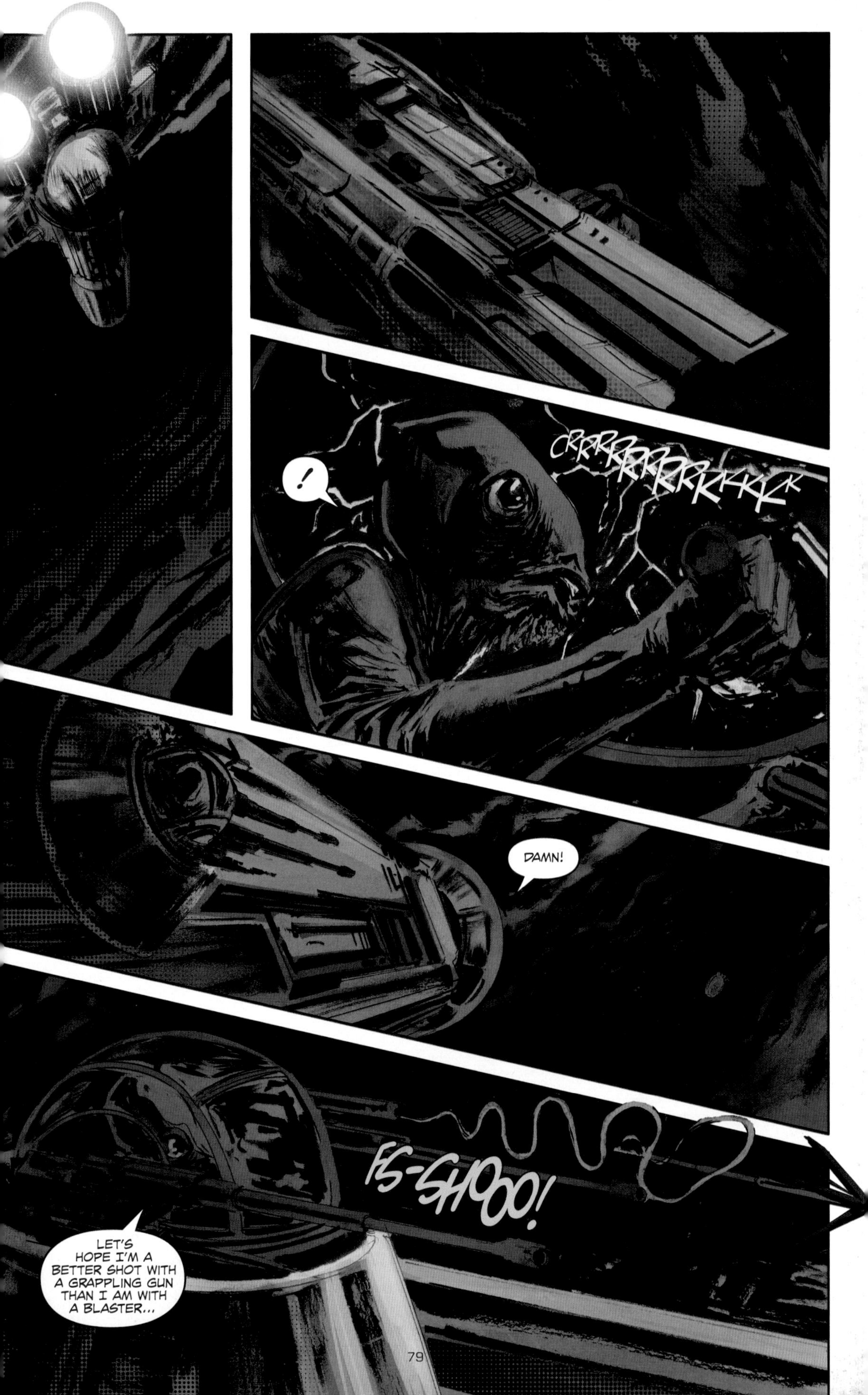
!
CRRRRRRRRRRRKKKK
DAMN!
FS-SHOOO!
LET'S HOPE I'M A BETTER SHOT WITH A GRAPPLING GUN THAN I AM WITH A BLASTER...

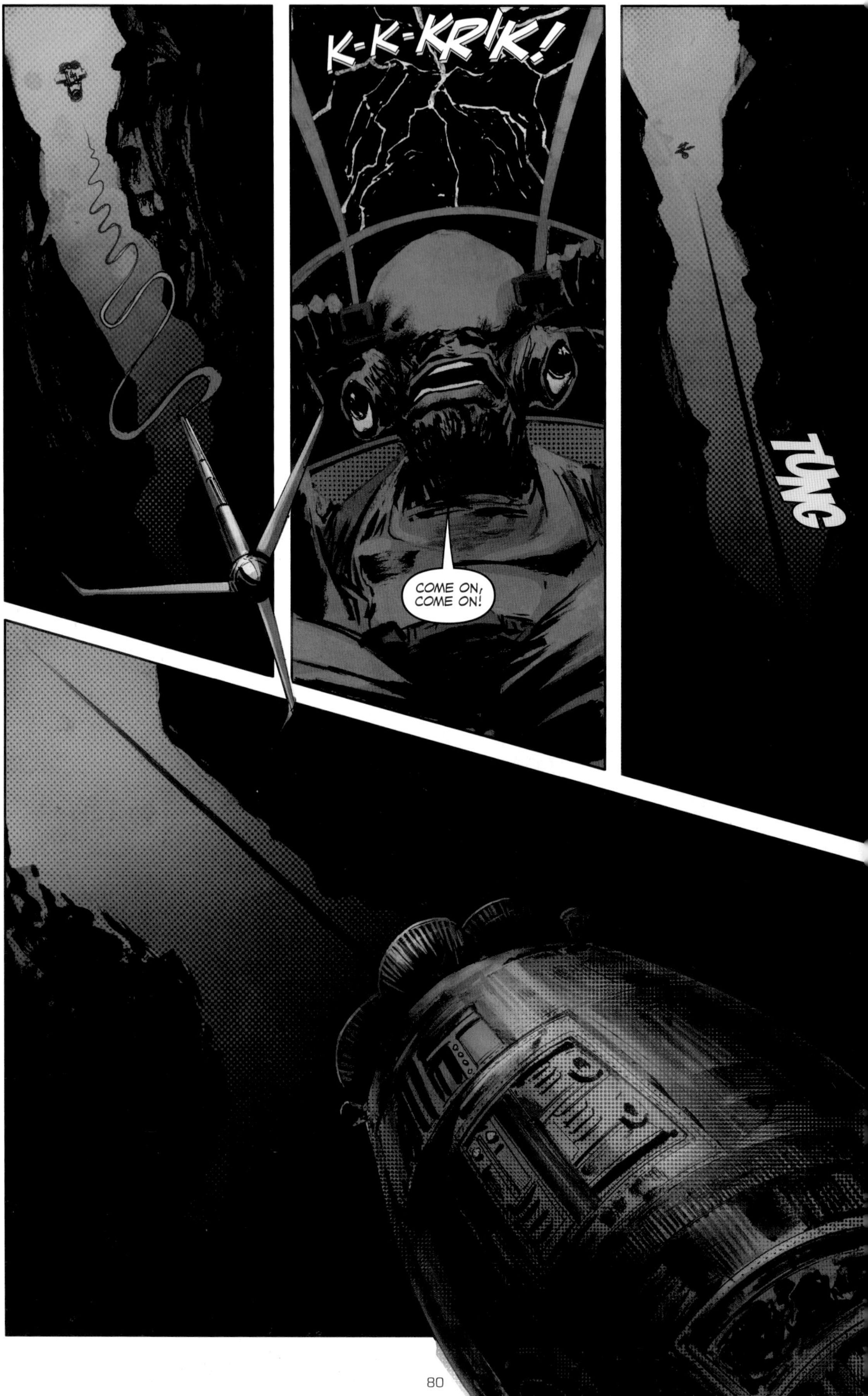
K-K-KRIK!
COME ON, COME ON!
TUNG

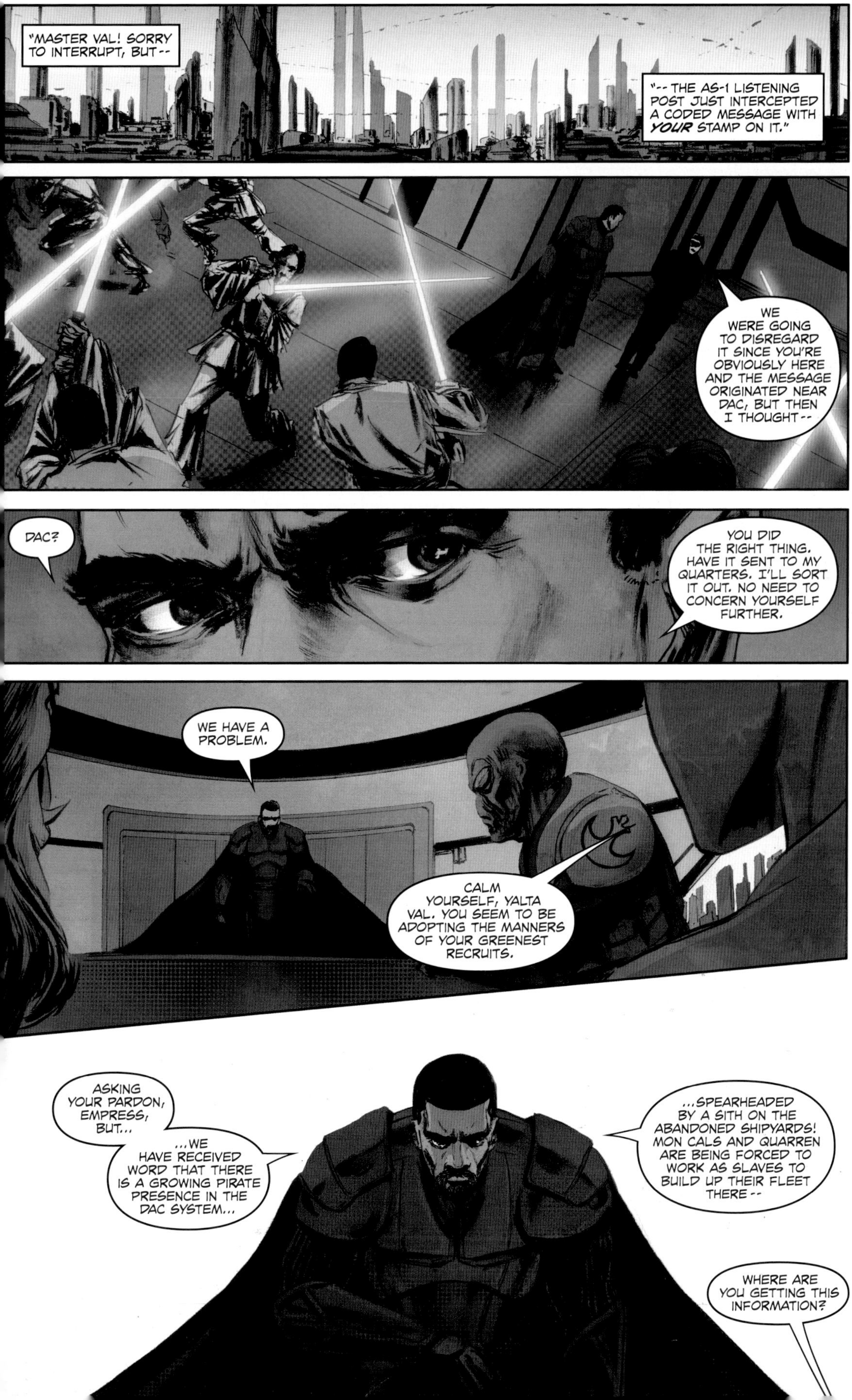
"MASTER VAL! SORRY TO INTERRUPT, BUT--
"-- THE AS-1 LISTENING POST JUST INTERCEPTED A CODED MESSAGE WITH YOUR STAMP ON IT."
WE WERE GOING TO DISREGARD IT SINCE YOU'RE OBVIOUSLY HERE AND THE MESSAGE ORIGINATED NEAR DAC, BUT THEN I THOUGHT--
DAC?
YOU DID THE RIGHT THING. HAVE IT SENT TO MY QUARTERS. I'LL SORT IT OUT. NO NEED TO CONCERN YOURSELF FURTHER.
WE HAVE A PROBLEM.
CALM YOURSELF, YALTA VAL. YOU SEEM TO BE ADOPTING THE MANNERS OF YOUR GREENEST RECRUITS.
ASKING YOUR PARDON, EMPRESS, BUT...
...WE HAVE RECEIVED WORD THAT THERE IS A GROWING PIRATE PRESENCE IN THE DAC SYSTEM...
...SPEARHEADED BY A SITH ON THE ABANDONED SHIPYARDS! MON CALS AND QUARREN ARE BEING FORCED TO WORK AS SLAVES TO BUILD UP THEIR FLEET THERE--
WHERE ARE YOU GETTING THIS INFORMATION?

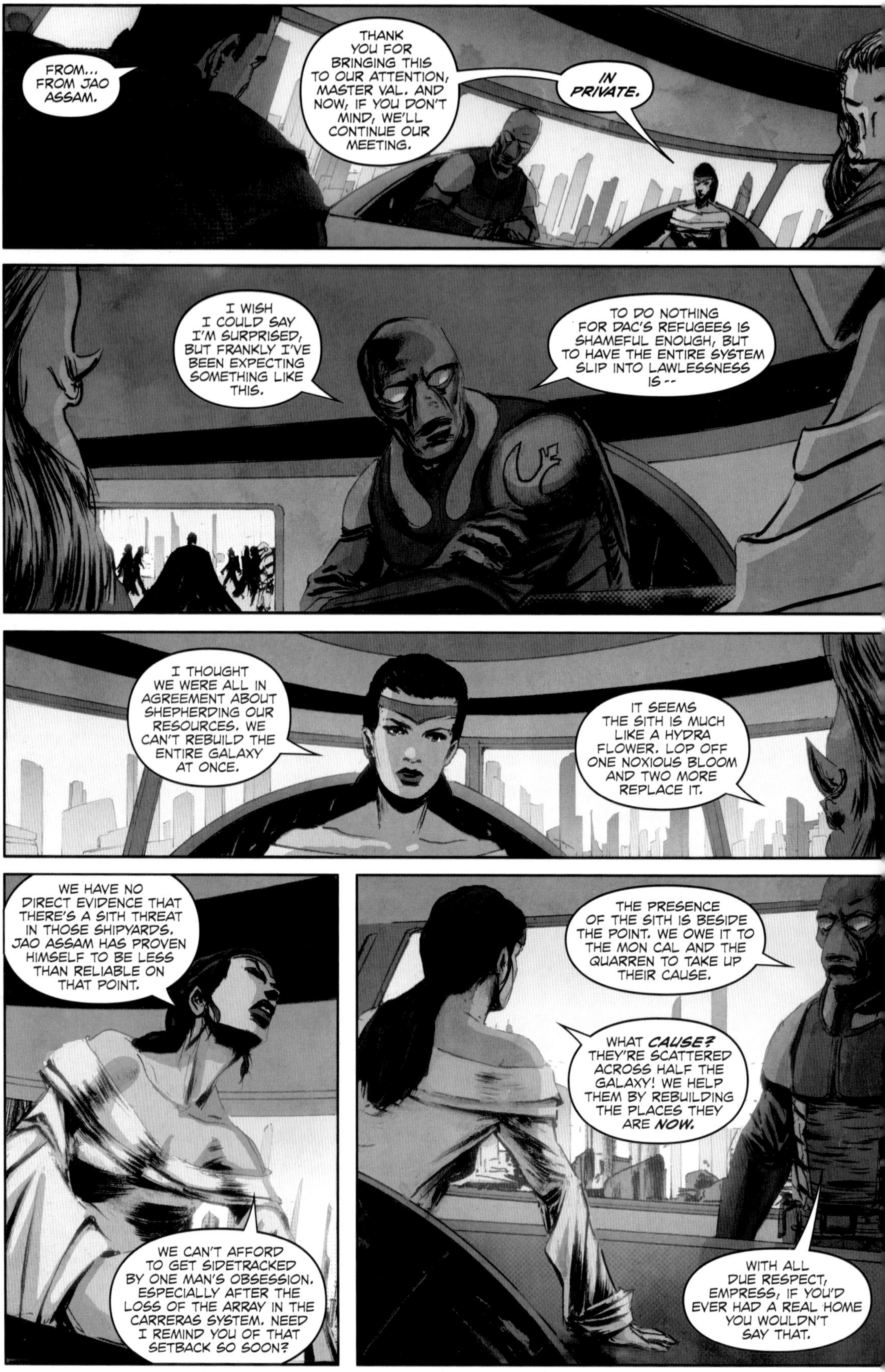
FROM... FROM JAO ASSAM.
THANK YOU FOR BRINGING THIS TO OUR ATTENTION, MASTER VAL. AND NOW, IF YOU DON'T MIND, WE'LL CONTINUE OUR MEETING.
IN PRIVATE.
I WISH I COULD SAY I'M SURPRISED, BUT FRANKLY I'VE BEEN EXPECTING SOMETHING LIKE THIS.
TO DO NOTHING FOR DAC'S REFUGEES IS SHAMEFUL ENOUGH, BUT TO HAVE THE ENTIRE SYSTEM SLIP INTO LAWLESSNESS IS--
I THOUGHT WE WERE ALL IN AGREEMENT ABOUT SHEPHERDING OUR RESOURCES. WE CAN'T REBUILD THE ENTIRE GALAXY AT ONCE.
IT SEEMS THE SITH IS MUCH LIKE A HYDRA FLOWER. LOP OFF ONE NOXIOUS BLOOM AND TWO MORE REPLACE IT.
WE HAVE NO DIRECT EVIDENCE THAT THERE'S A SITH THREAT IN THOSE SHIPYARDS. JAO ASSAM HAS PROVEN HIMSELF TO BE LESS THAN RELIABLE ON THAT POINT.
WE CAN'T AFFORD TO GET SIDETRACKED BY ONE MAN'S OBSESSION. ESPECIALLY AFTER THE LOSS OF THE ARRAY IN THE CARRERAS SYSTEM. NEED I REMIND YOU OF THAT SETBACK SO SOON?
THE PRESENCE OF THE SITH IS BESIDE THE POINT. WE OWE IT TO THE MON CAL AND THE QUARREN TO TAKE UP THEIR CAUSE.
WHAT *CAUSE?* THEY'RE SCATTERED ACROSS HALF THE GALAXY! WE HELP THEM BY REBUILDING THE PLACES THEY ARE *NOW.*
WITH ALL DUE RESPECT, EMPRESS, IF YOU'D EVER HAD A REAL HOME YOU WOULDN'T SAY THAT.

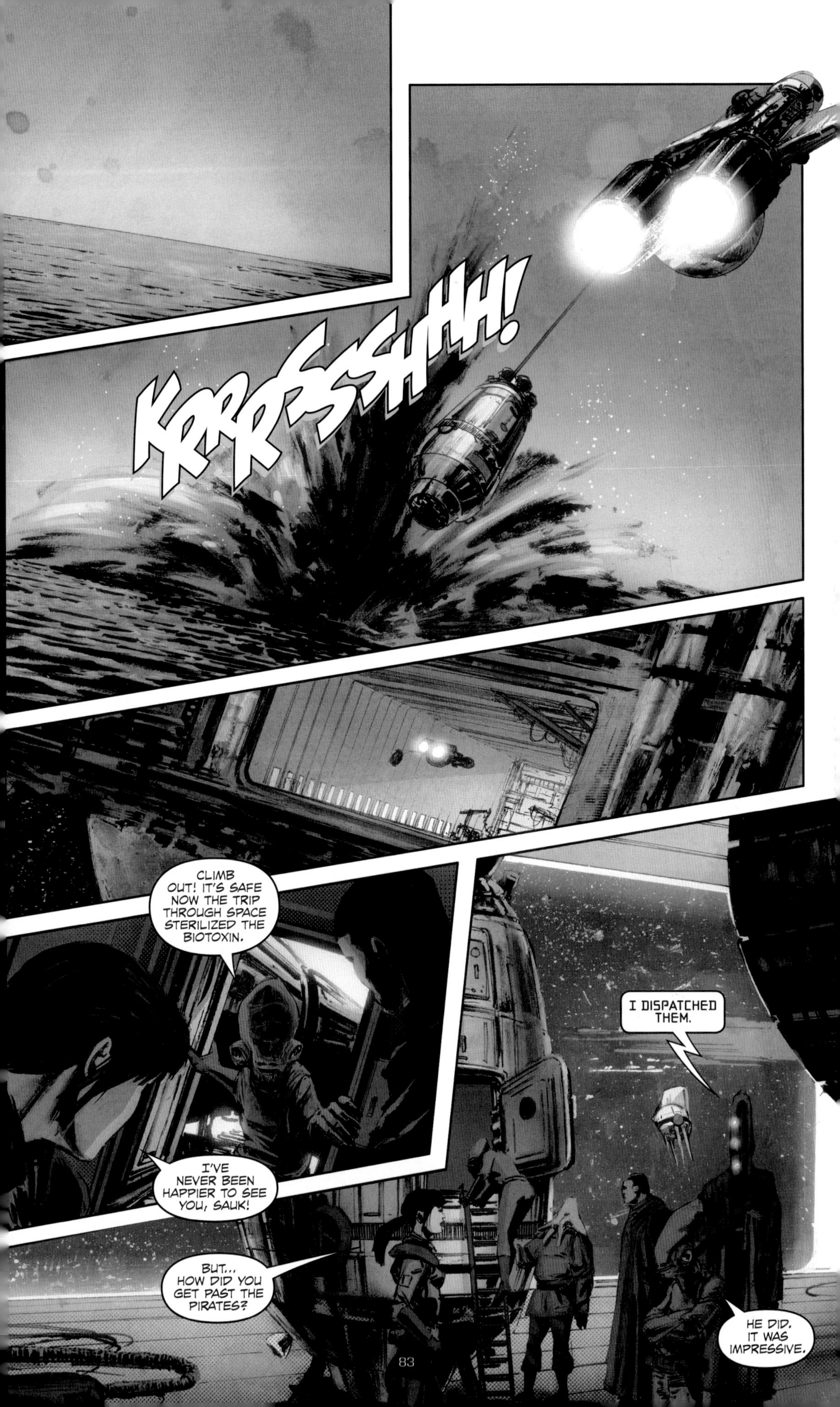
KRRRSSSHHH!
CLIMB OUT! IT'S SAFE NOW THE TRIP THROUGH SPACE STERILIZED THE BIOTOXIN.
I'VE NEVER BEEN HAPPIER TO SEE YOU, SAUK!
I DISPATCHED THEM.
BUT... HOW DID YOU GET PAST THE PIRATES?
HE DID. IT WAS IMPRESSIVE.

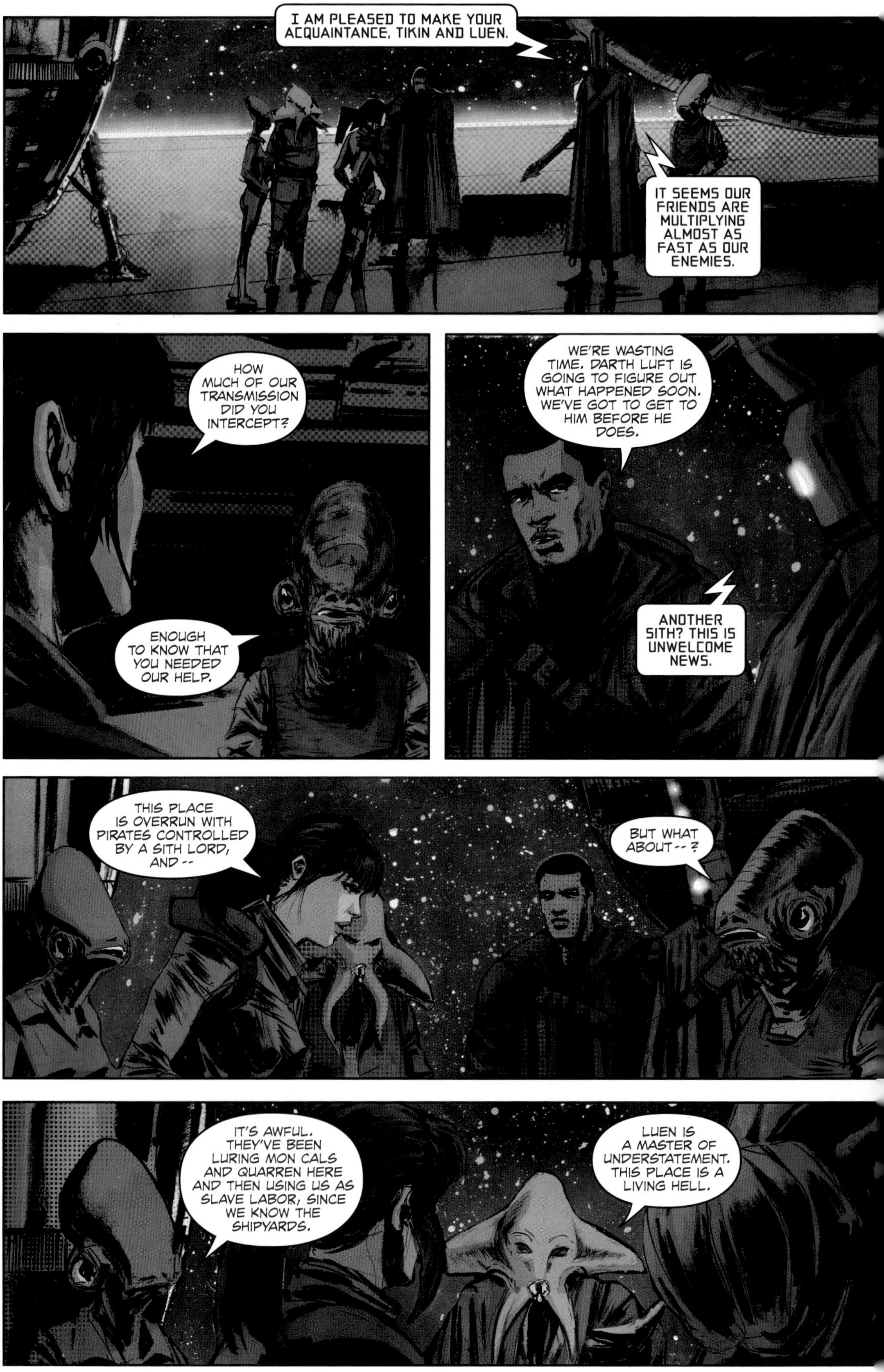
I AM PLEASED TO MAKE YOUR ACQUAINTANCE, TIKIN AND LUEN.
IT SEEMS OUR FRIENDS ARE MULTIPLYING ALMOST AS FAST AS OUR ENEMIES.
HOW MUCH OF OUR TRANSMISSION DID YOU INTERCEPT?
ENOUGH TO KNOW THAT YOU NEEDED OUR HELP.
WE'RE WASTING TIME. DARTH LUFT IS GOING TO FIGURE OUT WHAT HAPPENED SOON. WE'VE GOT TO GET TO HIM BEFORE HE DOES.
ANOTHER SITH? THIS IS UNWELCOME NEWS.
THIS PLACE IS OVERRUN WITH PIRATES CONTROLLED BY A SITH LORD, AND --
BUT WHAT ABOUT -- ?
IT'S AWFUL. THEY'VE BEEN LURING MON CALS AND QUARREN HERE AND THEN USING US AS SLAVE LABOR, SINCE WE KNOW THE SHIPYARDS.
LUEN IS A MASTER OF UNDERSTATEMENT. THIS PLACE IS A LIVING HELL.

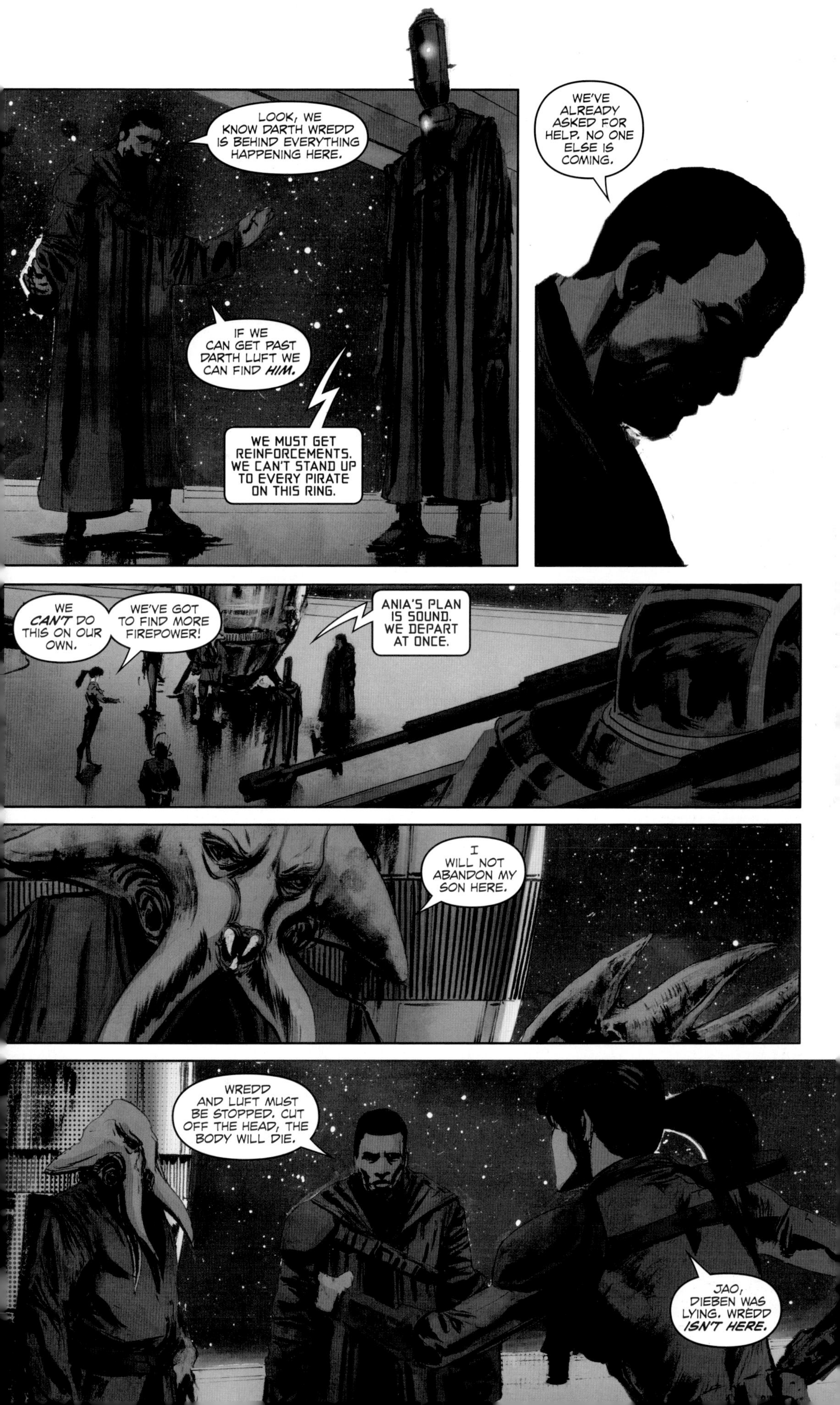

LOOK, WE KNOW DARTH WREDD IS BEHIND EVERYTHING HAPPENING HERE.
IF WE CAN GET PAST DARTH LUFT WE CAN FIND *HIM.*
WE MUST GET REINFORCEMENTS. WE CAN'T STAND UP TO EVERY PIRATE ON THIS RING.
WE'VE ALREADY ASKED FOR HELP. NO ONE ELSE IS COMING.
WE *CAN'T* DO THIS ON OUR OWN.
WE'VE GOT TO FIND MORE FIREPOWER!
ANIA'S PLAN IS SOUND. WE DEPART AT ONCE.
I WILL NOT ABANDON MY SON HERE.
WREDD AND LUFT MUST BE STOPPED. CUT OFF THE HEAD, THE BODY WILL DIE.
JAO, DIEBEN WAS LYING. WREDD *ISN'T HERE.*

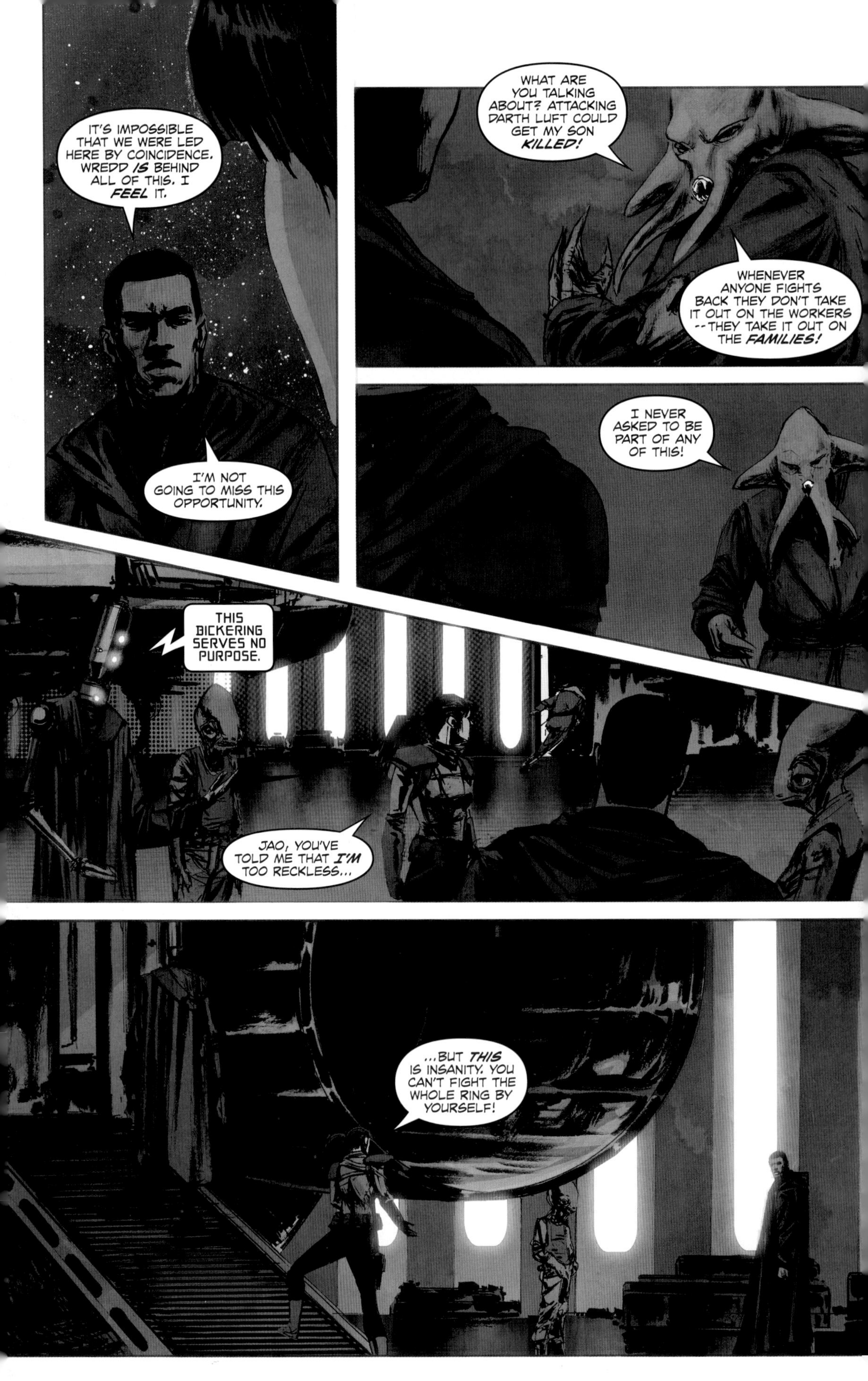

IT'S IMPOSSIBLE THAT WE WERE LED HERE BY COINCIDENCE. WREDD *IS* BEHIND ALL OF THIS. I *FEEL* IT.
I'M NOT GOING TO MISS THIS OPPORTUNITY.
WHAT ARE YOU TALKING ABOUT? ATTACKING DARTH LUFT COULD GET MY SON *KILLED!*
WHENEVER ANYONE FIGHTS BACK THEY DON'T TAKE IT OUT ON THE WORKERS --THEY TAKE IT OUT ON THE *FAMILIES!*
I NEVER ASKED TO BE PART OF ANY OF THIS!
THIS BICKERING SERVES NO PURPOSE.
JAO, YOU'VE TOLD ME THAT *I'M* TOO RECKLESS...
...BUT *THIS* IS INSANITY. YOU CAN'T FIGHT THE WHOLE RING BY YOURSELF!

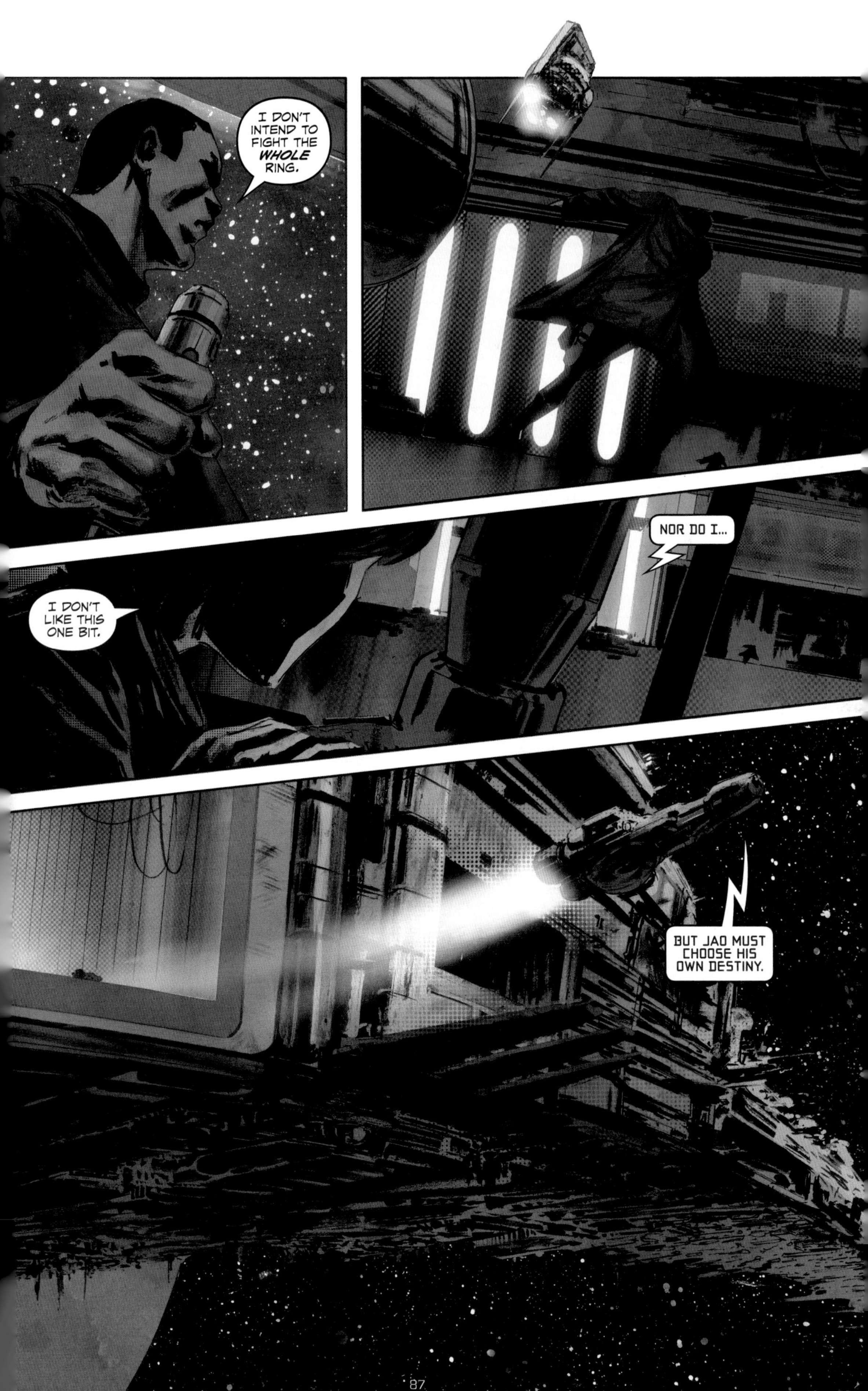

I DON'T INTEND TO FIGHT THE WHOLE RING.
I DON'T LIKE THIS ONE BIT.
NOR DO I...
BUT JAO MUST CHOOSE HIS OWN DESTINY.

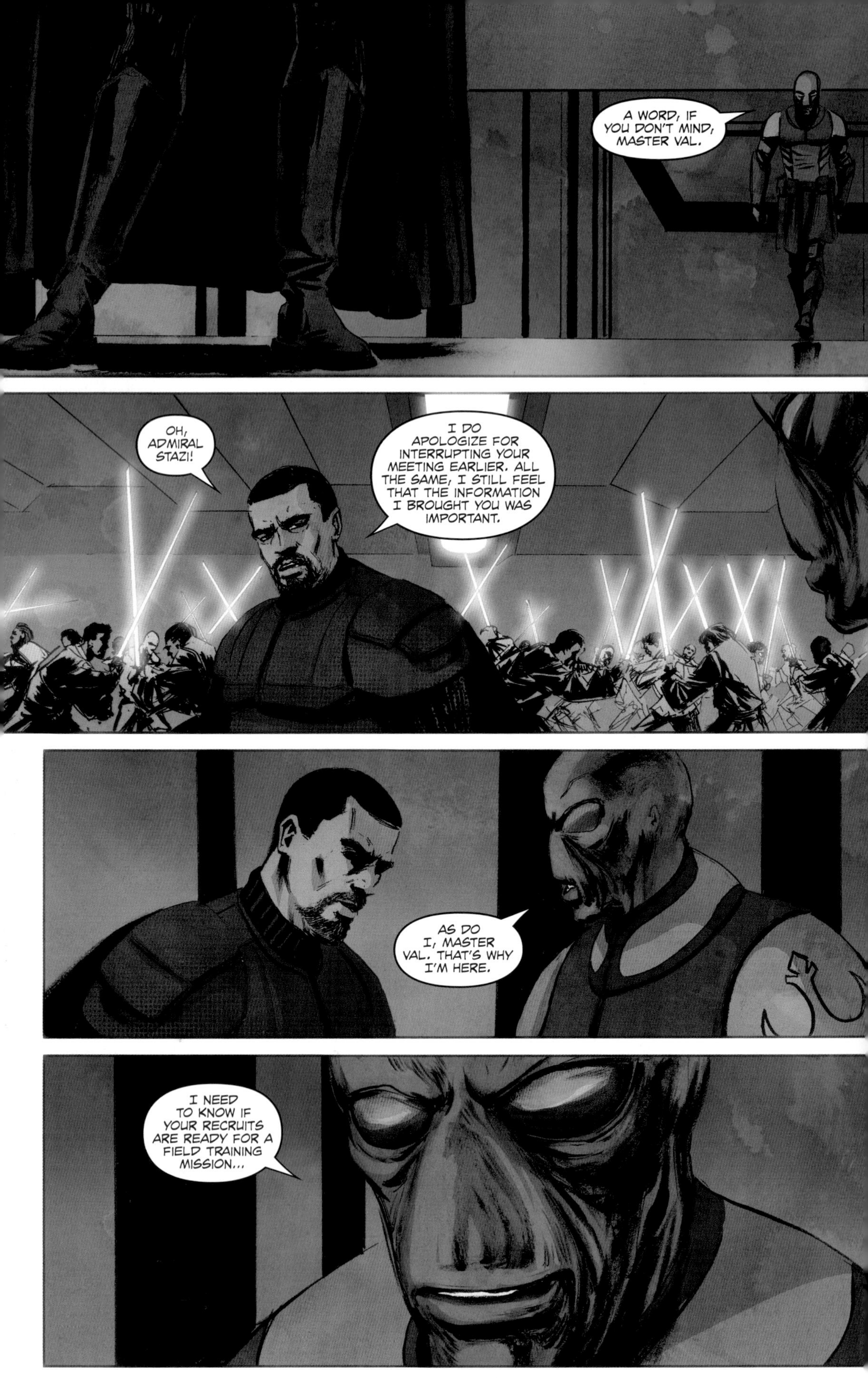
A WORD, IF YOU DON'T MIND, MASTER VAL.
OH, ADMIRAL STAZI!
I DO APOLOGIZE FOR INTERRUPTING YOUR MEETING EARLIER. ALL THE SAME, I STILL FEEL THAT THE INFORMATION I BROUGHT YOU WAS IMPORTANT.
AS DO I, MASTER VAL. THAT'S WHY I'M HERE.
I NEED TO KNOW IF YOUR RECRUITS ARE READY FOR A FIELD TRAINING MISSION...

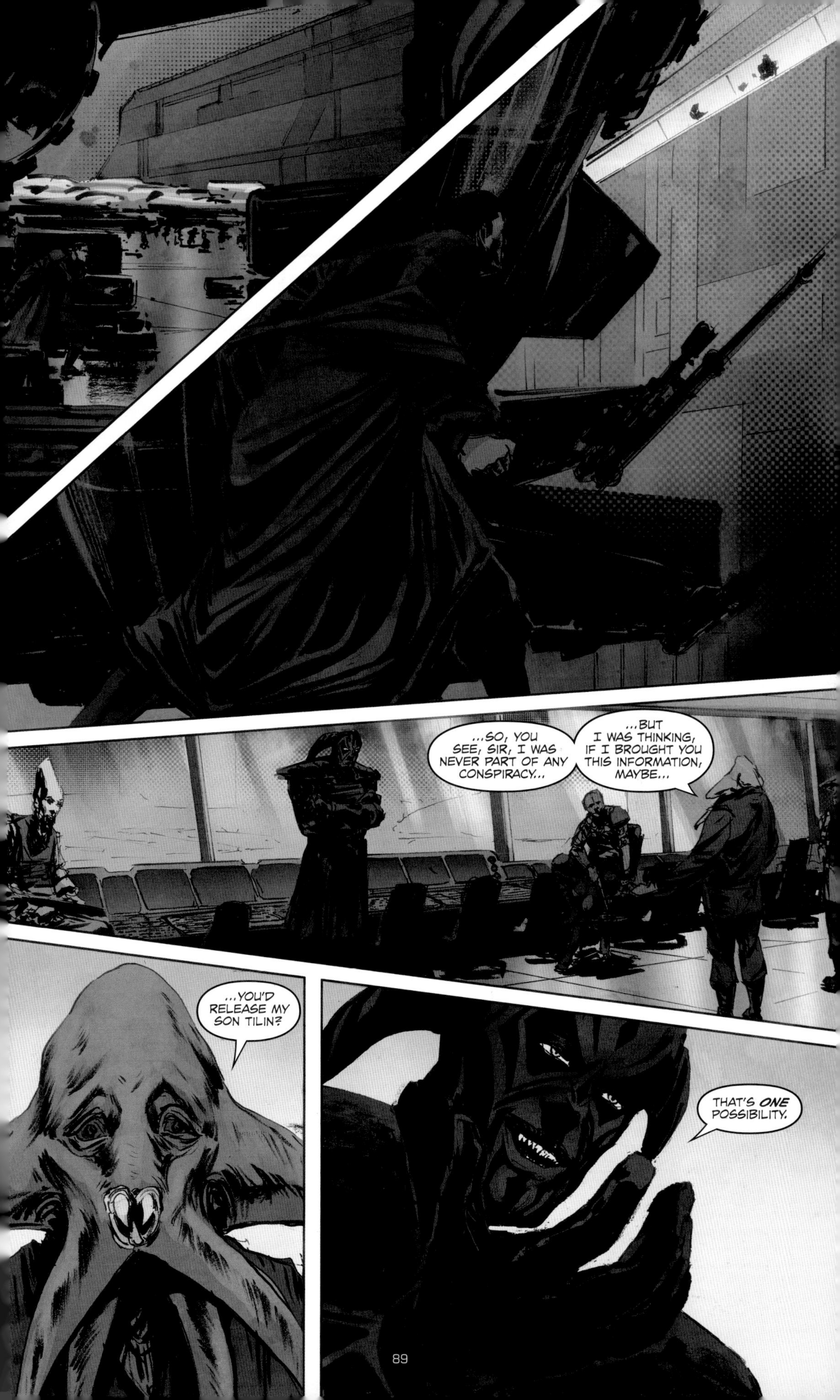
...SO, YOU SEE, SIR, I WAS NEVER PART OF ANY CONSPIRACY...
...BUT I WAS THINKING, IF I BROUGHT YOU THIS INFORMATION, MAYBE...
...YOU'D RELEASE MY SON TILIN?
THAT'S *ONE* POSSIBILITY.

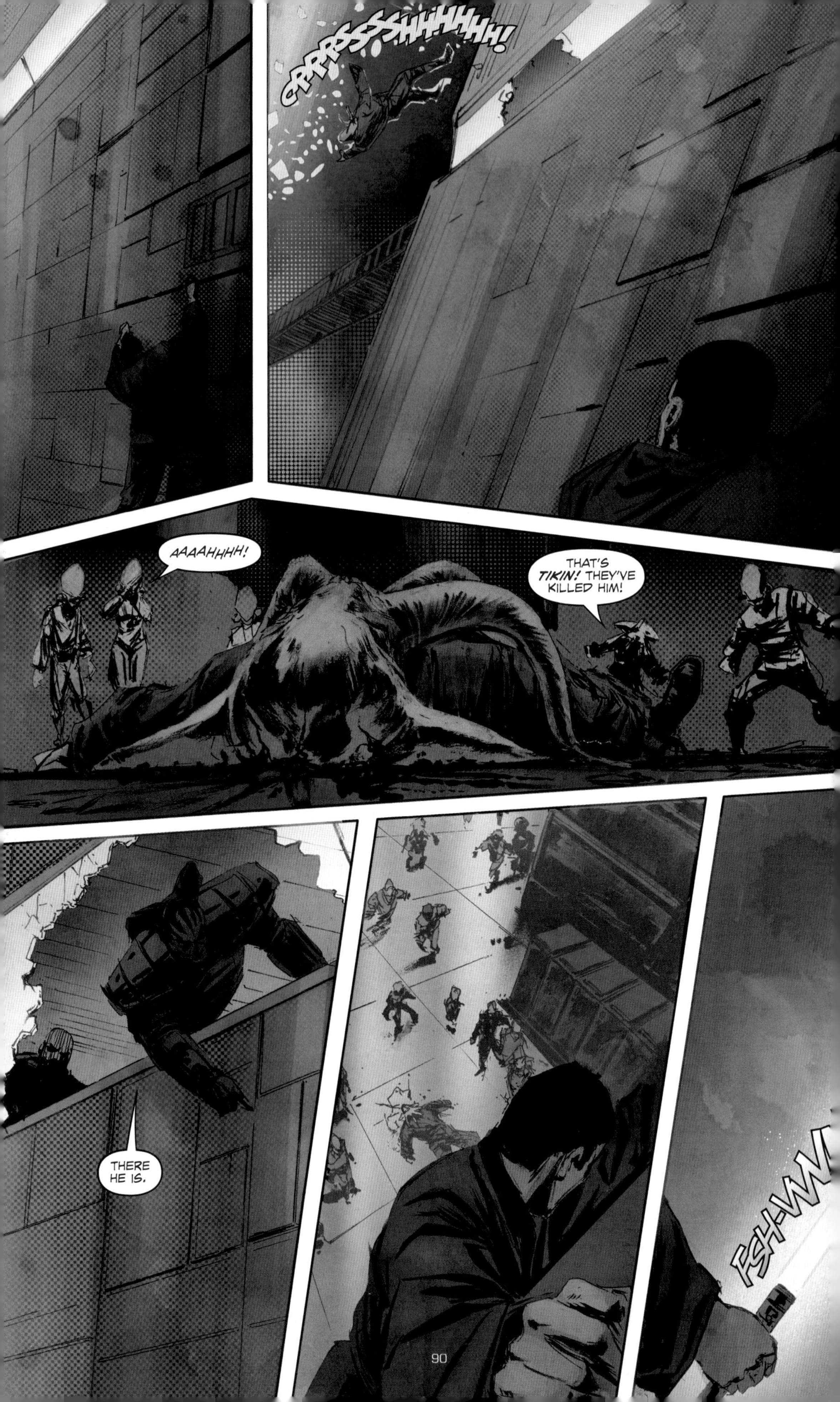

CPRRSSSSHHHHHH!
AAAAHHHH!
THAT'S TIKIN! THEY'VE KILLED HIM!
THERE HE IS.
FSH-WW

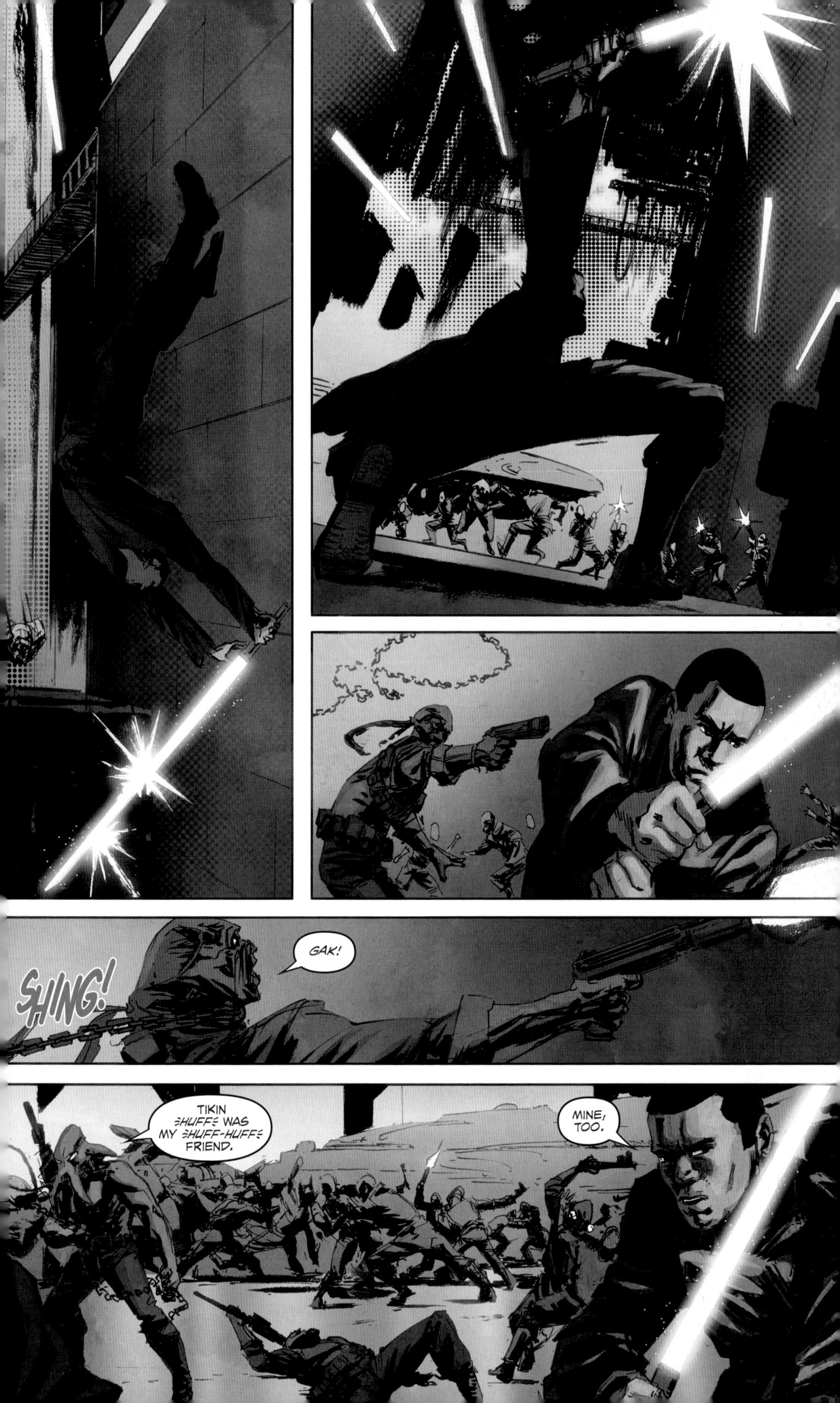

SHING!
GAK!
TIKIN =HUFF= WAS MY =HUFF-HUFF= FRIEND.
MINE, TOO.

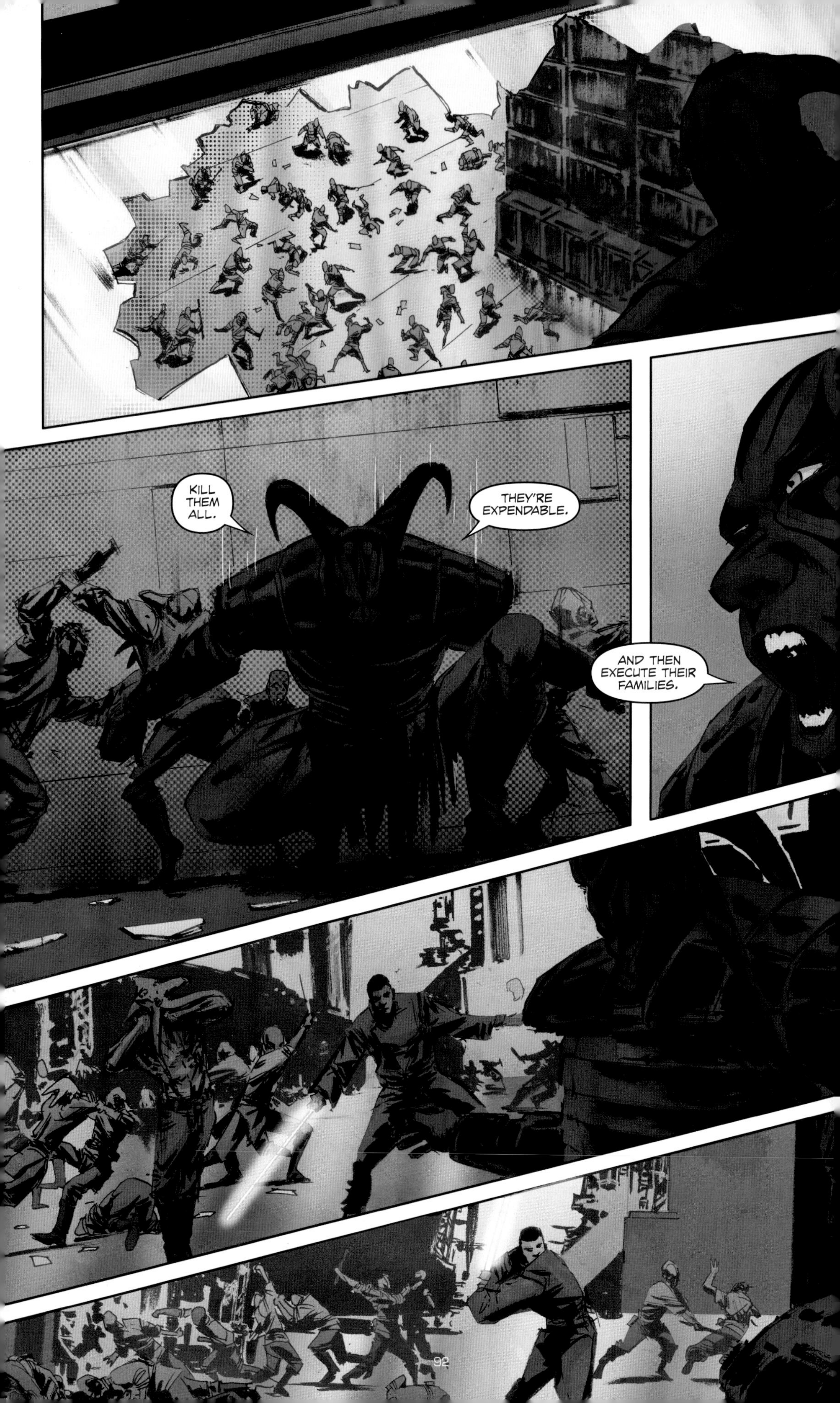
KILL THEM ALL.
THEY'RE EXPENDABLE.
AND THEN EXECUTE THEIR FAMILIES.

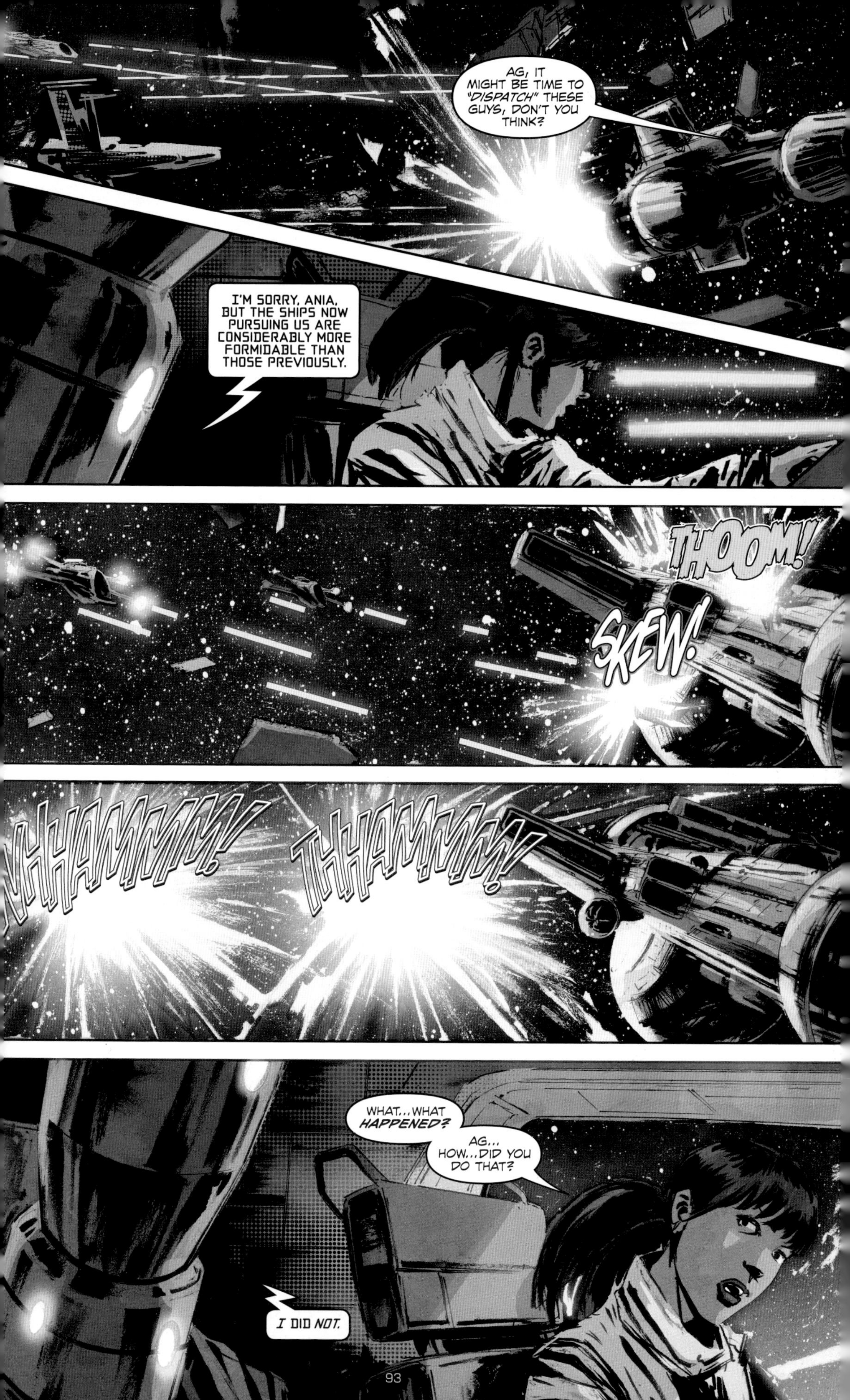
AG, IT MIGHT BE TIME TO "DISPATCH" THESE GUYS, DON'T YOU THINK?
I'M SORRY, ANIA, BUT THE SHIPS NOW PURSUING US ARE CONSIDERABLY MORE FORMIDABLE THAN THOSE PREVIOUSLY.
THOOM!
SKEW!
THHAMMM!
THHAMMM!
WHAT...WHAT HAPPENED?
AG... HOW...DID YOU DO THAT?
I DID NOT.

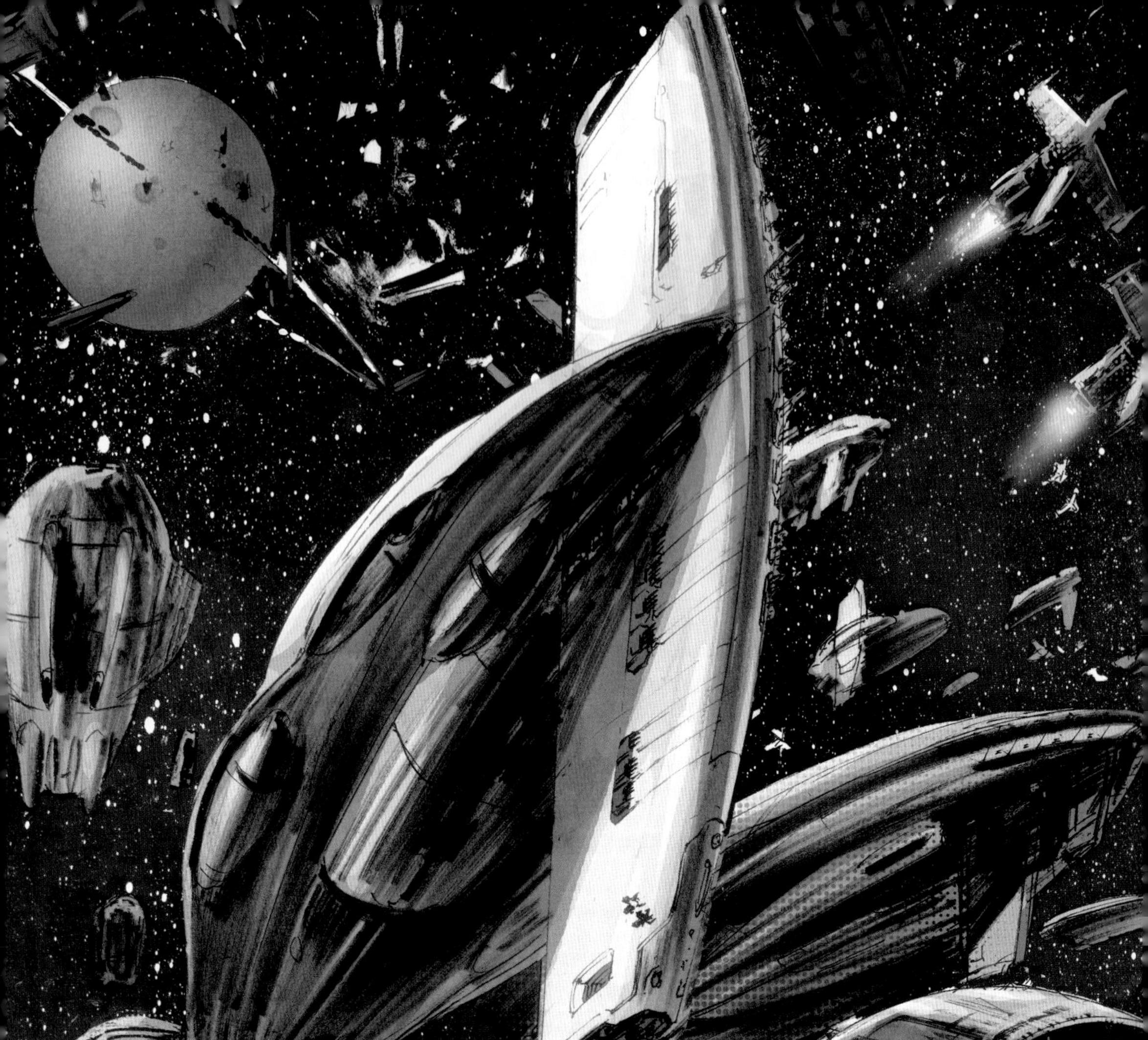

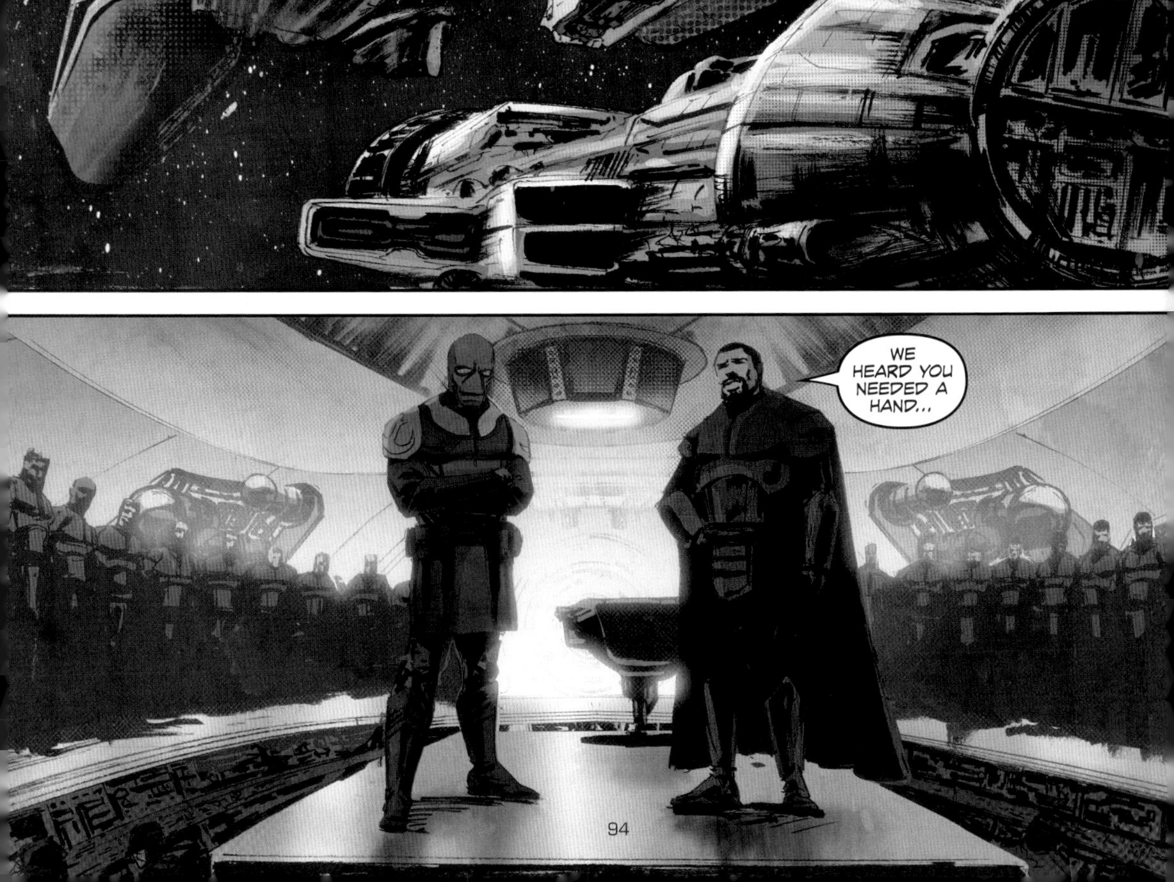
WE HEARD YOU NEEDED A HAND...

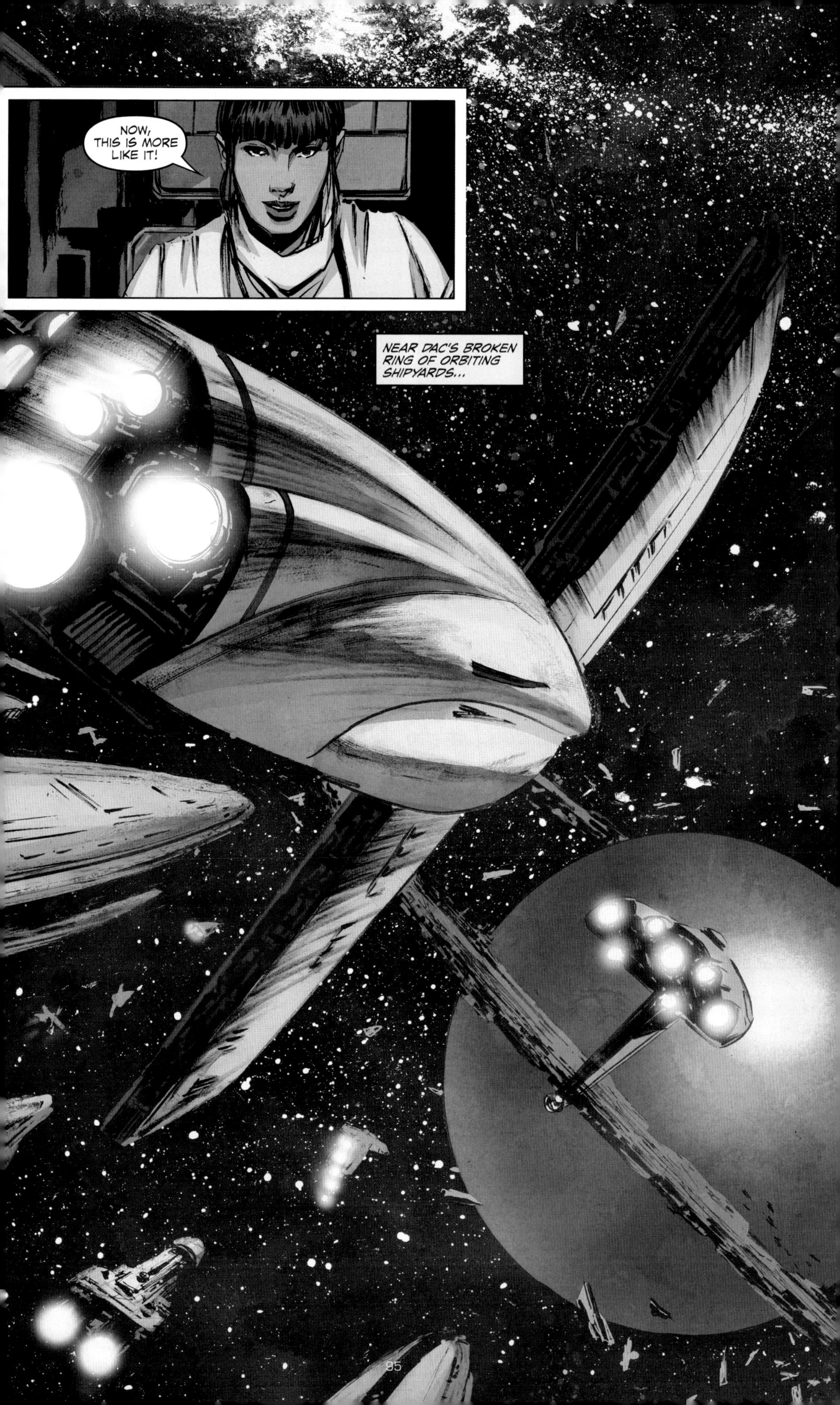
NOW, THIS IS MORE LIKE IT!
NEAR DAC'S BROKEN RING OF ORBITING SHIPYARDS...

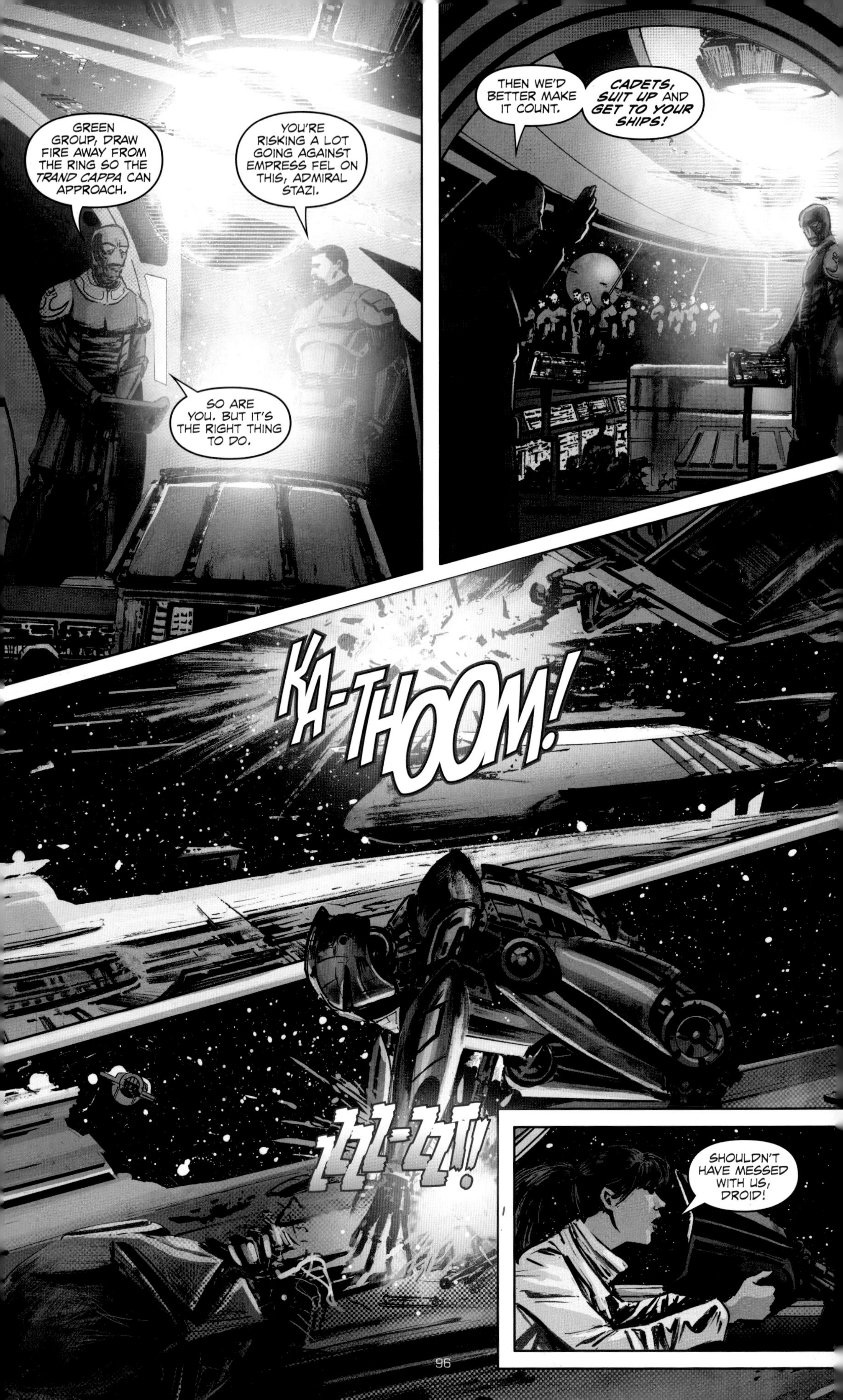

GREEN GROUP, DRAW FIRE AWAY FROM THE RING SO THE *TRAND CAPPA* CAN APPROACH.
YOU'RE RISKING A LOT GOING AGAINST EMPRESS FEL ON THIS, ADMIRAL STAZI.
SO ARE YOU. BUT IT'S THE RIGHT THING TO DO.
THEN WE'D BETTER MAKE IT COUNT.
CADETS, SUIT UP AND *GET TO YOUR SHIPS!*
KA-THOOM!
ZZZ-ZZT!
SHOULDN'T HAVE MESSED WITH US, DROID!

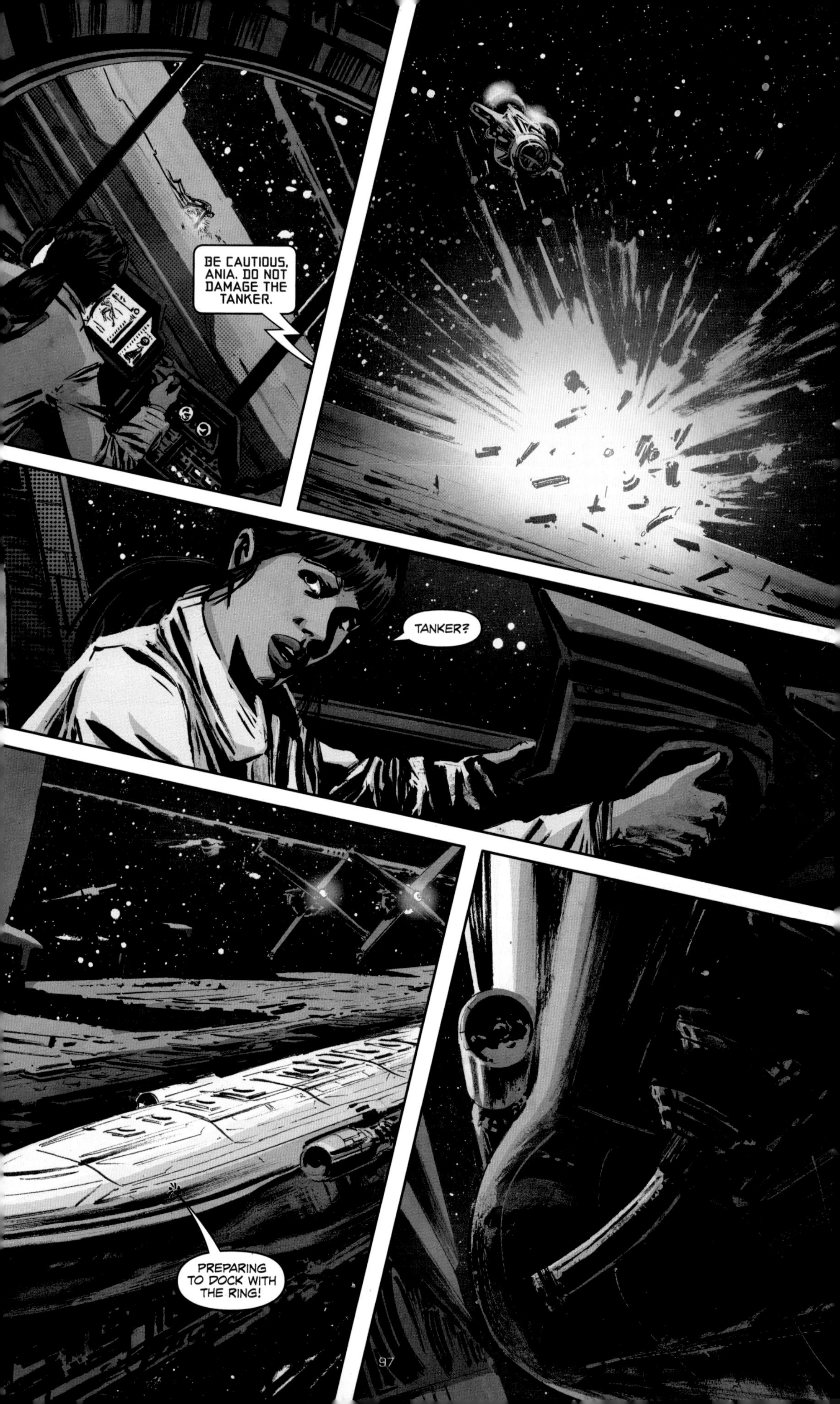

BE CAUTIOUS, ANIA. DO NOT DAMAGE THE TANKER.
TANKER?
PREPARING TO DOCK WITH THE RING!

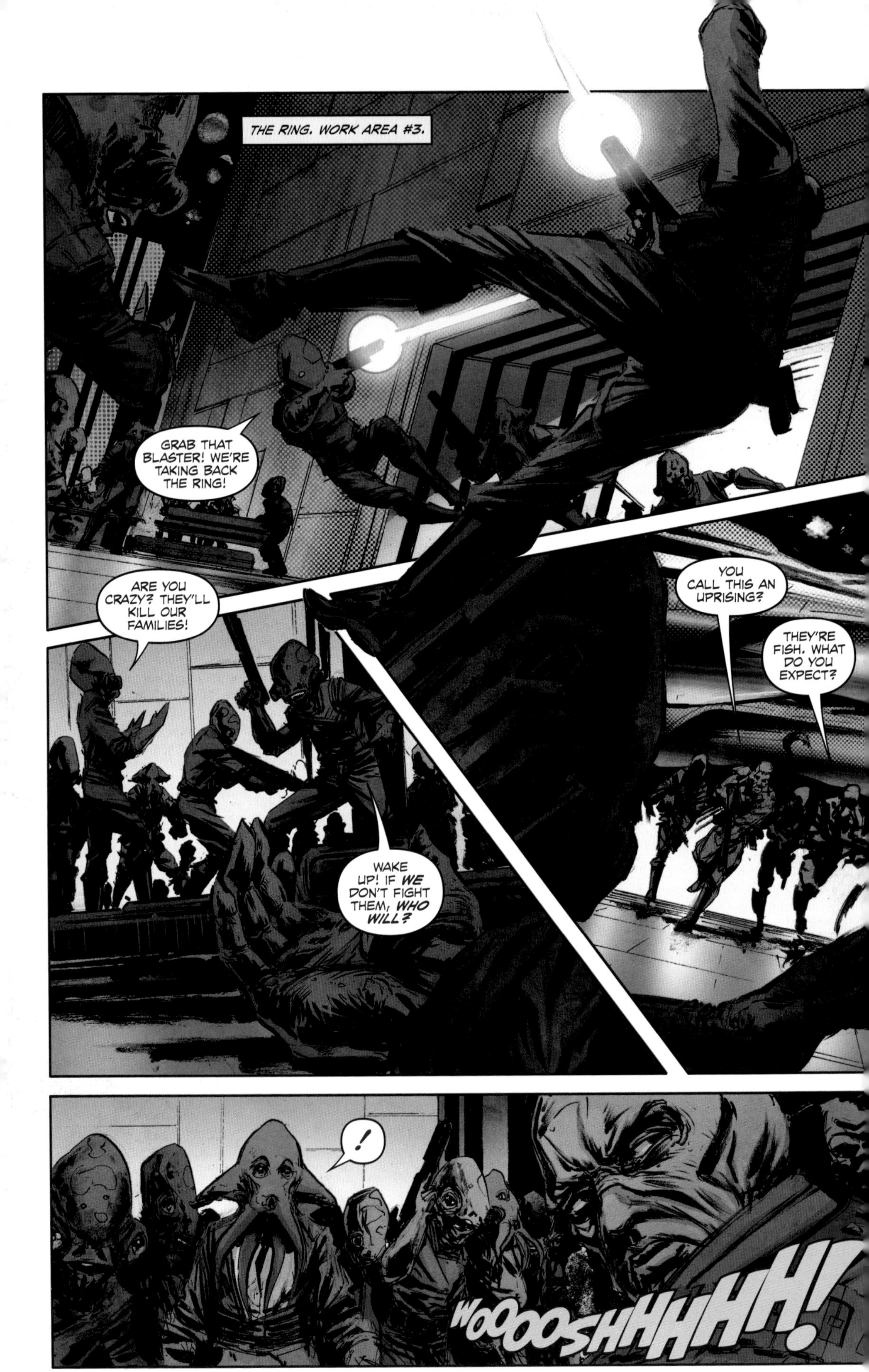
THE RING. WORK AREA #3.
GRAB THAT BLASTER! WE'RE TAKING BACK THE RING!
ARE YOU CRAZY? THEY'LL KILL OUR FAMILIES!
WAKE UP! IF WE DON'T FIGHT THEM, WHO WILL?
YOU CALL THIS AN UPRISING?
THEY'RE FISH. WHAT DO YOU EXPECT?
!
WOOOOSHHHHHH!

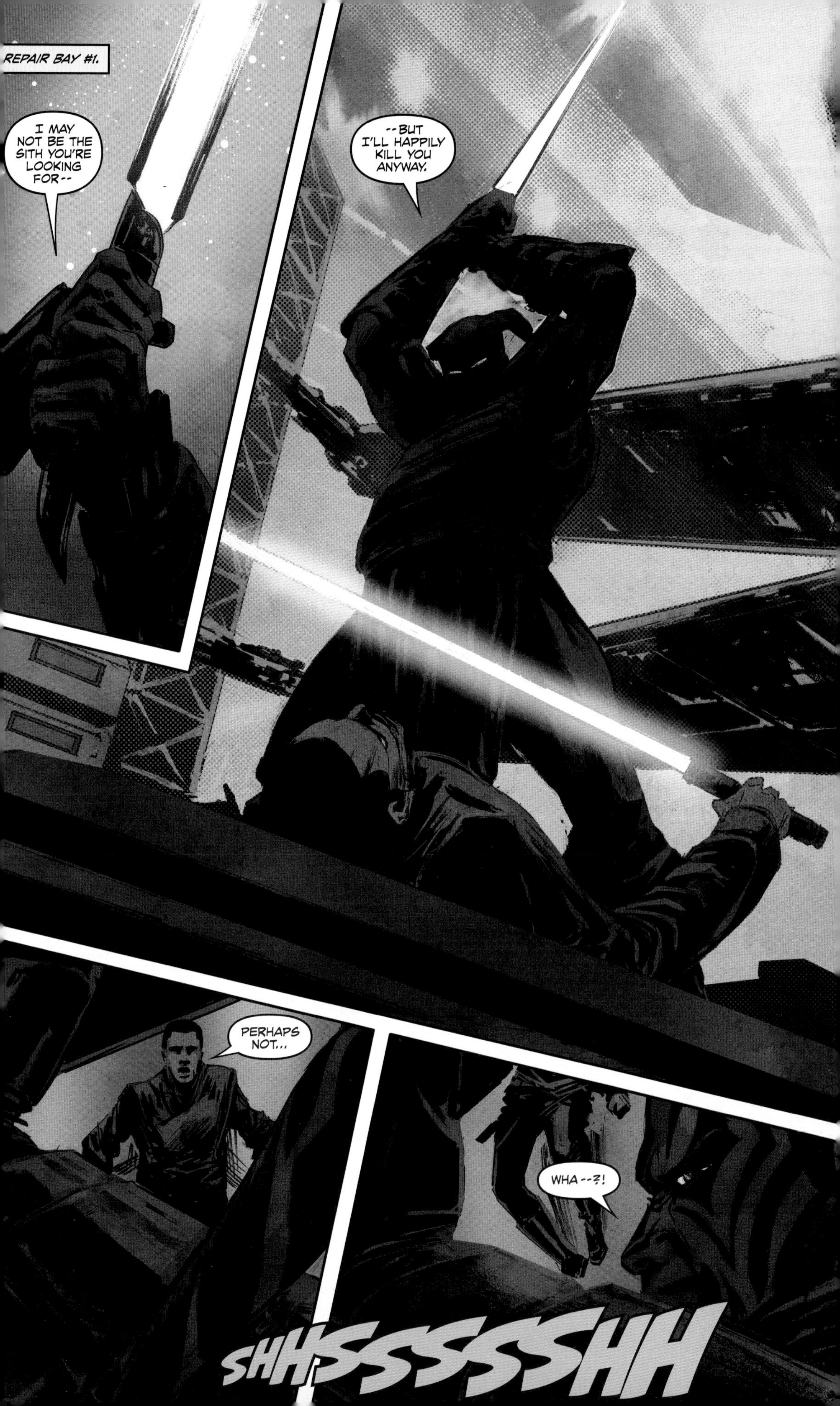
REPAIR BAY #1.
I MAY NOT BE THE SITH YOU'RE LOOKING FOR--
--BUT I'LL HAPPILY KILL YOU ANYWAY.
PERHAPS NOT...
WHA--?!
SHHSSSSSSHH

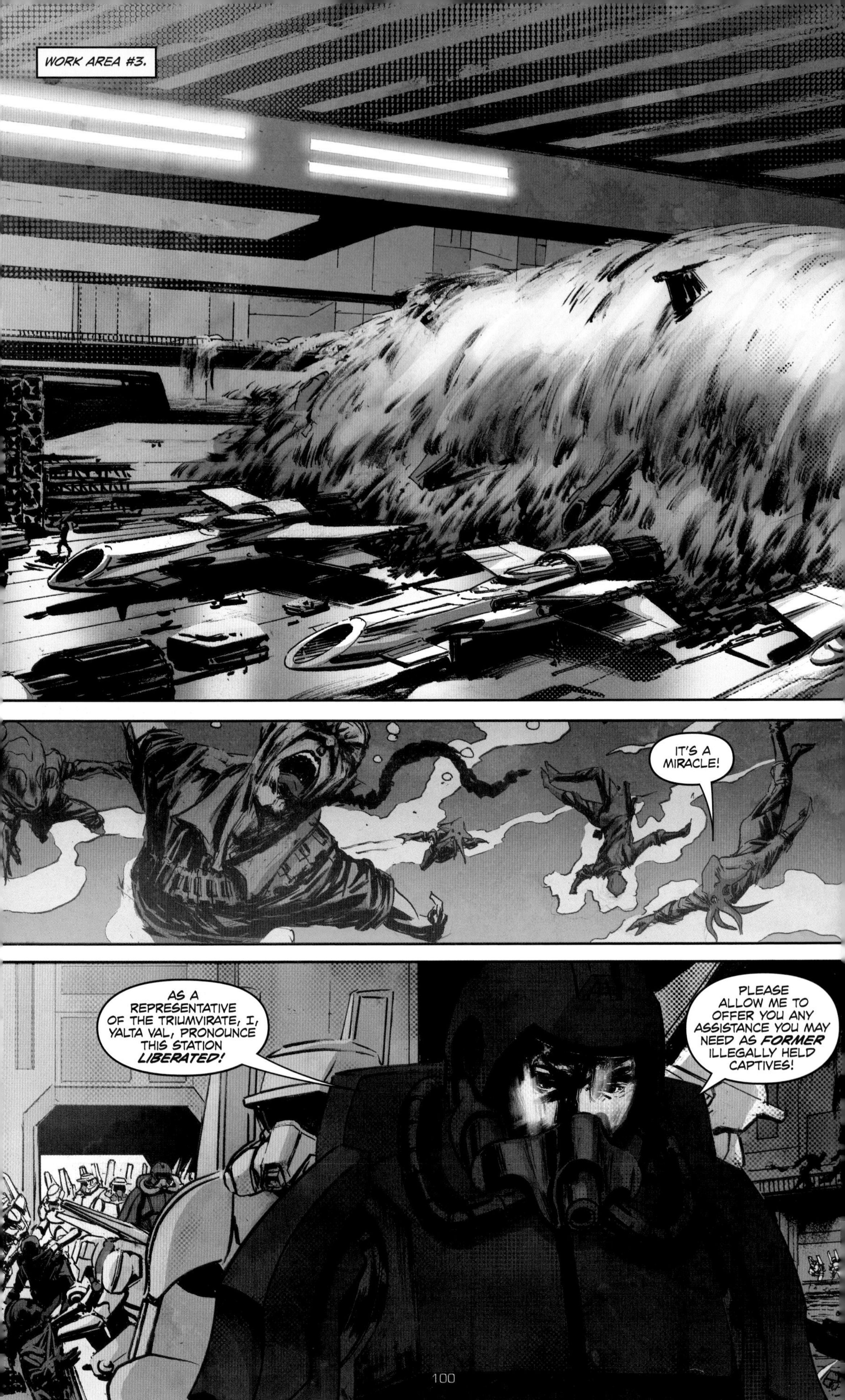
WORK AREA #3.
IT'S A MIRACLE!
AS A REPRESENTATIVE OF THE TRIUMVIRATE, I, YALTA VAL, PRONOUNCE THIS STATION LIBERATED!
PLEASE ALLOW ME TO OFFER YOU ANY ASSISTANCE YOU MAY NEED AS FORMER ILLEGALLY HELD CAPTIVES!

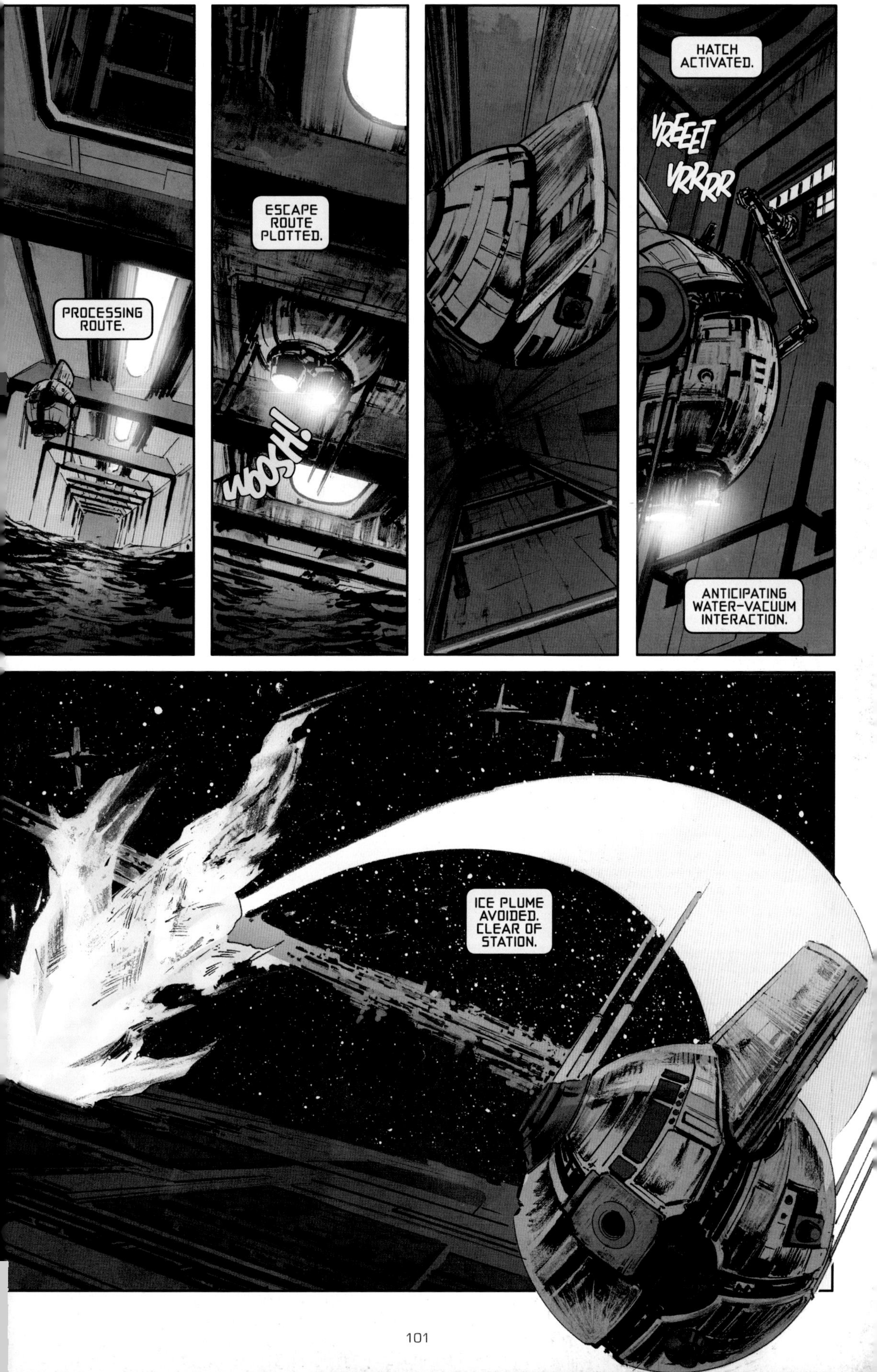
PROCESSING ROUTE.
ESCAPE ROUTE PLOTTED.
WOOSH!
HATCH ACTIVATED.
VREEEET
VRRRR
ANTICIPATING WATER–VACUUM INTERACTION.
ICE PLUME AVOIDED. CLEAR OF STATION.

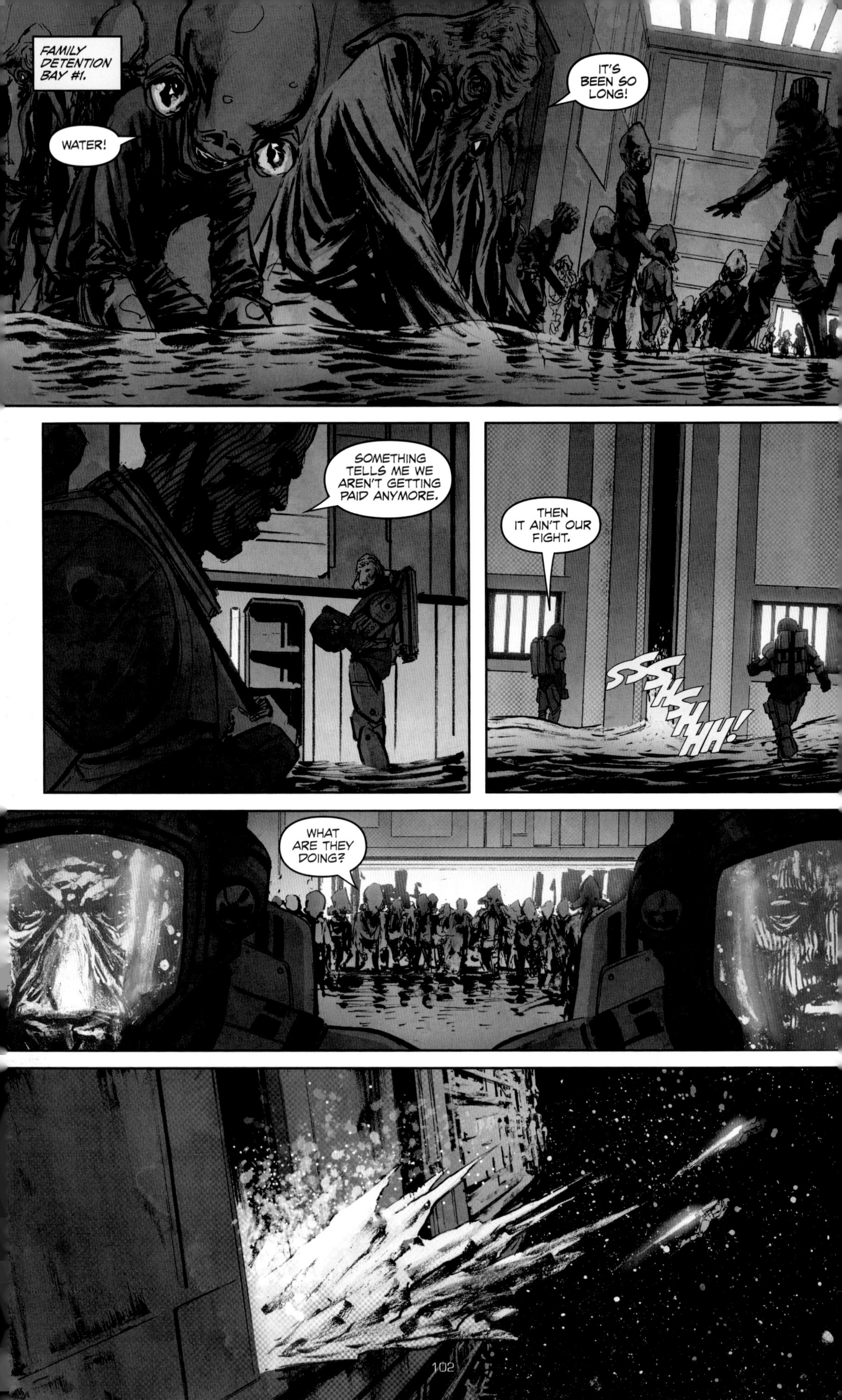
FAMILY DETENTION BAY #1.
WATER!
IT'S BEEN SO LONG!
SOMETHING TELLS ME WE AREN'T GETTING PAID ANYMORE.
THEN IT AIN'T OUR FIGHT.
SSSHSHHH!
WHAT ARE THEY DOING?

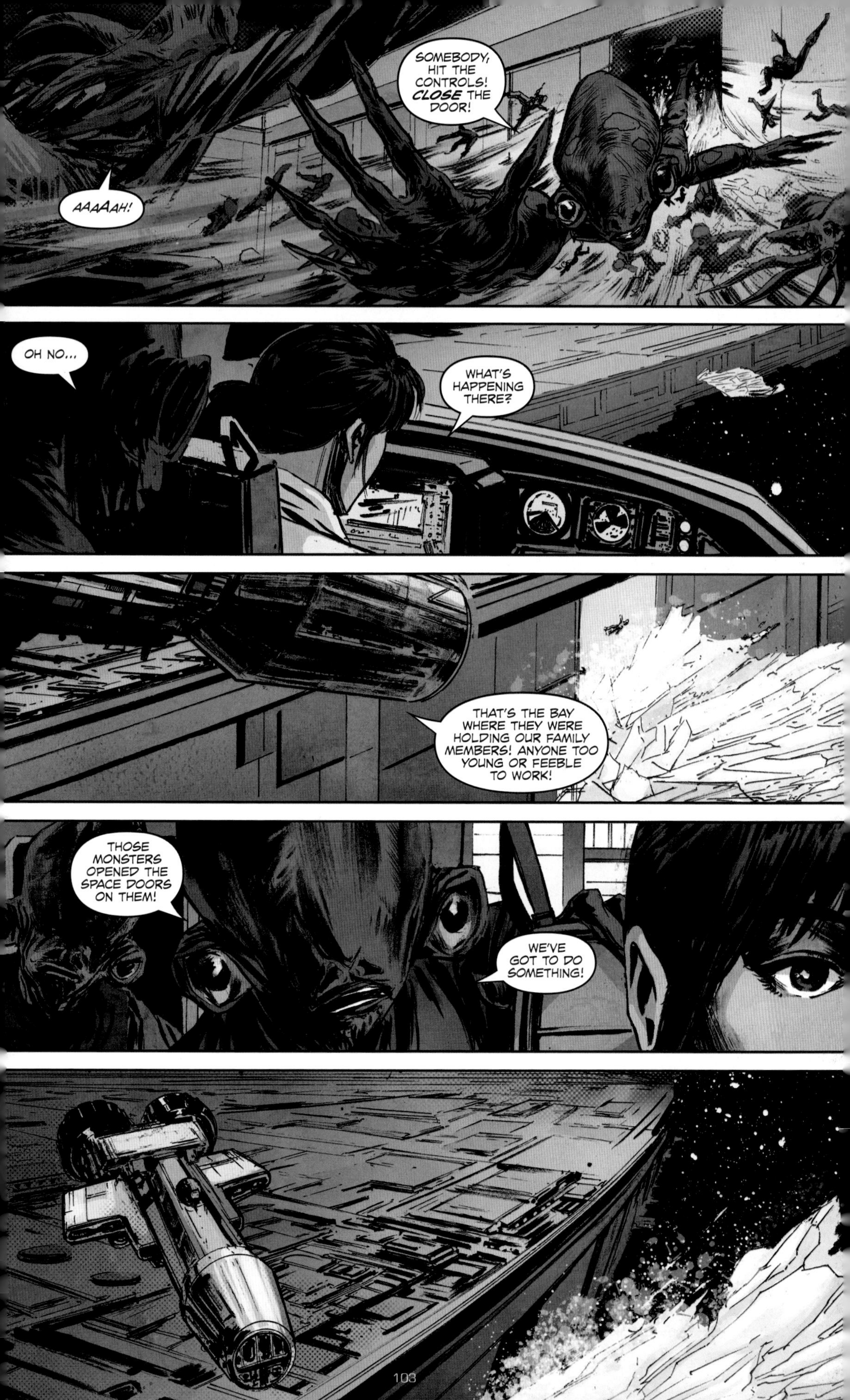
SOMEBODY, HIT THE CONTROLS! CLOSE THE DOOR!
AAAAAH!
OH NO...
WHAT'S HAPPENING THERE?
THAT'S THE BAY WHERE THEY WERE HOLDING OUR FAMILY MEMBERS! ANYONE TOO YOUNG OR FEEBLE TO WORK!
THOSE MONSTERS OPENED THE SPACE DOORS ON THEM!
WE'VE GOT TO DO SOMETHING!

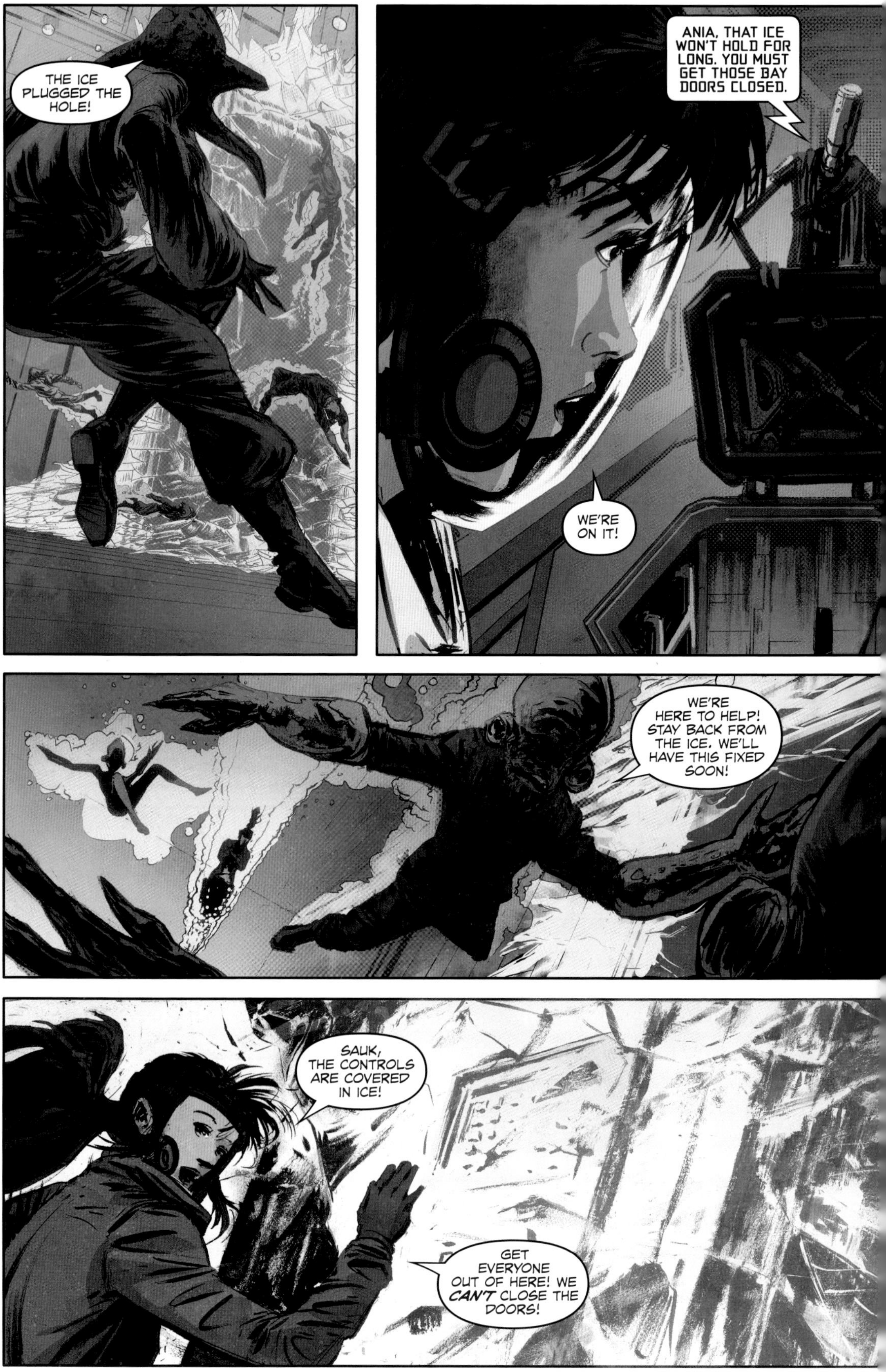
THE ICE PLUGGED THE HOLE!
ANIA, THAT ICE WON'T HOLD FOR LONG. YOU MUST GET THOSE BAY DOORS CLOSED.
WE'RE ON IT!
WE'RE HERE TO HELP! STAY BACK FROM THE ICE. WE'LL HAVE THIS FIXED SOON!
SAUK, THE CONTROLS ARE COVERED IN ICE!
GET EVERYONE OUT OF HERE! WE *CAN'T* CLOSE THE DOORS!

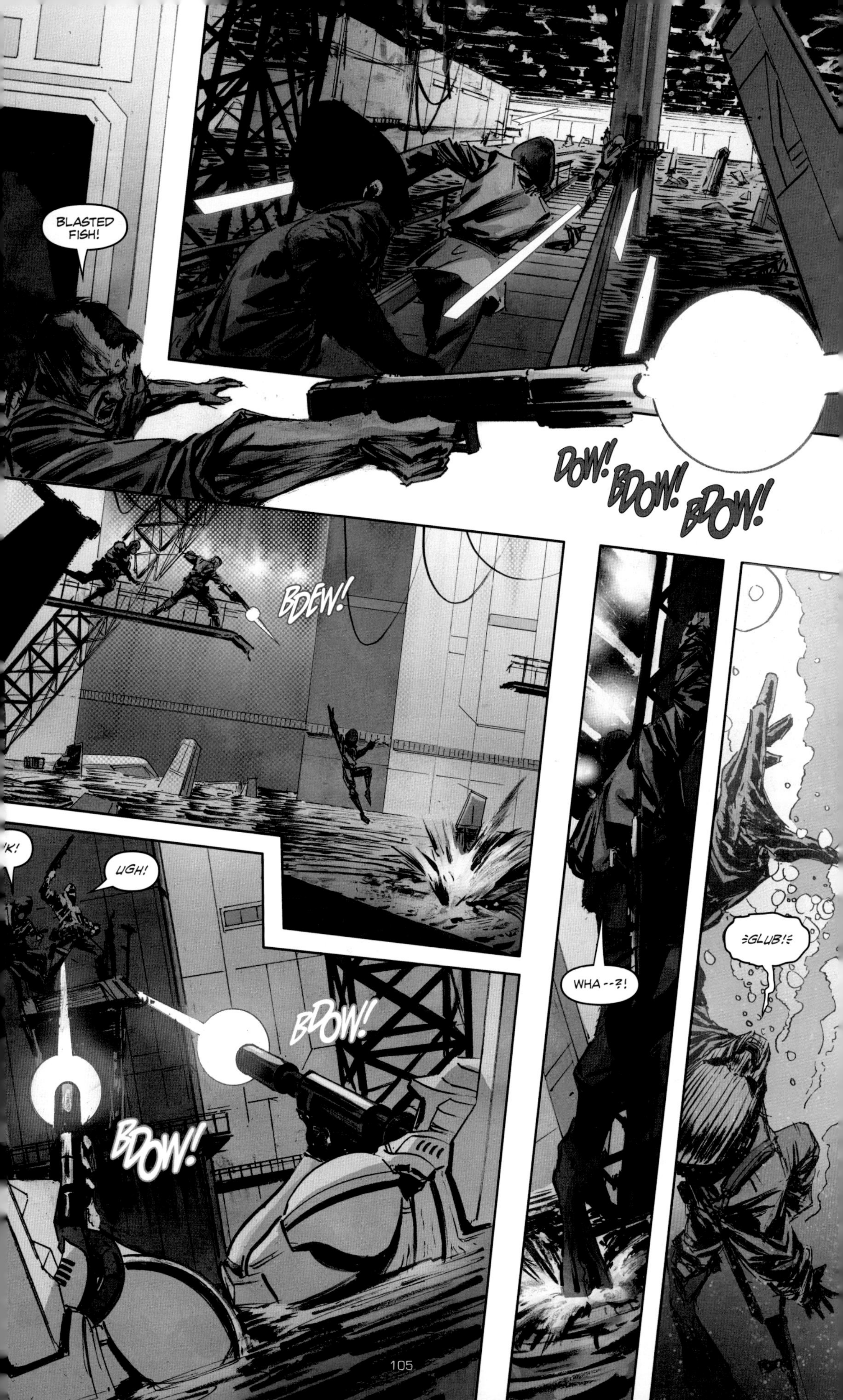
BLASTED FISH!
DOW! BDOW! BDOW!
BDEW!
UGH!
BDOW!
BDOW!
WHA--?!
GLUB!

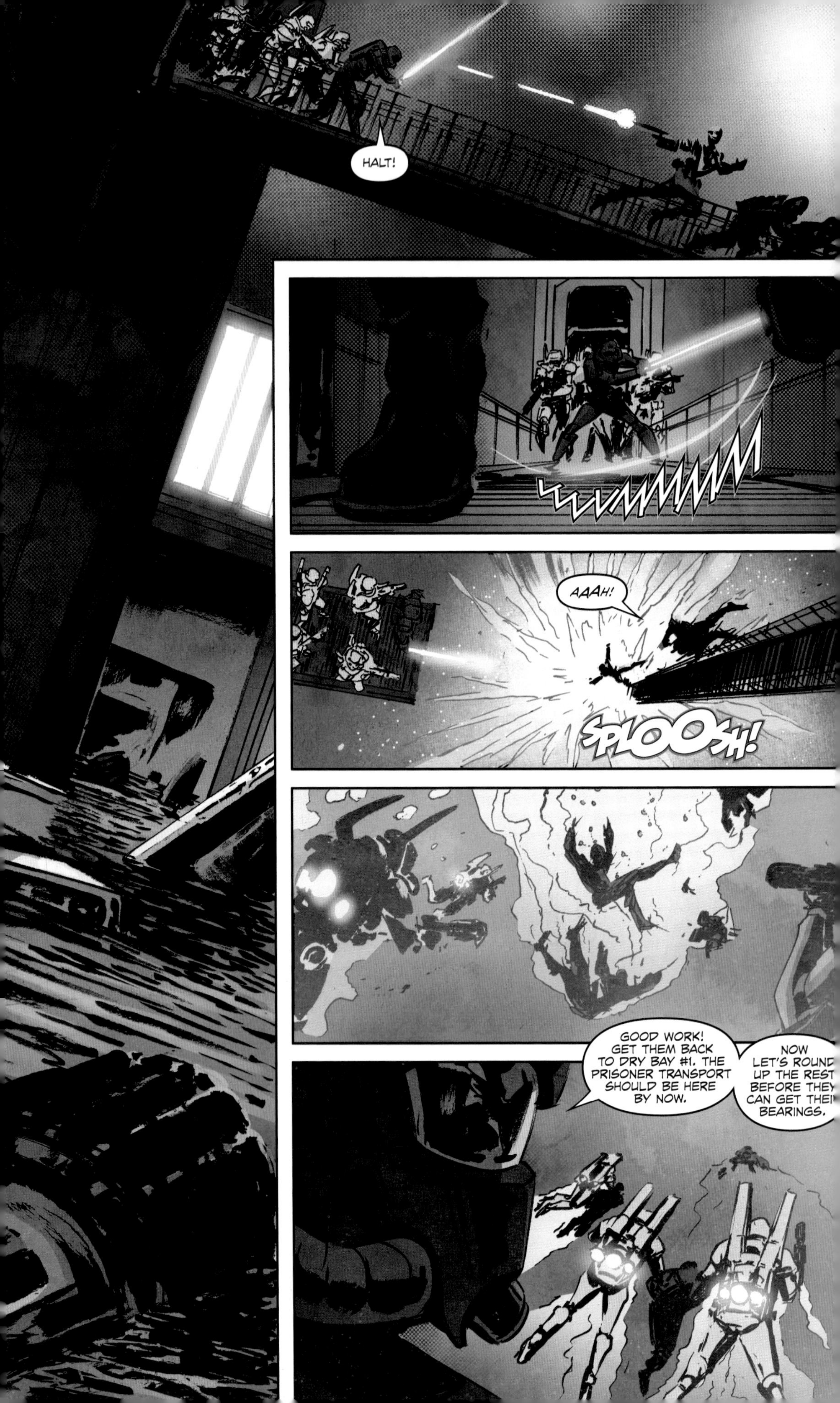
HALT!
AAAH!
SPLOOSH!
GOOD WORK! GET THEM BACK TO DRY BAY #1. THE PRISONER TRANSPORT SHOULD BE HERE BY NOW.
NOW LET'S ROUND UP THE REST BEFORE THEY CAN GET THEI BEARINGS.

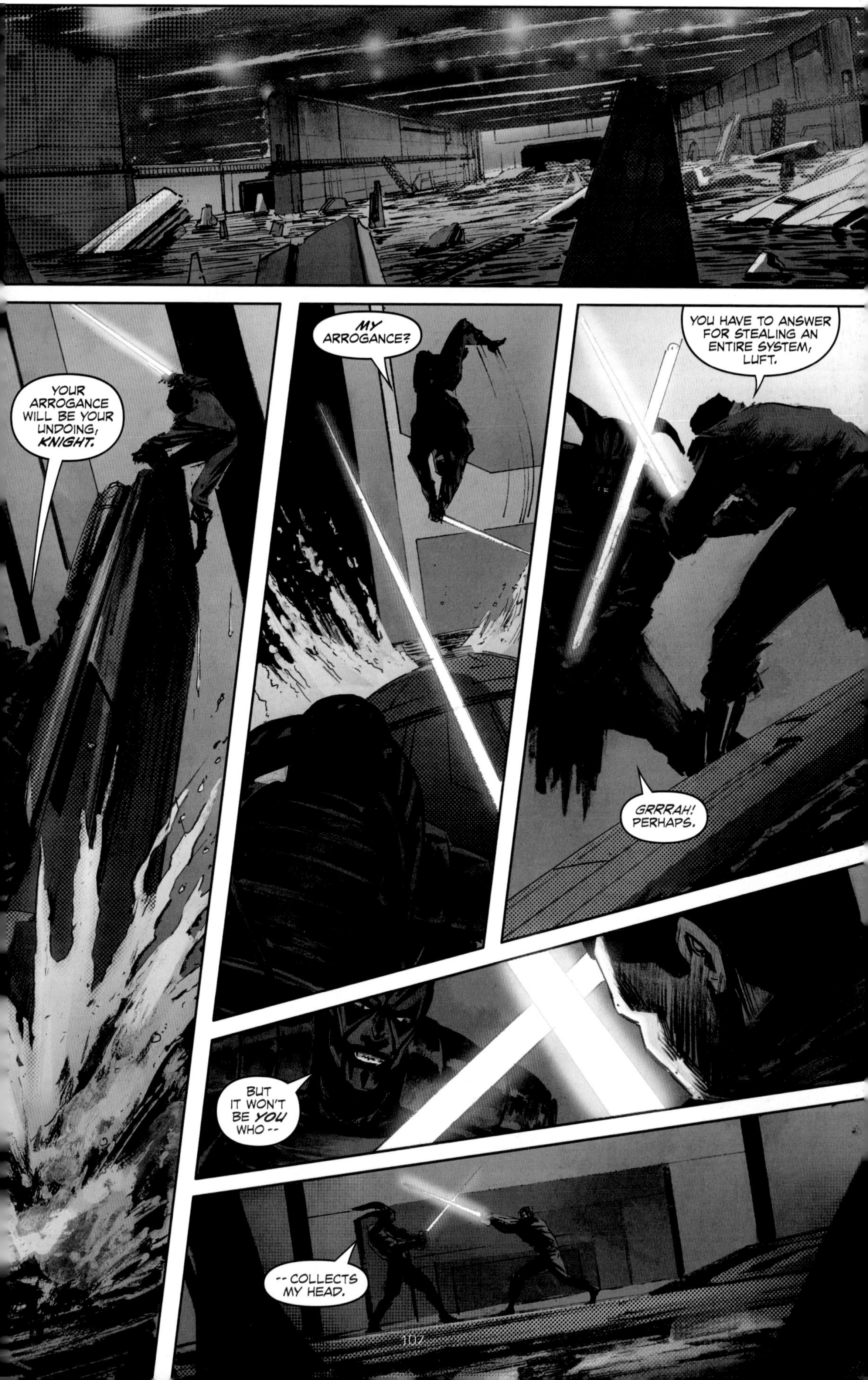

YOUR ARROGANCE WILL BE YOUR UNDOING, KNIGHT.
MY ARROGANCE?
YOU HAVE TO ANSWER FOR STEALING AN ENTIRE SYSTEM, LUFT.
GRRRAH! PERHAPS.
BUT IT WON'T BE YOU WHO --
-- COLLECTS MY HEAD.

ANIA, I CANNOT STAY. I AM BLASTER FODDER OUT HERE.

I WILL LOOP AROUND AND RETURN FOR YOU --

-- ONCE I AM CLEAR.

BUT DON'T TAKE TOO LONG. WE'VE --

KRRKKRK

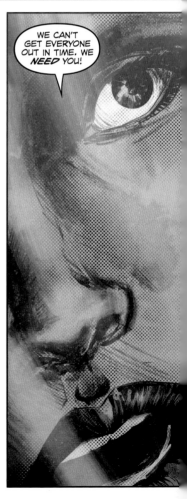

WE CAN'T GET EVERYONE OUT IN TIME. WE NEED YOU!

OH... NO...

AG, THE ICE IS CRACKING!

K-KRAKK

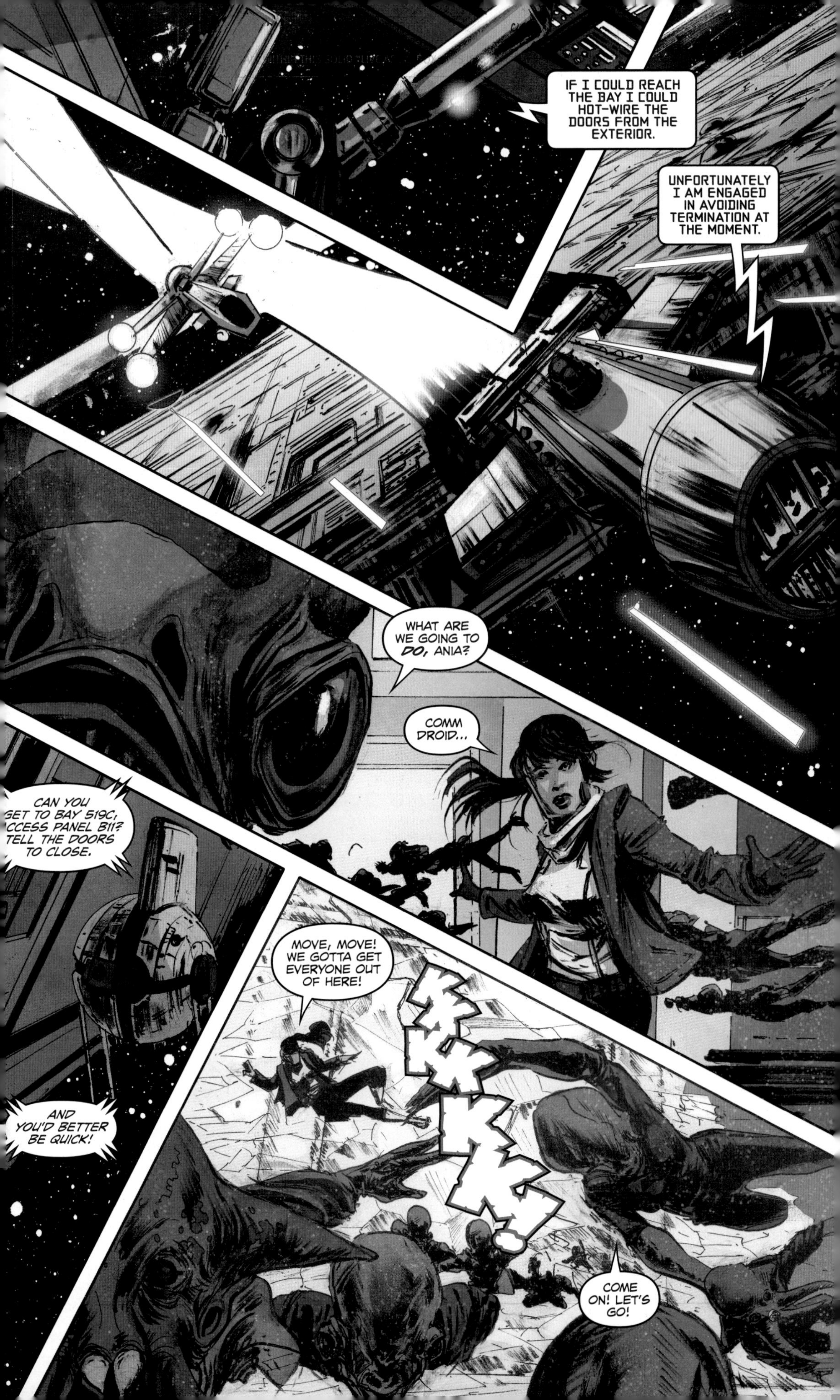

IF I COULD REACH THE BAY I COULD HOT-WIRE THE DOORS FROM THE EXTERIOR.
UNFORTUNATELY I AM ENGAGED IN AVOIDING TERMINATION AT THE MOMENT.
WHAT ARE WE GOING TO *DO*, ANIA?
COMM DROID...
CAN YOU GET TO BAY 519C, ACCESS PANEL B11? TELL THE DOORS TO CLOSE.
AND YOU'D BETTER BE QUICK!
MOVE, MOVE! WE GOTTA GET EVERYONE OUT OF HERE!
KKKK!
COME ON! LET'S GO!

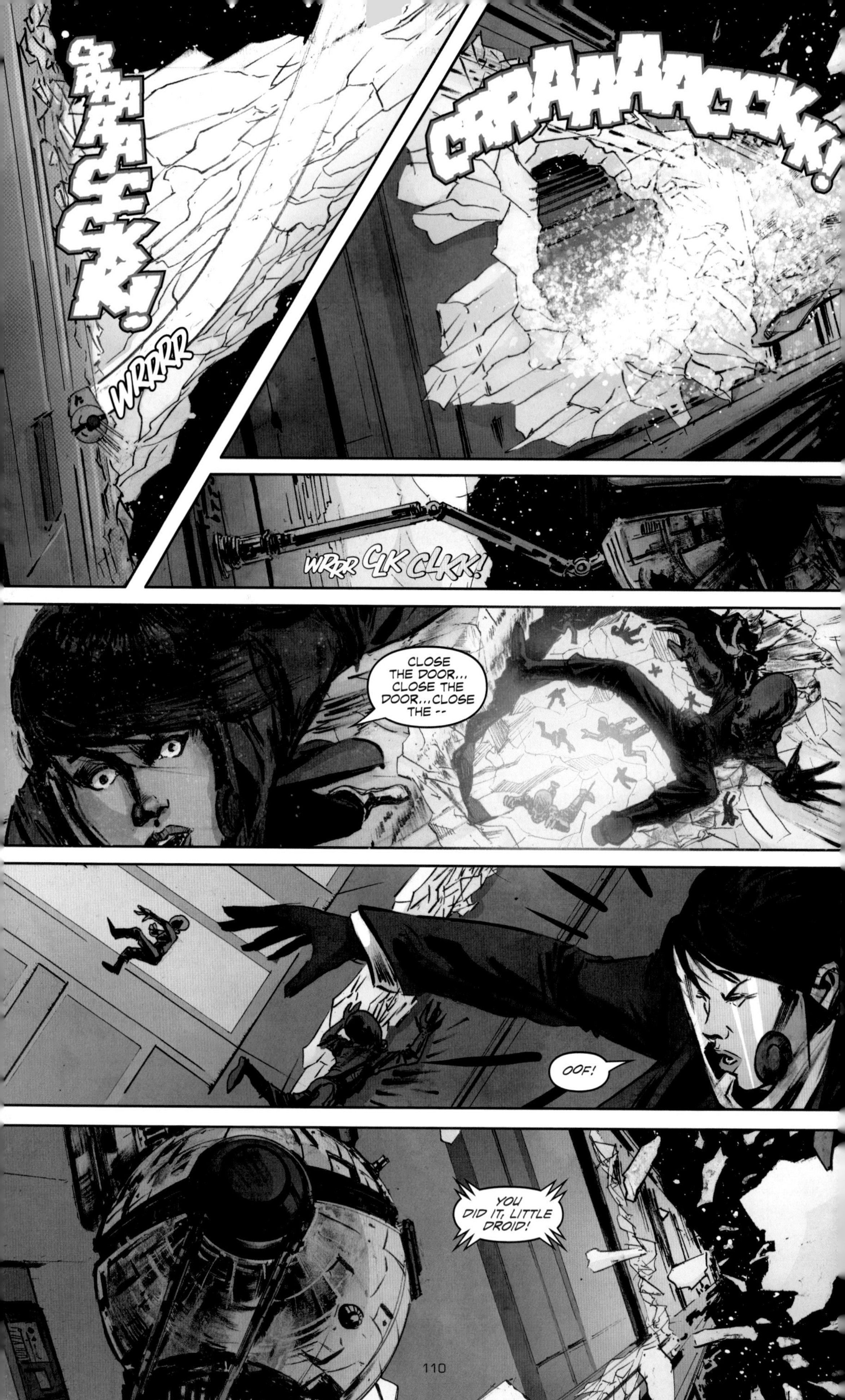
CRRRAAACCK!
CRRAAAAACCKK!
WRRRRR
WRRR CLK CLKK!
CLOSE THE DOOR... CLOSE THE DOOR... CLOSE THE --
OOF!
YOU DID IT, LITTLE DROID!

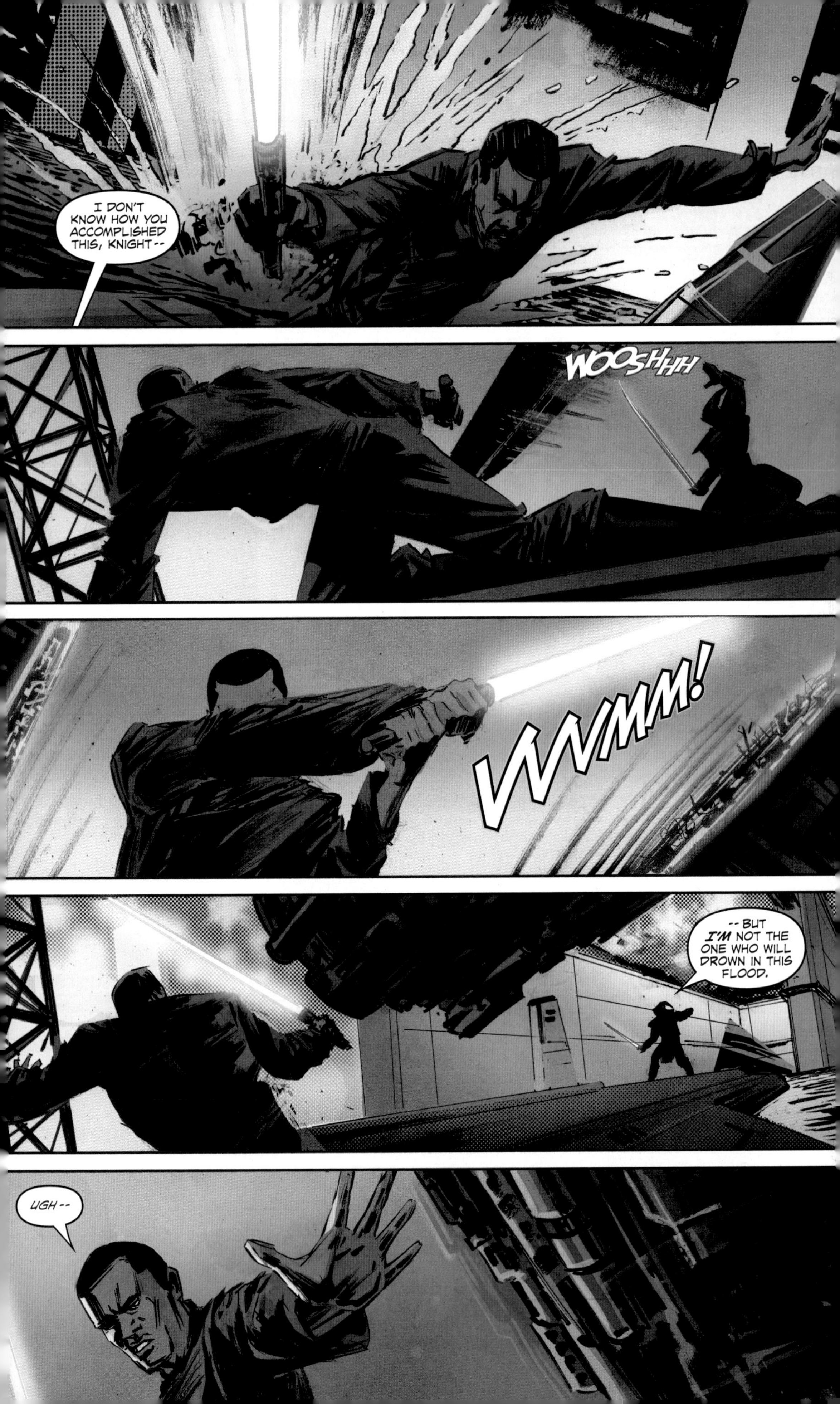
I DON'T KNOW HOW YOU ACCOMPLISHED THIS, KNIGHT--
WOOSHHH
VVVMM!
--BUT I'M NOT THE ONE WHO WILL DROWN IN THIS FLOOD.
UGH--

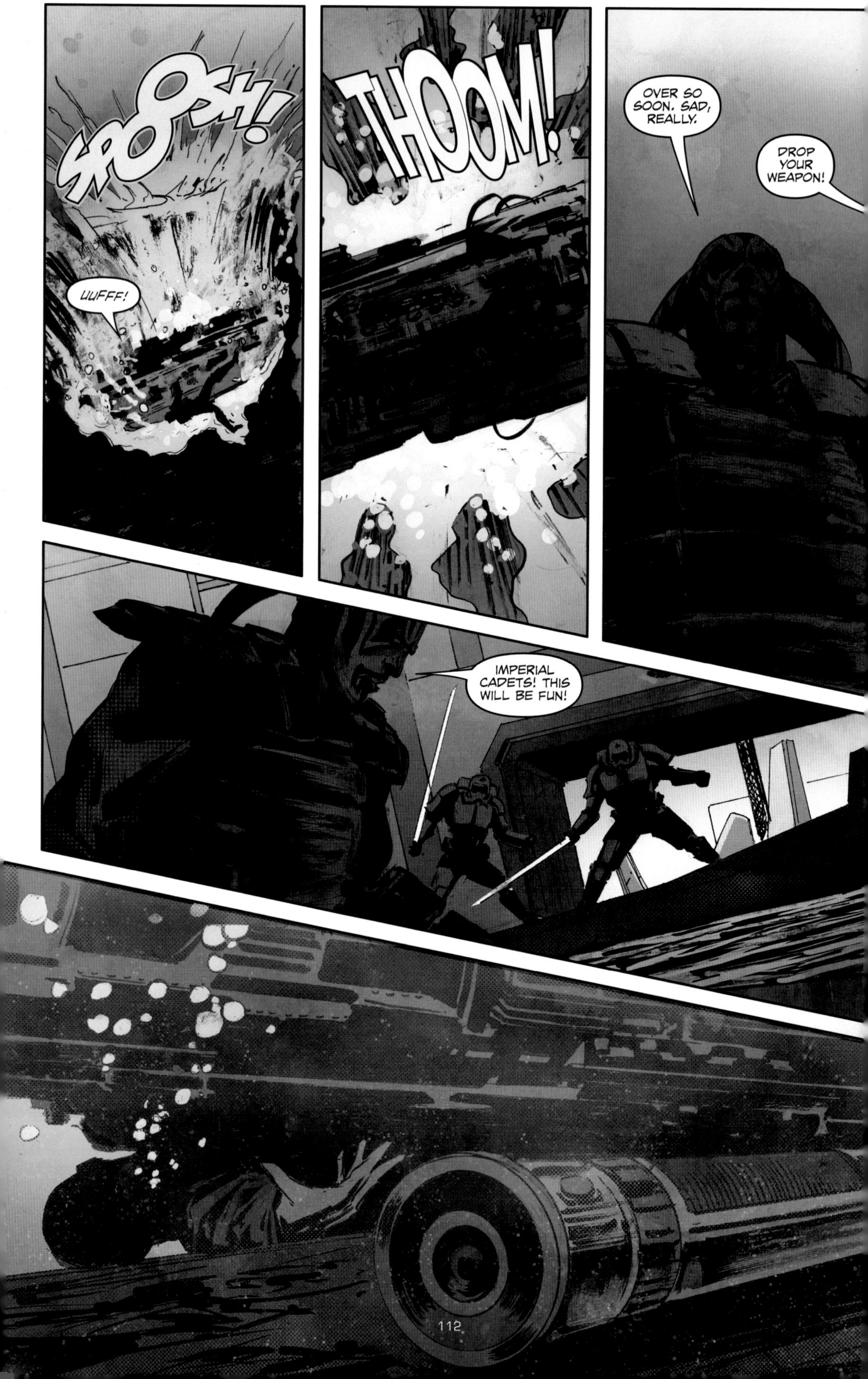
SPOOSH!
UUFFF!
THOOM!
OVER SO SOON. SAD, REALLY.
DROP YOUR WEAPON!
IMPERIAL CADETS! THIS WILL BE FUN!

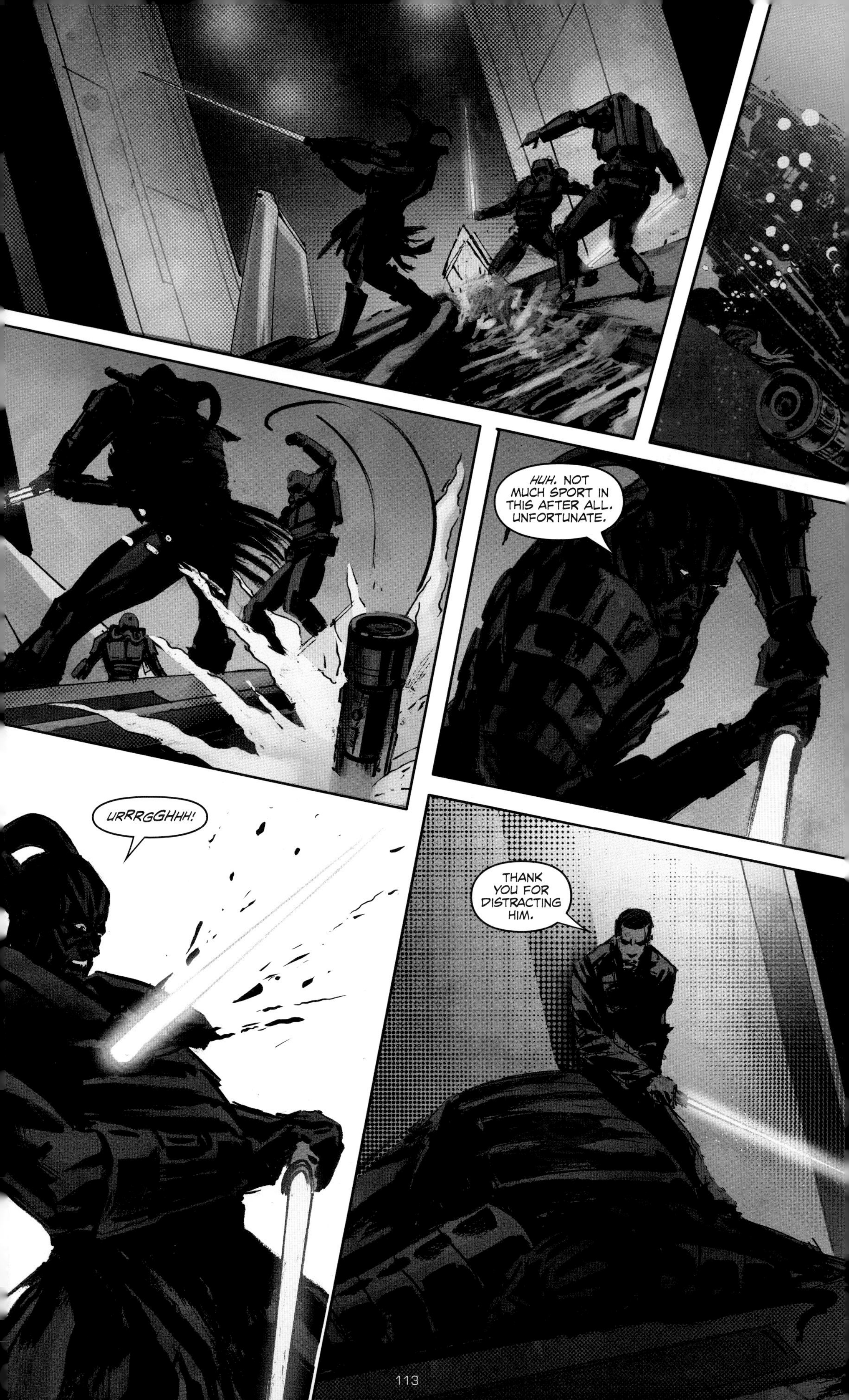
HUH. NOT MUCH SPORT IN THIS AFTER ALL. UNFORTUNATE.
URRRGGHHH!
THANK YOU FOR DISTRACTING HIM.

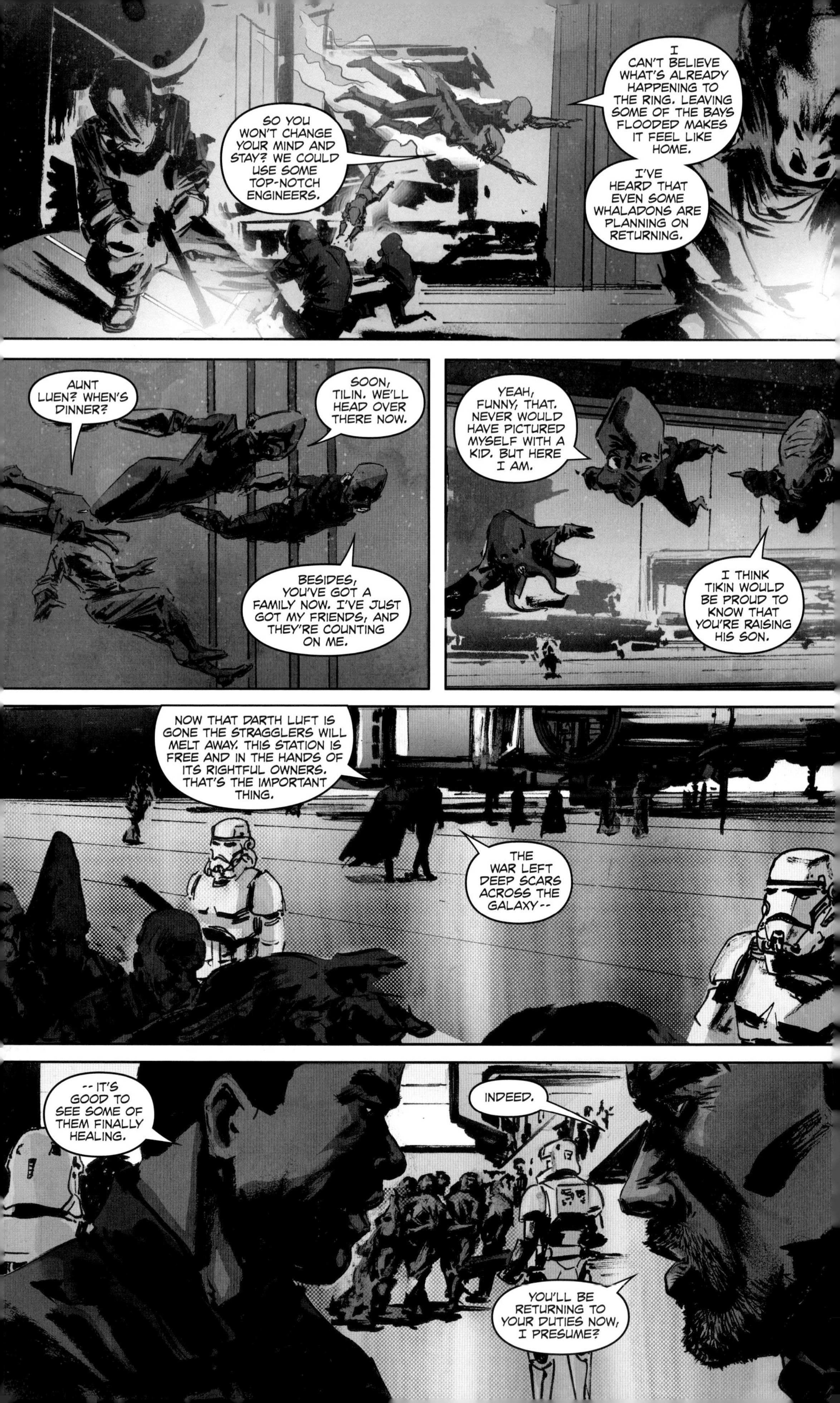
SO YOU WON'T CHANGE YOUR MIND AND STAY? WE COULD USE SOME TOP-NOTCH ENGINEERS.
I CAN'T BELIEVE WHAT'S ALREADY HAPPENING TO THE RING. LEAVING SOME OF THE BAYS FLOODED MAKES IT FEEL LIKE HOME.
I'VE HEARD THAT EVEN SOME WHALADONS ARE PLANNING ON RETURNING.
AUNT LUEN? WHEN'S DINNER?
SOON, TILIN. WE'LL HEAD OVER THERE NOW.
BESIDES, YOU'VE GOT A FAMILY NOW. I'VE JUST GOT MY FRIENDS, AND THEY'RE COUNTING ON ME.
YEAH, FUNNY, THAT. NEVER WOULD HAVE PICTURED MYSELF WITH A KID. BUT HERE I AM.
I THINK TIKIN WOULD BE PROUD TO KNOW THAT YOU'RE RAISING HIS SON.
NOW THAT DARTH LUFT IS GONE THE STRAGGLERS WILL MELT AWAY. THIS STATION IS FREE AND IN THE HANDS OF ITS RIGHTFUL OWNERS. THAT'S THE IMPORTANT THING.
THE WAR LEFT DEEP SCARS ACROSS THE GALAXY--
--IT'S GOOD TO SEE SOME OF THEM FINALLY HEALING.
INDEED.
YOU'LL BE RETURNING TO YOUR DUTIES NOW, I PRESUME?

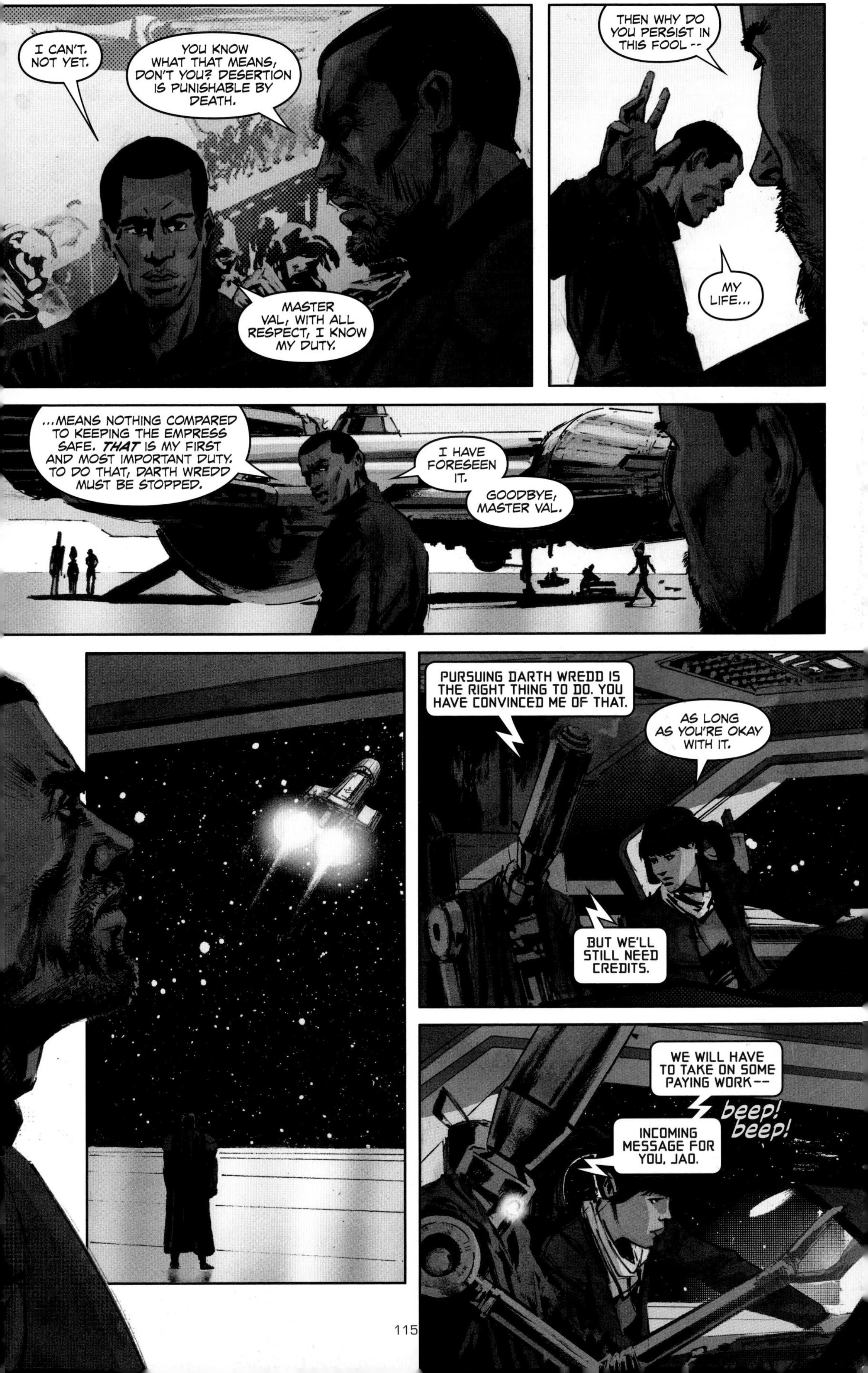
I CAN'T. NOT YET.
YOU KNOW WHAT THAT MEANS, DON'T YOU? DESERTION IS PUNISHABLE BY DEATH.
MASTER VAL, WITH ALL RESPECT, I KNOW MY DUTY.
THEN WHY DO YOU PERSIST IN THIS FOOL --
MY LIFE...
...MEANS NOTHING COMPARED TO KEEPING THE EMPRESS SAFE. *THAT* IS MY FIRST AND MOST IMPORTANT DUTY. TO DO THAT, DARTH WREDD MUST BE STOPPED.
I HAVE FORESEEN IT.
GOODBYE, MASTER VAL.
PURSUING DARTH WREDD IS THE RIGHT THING TO DO. YOU HAVE CONVINCED ME OF THAT.
AS LONG AS YOU'RE OKAY WITH IT.
BUT WE'LL STILL NEED CREDITS.
WE WILL HAVE TO TAKE ON SOME PAYING WORK--
beep! beep!
INCOMING MESSAGE FOR YOU, JAO.

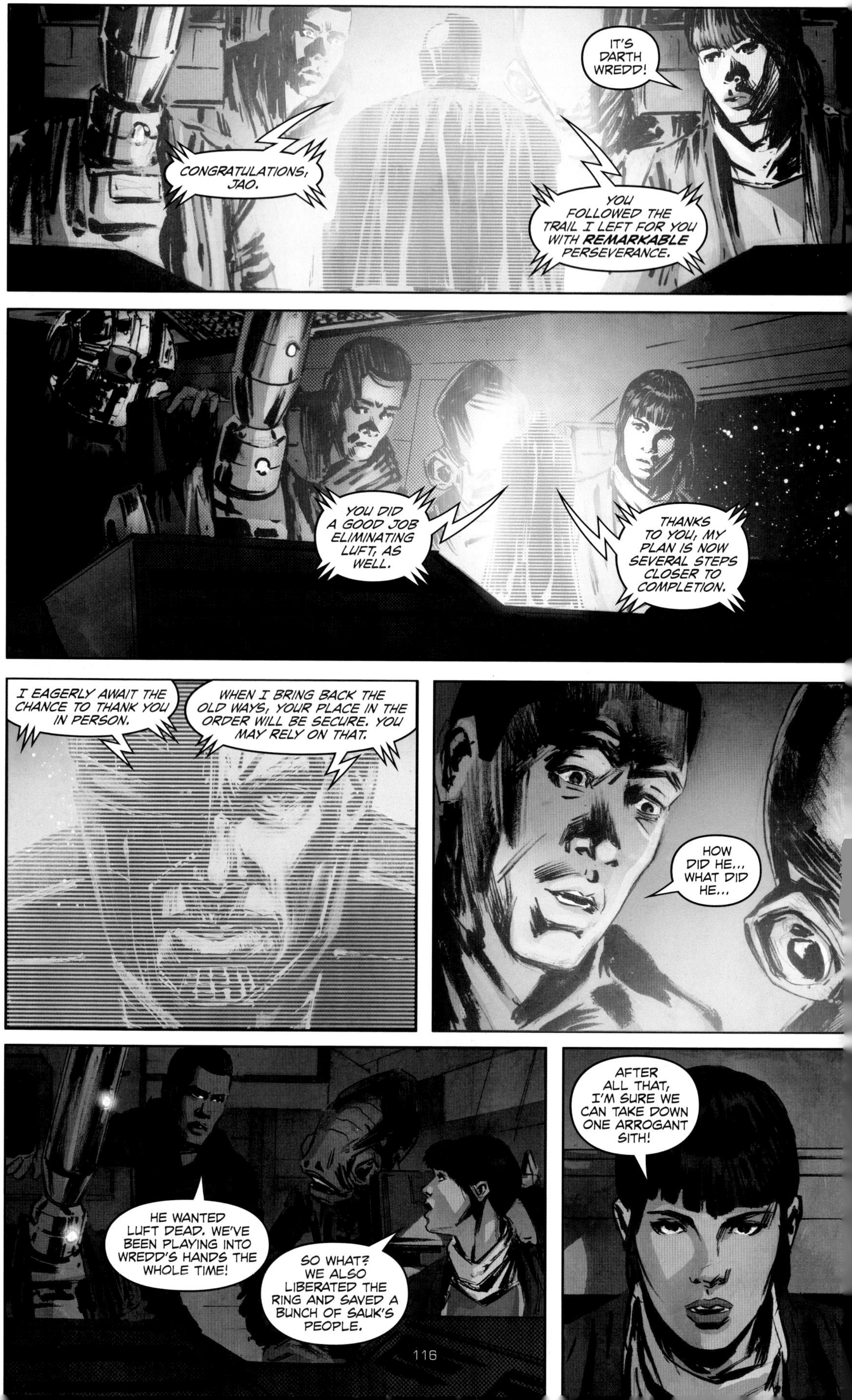
IT'S DARTH WREDD!
CONGRATULATIONS, JAO.
YOU FOLLOWED THE TRAIL I LEFT FOR YOU WITH **REMARKABLE** PERSEVERANCE.
YOU DID A GOOD JOB ELIMINATING LUFT, AS WELL.
THANKS TO YOU, MY PLAN IS NOW SEVERAL STEPS CLOSER TO COMPLETION.
I EAGERLY AWAIT THE CHANCE TO THANK YOU IN PERSON.
WHEN I BRING BACK THE OLD WAYS, YOUR PLACE IN THE ORDER WILL BE SECURE. YOU MAY RELY ON THAT.
HOW DID HE... WHAT DID HE...
HE WANTED LUFT DEAD. WE'VE BEEN PLAYING INTO WREDD'S HANDS THE WHOLE TIME!
SO WHAT? WE ALSO LIBERATED THE RING AND SAVED A BUNCH OF SAUK'S PEOPLE.
AFTER ALL THAT, I'M SURE WE CAN TAKE DOWN ONE ARROGANT SITH!

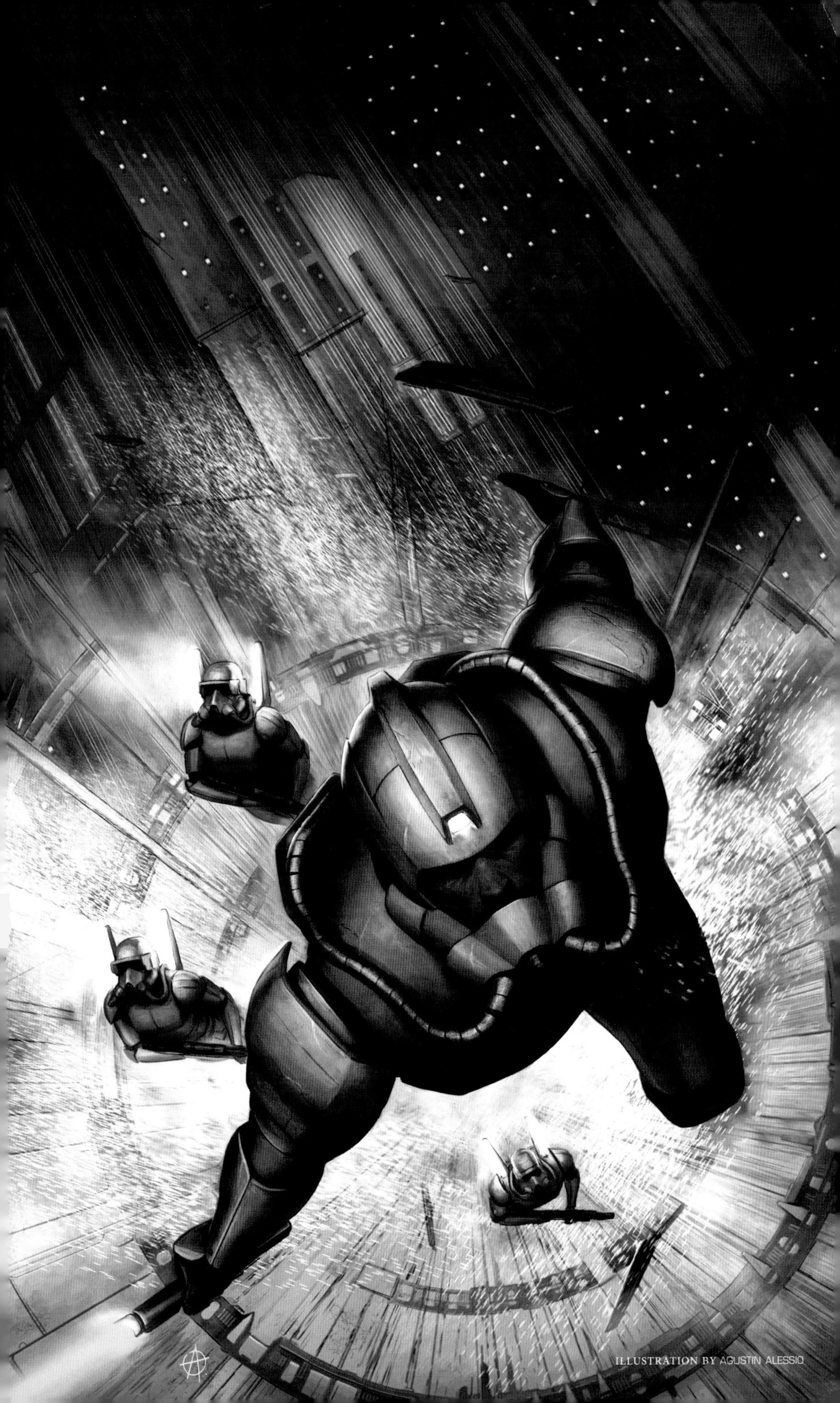

ILLUSTRATION BY AGUSTIN ALESSIO

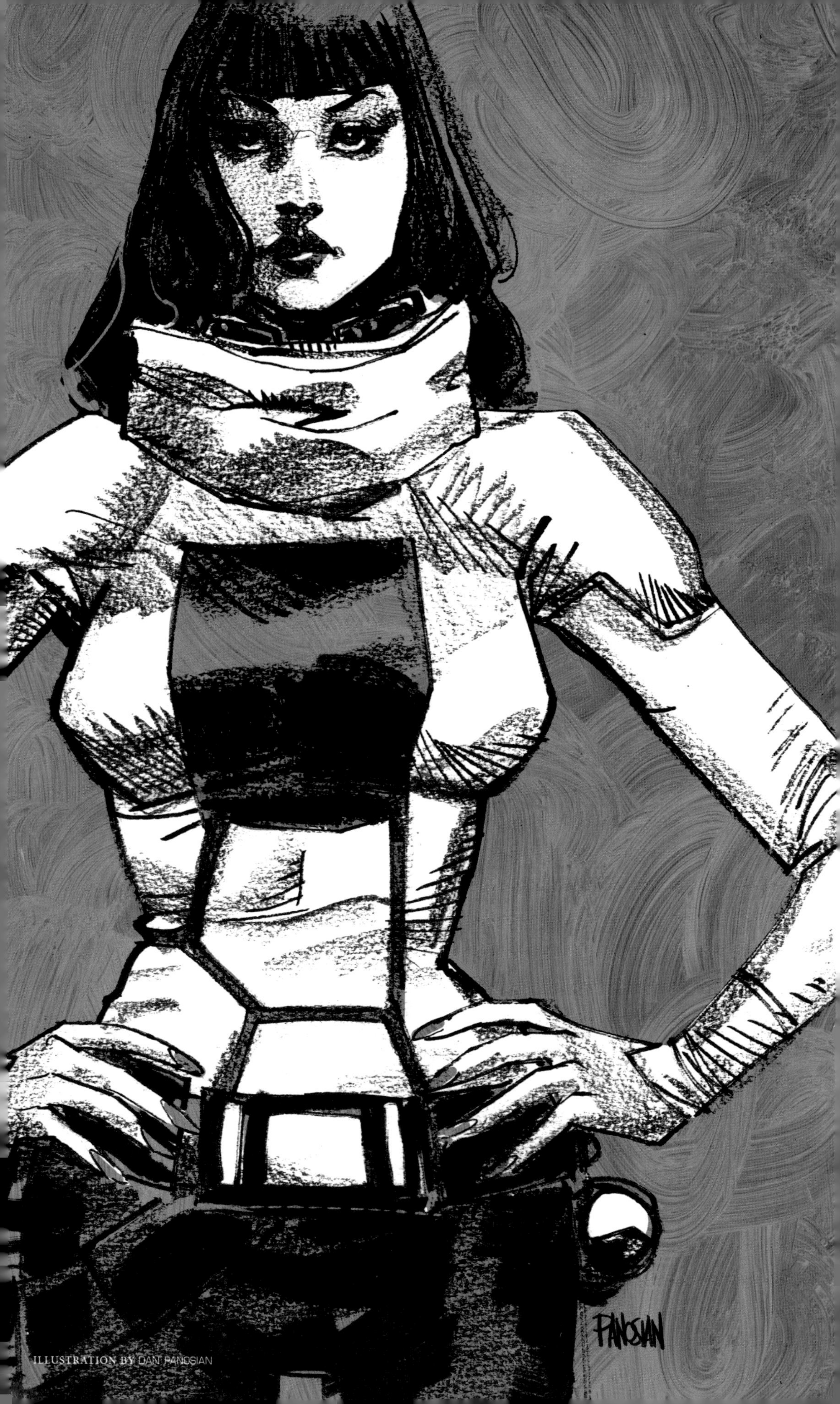
PANOSIAN

ILLUSTRATION BY DAN PANOSIAN

STAR WARS GRAPHIC NOVEL TIMELINE (IN YEARS)

Dawn of the Jedi—36,000–25,000 BSW4

Omnibus: Tales of the Jedi—5,000–3,986 BSW4

Knights of the Old Republic—3,964–3,963 BSW4

The Old Republic—3678, 3653, 3600 BSW4

Lost Tribe of the Sith—2974 BSW4

Knight Errant—1,032 BSW4

Jedi vs. Sith—1,000 BSW4

Jedi: The Dark Side—53 BSW4

Omnibus: Rise of the Sith—33 BSW4

Episode I: The Phantom Menace—32 BSW4

Omnibus: Emissaries and Assassins—32 BSW4

Omnibus: Quinlan Vos—Jedi in Darkness—31–30 BSW4

Omnibus: Menace Revealed—31–22 BSW4

Honor and Duty—22 BSW4

Blood Ties—22 BSW4

Episode II: Attack of the Clones—22 BSW4

Clone Wars—22–19 BSW4

Omnibus: Clone Wars—22–19 BSW4

Clone Wars Adventures—22–19 BSW4

Darth Maul: Death Sentence—20 BSW4

Episode III: Revenge of the Sith—19 BSW4

Purge—19 BSW4

Dark Times—19 BSW4

Darth Vader—19 BSW4

Omnibus: Droids and Ewoks—15 BSW4–3.5 ASW4

Omnibus: Droids—5.5 BSW4

Omnibus: Boba Fett—3 BSW4–10 ASW4

Agent of the Empire—3 BSW4

The Force Unleashed—2 BSW4

Omnibus: At War with the Empire—1 BSW4

Episode IV: A New Hope—SW4

Star Wars—0 ASW4

Classic Star Wars—0–3 ASW4

Omnibus: A Long Time Ago. . . .—0–4 ASW4

Omnibus: Wild Space—0–4 ASW4

Empire—0 ASW4

Omnibus: The Other Sons of Tatooine—0 ASW4

Omnibus: Early Victories—0–3 ASW4

Jabba the Hutt: The Art of the Deal—1 ASW4

Episode V: The Empire Strikes Back—3 ASW4

Ewoks: Shadows of Endor—3.5–4 ASW4

Omnibus: Shadows of the Empire—3.5–4.5 ASW4

Episode VI: Return of the Jedi—4 ASW4

Omnibus: X-Wing Rogue Squadron—4–5 ASW4

The Thrawn Trilogy—9 ASW4

Dark Empire—10 ASW4

Crimson Empire—11 ASW4

Jedi Academy: Leviathan—12 ASW4

Union—19 ASW4

Chewbacca—25 ASW4

Invasion—25 ASW4

Legacy—130–138 ASW4

Dawn of the Jedi
36,000 years before
Star Wars: A New Hope

Old Republic Era
25,000–1000 years before
Star Wars: A New Hope

Rise of the Empire Era
1000–0 years before Star
Wars: A New Hope

Rebellion Era
0–5 years after
Star Wars: A New Hope

New Republic Era
5–25 years after
Star Wars: A New Hope

New Jedi Order Era
25+ years after
Star Wars: A New Hope

Legacy Era
130+ years after
Star Wars: A New Hope

Vector
Crosses four eras in timeline

Volume 1 contains:
Knights of the Old Republic Volume 5
Dark Times Volume 3
Volume 2 contains:
Rebellion Volume 4
Legacy Volume 6

Infinities
Does not apply to timeline
Star Wars Tales
Omnibus: Infinities
Omnibus: Wild Space Volume 2

BSW4 = before *Episode IV: A New Hope*. ASW4 = after *Episode IV: A New Hope*.

R WARS OMNIBUS COLLECTIONS

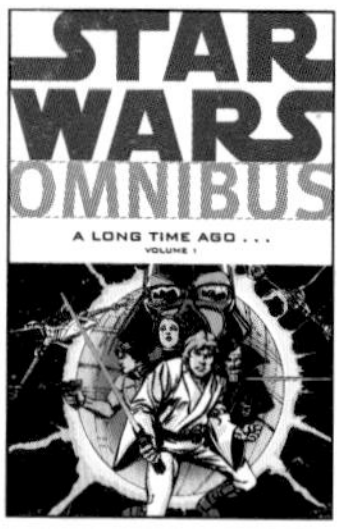

STAR WARS: BOBA FETT

Boba Fett, the most feared, most respected, and most loved bounty hunter in the galaxy, now has all of his comics stories collected into one massive volume!
ISBN 978-1-59582-418-9 | $24.99

STAR WARS: INFINITIES

Three different tales where *one thing* happens differently than it did in the original trilogy of *Star Wars* films. Luke Skywalker, Princess Leia, Han Solo, and Darth Vader are launched onto new trajectories!
ISBN 978-1-61655-078-3 | $24.99

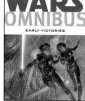

STAR WARS: A LONG TIME AGO. . . .

Star Wars: A Long Time Ago. . . . omnibus volumes feature classic *Star Wars* stories not seen in over twenty years! Originally printed by Marvel Comics, these recolored stories are sure to please Star Wars fans both new and old.
Volume 1: ISBN 978-1-59582-486-8 | $24.99   Volume 4: ISBN 978-1-59582-640-4 | $24.99
Volume 2: ISBN 978-1-59582-554-4 | $24.99   Volume 5: ISBN 978-1-59582-801-9 | $24.99
Volume 3: ISBN 978-1-59582-639-8 | $24.99

STAR WARS: WILD SPACE

Rare and previously uncollected stories! Contains work from some of comics' most famous writers and artists (including Alan Moore, Chris Claremont, Archie Goodwin, Walt Simonson, and Alan Davis), plus stories featuring the greatest heroes and villains of *Star Wars*!
Volume 1: ISBN 978-1-61655-146-9 | $24.99   Volume 2: ISBN 978-1-61655-147-6 | $24.99

STAR WARS: EARLY VICTORIES

Following the destruction of the first Death Star, Luke Skywalker and Princess Leia find there are many more battles to be fought against the Empire and Darth Vader!
ISBN 978-1-59582-172-0 | $24.99

STAR WARS: AT WAR WITH THE EMPIRE

Stories of the early days of the Rebel Alliance and the beginnings of its war with the Empire—tales of the *Star Wars* galaxy set before, during, and after the events in *Star Wars: A New Hope!*
Volume 1: ISBN 978-1-59582-699-2 | $24.99   Volume 2: ISBN 978-1-59582-777-7 | $24.99

STAR WARS: THE OTHER SONS OF TATOOINE

Luke's story has been told time and again, but what about the journeys of his boyhood friends, Biggs Darklighter and Janek "Tank" Sunber? Both are led to be heroes in their own right: one of the Rebellion, the other of the Empire . . .
ISBN 978-1-59582-866-8 | $24.99

STAR WARS: SHADOWS OF THE EMPIRE

Featuring all your favorite characters from the *Star Wars* trilogy—Luke Skywalker, Princess Leia, and Han Solo—this volume includes stories written by acclaimed novelists Timothy Zahn and Steve Perry!
ISBN 978-1-59582-434-9 | $24.99

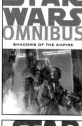

STAR WARS: X-WING ROGUE SQUADRON

The starfighters of the Rebel Alliance become the defenders of a new Republic in these stories featuring Wedge Antilles and his team of ace pilots known throughout the galaxy as Rogue Squadron.
Volume 1: ISBN 978-1-59307-572-9 | $24.99   Volume 3: ISBN 978-1-59307-776-1 | $24.99
Volume 2: ISBN 978-1-59307-619-1 | $24.99

AVAILABLE AT YOUR LOCAL COMICS SHOP OR BOOKSTORE!
To find a comics shop in your area, call 1-888-266-4226
For more information or to order direct: • On the web: DarkHorse.com • E-mail: mailorder@darkhorse.com
• Phone: 1-800-862-0052 Mon.–Fri. 9 AM to 5 PM Pacific Time • STAR WARS © Lucasfilm Ltd. & ™ (BL 8001)